Teaching Essential Units of Language

This textbook provides a practical and research-based foundation for teaching second language (L2) multiword units (also commonly called collocations). Multiword units – such as *strong tea*, *beautiful weather*, or *would you mind* – cannot be readily understood or predicted by the meanings of their component parts, and prove particularly challenging for English language learners. With contributions from top scholars, this text presents a thorough and rounded overview of the principles and practices currently dominant in teaching L2 phrases in a variety of instructional settings around the world. Divided into two sections, Part I examines the pedagogical foundations of teaching the essential units of language. Part II covers a range of techniques and classroom activities for implementing instruction. Intended for students and teacher educators, this accessible volume integrates the key principles, strategies, and applications of current and effective English language instruction for both vocabulary and grammar.

Eli Hinkel is Professor of Linguistics and MA-TESL Programs, Seattle Pacific University, USA.

ESL & Applied Linguistics Professional Series

Eli Hinkel, Series Editor

Teacher Training and Professional Development of Chinese English Language Teachers
Changing From Fish to Dragon
Faridah Pawan, Wenfang Fan, Pei Miao

Research on Reflective Practice in TESOL
Thomas S. C. Farrell

Teaching English to Second Language Learners in Academic Contexts
Reading, Writing, Listening, Speaking
Jonathan M. Newton, Dana R. Ferris, Christine C. M. Goh, William Grabe, Fredricka L. Stoller, Larry Vandergrift

The Politics of English Second Language Writing Assessment in Global Contexts
Edited by Todd Ruecker, Deborah Crusan

Transnational Writing Education
Theory, History, and Practice
Edited by Xiaoye You

Understanding and Teaching English Spelling
A Strategic Guide
Adam Brown

Teaching Essential Units of Language
Beyond Single-word Vocabulary
Edited by Eli Hinkel

For more information about this series, please visit: www.routledge.com/ESL--Applied-Linguistics-Professional-Series/book-series/LEAESLALP

Teaching Essential Units of Language

Beyond Single-word Vocabulary

Edited by Eli Hinkel

Routledge
Taylor & Francis Group

NEW YORK AND LONDON

First published 2019
by Routledge
711 Third Avenue, New York, NY 10017

and by Routledge
2 Park Square, Milton Park, Abingdon, Oxon, OX14 4RN

Routledge is an imprint of the Taylor & Francis Group, an informa business

Library of Congress Cataloging-in-Publication Data
A catalog record has been requested for this book

ISBN: 978-1-138-47876-3 (hbk)
ISBN: 978-1-138-47877-0 (pbk)
ISBN: 978-1-351-06773-7 (ebk)

Typeset in Bembo and Gill Sans
by Out of House Publishing

Printed and bound in Great Britain by
TJ International Ltd, Padstow, Cornwall

Contents

Preface   vii

Acknowledgements   x

A Short Preamble: A Bit of History in the Life of
Phrases and Multiword Units   1
ELI HINKEL

Part I: Key Considerations   **17**

1   Teaching Multiword Units: A Teacher's Perspective   19
PENNY UR

2   Working with Multiword Units in ESP/EAP   36
AVERIL COXHEAD

3   Teaching Idioms and Idiomatic Expressions Across the
Second Language Curriculum   55
JOHN I. LIONTAS

Part II: Teaching Practicalities **107**

4 Teaching Strategies and Techniques: Collocations and
  Multiword Units 109
  ELI HINKEL

5 Teaching and Assessing Multiword Expressions Using an
  Open Educational Resources Academic English Corpus 134
  BRENT A. GREEN

6 Functions of Formulaic Expressions at School: From the
  Coffee Shop to the Classroom 165
  CHERYL BOYD ZIMMERMAN

7 Teaching Lexical Bundles: Which Ones and How? 186
  RANDI REPPEN

Index 201

Preface

The goal of this book is to provide a practical and research-based foundation for teaching second language (L2) collocations and multiword units, by any name – more on the terminology conundrums in the Preamble that follows, and in chapter 4, which provides a thorough overview of the phraseology issues. The book presents principles, strategies and techniques, and applications of current and effective English instruction that extends to units of language longer and more complex than single-word vocabulary – in terms of both vocabulary and grammar (also referred to as lexico-grammar in linguistics). The aims are to present a thorough and rounded overview of the principles and techniques currently dominant in teaching L2 phrases in a range of instructional settings around the world. Examples of collocations and multiword units are countless, e.g. *two for lunch/dinner, long/nice/full/busy/final/present day, beautiful child/dress/face/hair/spot/weather, chilly day/night/wind/reception,* or *do you/would you mind.*

As an aside, at present, there are around a few dozen terms that refer to these multiword units, chunks, collocations, phrases, idioms, expressions, formulaic sequences, formulaic language, prefabricated constructions, lexical bundles, and the like. One of the reasons for this terminological disorder lies in the fact that pedagogical materials for teaching these units of language are virtually non-existent despite hundreds of research publications on their astounding frequencies and ubiquity in all manner of language, e.g.

informal conversations, news reports, formal speeches, university and academic lectures, email, fiction, blogs, and academic writing.

A key attribute of multiword units is that often their meanings cannot be readily understood or predicted from the meanings of their component parts. For example, knowing the meaning of the word "look" and the meaning of the word "after" does not indicate that you will know the meaning of the collocation "look after." In language teaching and learning, one of the crucial characteristics of multiword units is that it is not usually possible to translate them from one language to another by employing any type of grammar or vocabulary rules. Units of language that are longer than a single word represent a crucial – absolutely fundamental – area of instruction. They occur in all language uses, and they are not called "essential language units" for nothing: they are also enormously frequent. When it comes to language teaching and learning, there is not a moment to lose.

This book can serve as a source text or a supplementary textbook in courses on L2 vocabulary and grammar for pre-service and in-service teachers as well as for teacher educators who seek to develop their professional knowledge and skills in the course of their education. The aims are to present a concise overview of phraseological study, but most importantly, a compendium of teaching strategies, techniques, and activities that can be suitable and effective in a range of instructional settings around the world. It goes without saying that in the final count, classroom teachers anywhere are ultimately responsible for implementing language instruction in the best interests of their students. To this end, the book sets out to illuminate the options and choices in teaching multiword units from a contemporary perspective.

The book is divided into two parts. Part I, Key Considerations, examines the pedagogical foundations and instructional foci in teaching essential units of language. Part II on Teaching Practicalities is about strategies, techniques, and productive activities for classroom teaching. That is, the chapters demonstrate a range of options for teaching language units that can be implemented while keeping an eye on advantages and disadvantages of each technique.

The Book Structure

This text seeks to be expeditious, constructive, and down to earth. Chapters highlight key features of multiword expressions, the extraordinarily broad range of their occurrences, and teaching strategies and tactics.

Part I consists of three chapters. The first chapter (by Penny Ur) spotlights practical classroom teaching of multiword units in English, though most of its content is also relevant to the teaching of other languages. The second chapter (by Averil Coxhead) focuses on working with multiword units in English for Academic Purposes and English for Specific Purposes, beginning with a short discussion on why multiword units are important in these areas. Chapter 3 (by John I. Liontas) discusses the practical efficacy of teaching idioms and idiomatic language across the second or foreign language curriculum.

Part II also includes four chapters. Chapter 4 (by Eli Hinkel) presents several teaching strategies, techniques, and activities that can be implemented at any level of learners' proficiencies from beginning to advanced. The fifth chapter (by Brent Green) addresses specific ways teachers can access or create open educational resources corpora and engage their learners in specific multiword expressions acquisition tasks. Chapter 6 (by Cheryl Boyd Zimmerman) explores various pragmatic functions of formulaic sequences, that is, the practical purposes of these language units. The final chapter (by Randi Reppen) draws on results from previous studies of lexical bundles to identify four-word lexical bundles that are characteristic of conversation and of academic language (both spoken and written).

Acknowledgements

The terminology used today to refer to the countless units of language (literally countless – their exact or even approximate numbers are unknown) with which this book is concerned is confusing, somewhat redundant, and often complicated to the point of disarray (see Chapter 4). The book owes its concise, clear, and well-suited title to Naomi Silverman of Taylor & Francis at the time. Naomi has a gift, a true talent, for what she calls "calling a spade a spade" and coming up with tremendous titles for books when all hope of finally pinpointing one might seem to be lost. Naomi, thank you. The title of the book (and I personally) are forever in your debt. Karen Adler, Commissioning Editor, Taylor & Francis, has been open-minded, thoughtful, insightful, supportive, and enthusiastic in her role as the lead for this publication. Robert B. Kaplan has been more than generous, foresightful, astute, and gracious with his assistance through the years. Bob, thank you for all your help – definitely, above and beyond the call.

A Short Preamble

A Bit of History in the Life of Phrases and Multiword Units[1]

Eli Hinkel

Idioms and Phraseology in English

What represents an idiom, a proverb, a conventionalized expression, a chunk, a word cluster, or a grammatically irregular unit of language is notoriously – famously – difficult to define and hence to identify. Significant and ongoing lexicographic efforts to do so have been undertaken at least since the 1940s. Not surprisingly, multiword phrases and expressions can be challenging to explain in teaching, systematize for making and using learners' dictionaries, or thematically develop in textbooks. With the emergence of computer technology and the proliferation of large and analyzable language corpora in a range of texts and genres, broad expectations arose that the conundrum of defining and identifying multiword, idiomatic, and phrasal expressions could potentially be accorded a measure of systematicity. However, perhaps counter-intuitively, analyses of language corpora have further added to the typological and terminological stew: computerized examinations of both spoken and written language data have shed light on the enormity, variability, and complexity of idiomatic and recurrent expressions.

In the 1970s and 1980s, studies in phraseology and lexicology allowed for far-reaching insights into lexicon–grammar interconnectedness (Cowie,

1988; Cowie & Mackin, 1975). Unlike traditional grammars, analyses of idiomatic constructions do not assume that a clear-cut division between lexicon and grammar exists. All conventionalized expressions and phrases can be as small as single words or short phrases (e.g. *forwards, backwards, silence!, bling, whatever, in the bag, not on your life, a piece of cake*) or as long as complete sentences (e.g. *a fool and his money are soon parted, you don't say, actions speak louder than words,* or *every cloud has a silver lining*). Depending on their meanings and syntactic length, idiomatic phrases can form lexico-grammatical continua that can be treated as whole-unit structures (Cowie, 1998; Fillmore, Kay, & O'Connor, 1988; Kay & Fillmore, 1999; Howarth, 1998).

Language research and analyses have long established that a great number of linguistic combinations simply sound "right" to proficient users of English and that collocations are very common in both speaking and writing (Wilkins, 1972; Yorio, 1989). More importantly, however, combinations that are infrequent or hardly ever found may sound unnatural and wrong, even when they are grammatically correct (e.g. *?collect all your chickens in one basket, ?speed down, ?quick food,* or *?be upset over spilled milk*).

A formal and relatively early definition of idioms was advanced by Adam Makkai (1972), and was later adopted in several editions of the *Oxford English Dictionary* in the 1970s and 1980s:

> A form of expression, grammatical construction, phrase, etc., peculiar to a language; a peculiarity of phraseology approved by the usage of language, often having a significance other than its grammatical or logical one.
>
> (Makkai, 1972, p. 23)

In English language textbooks and dictionaries, this classical definition is still widely adopted, although usually not stated. Numerous examples of conventionalized and phrasal expressions that are typically provided tend to present them as "peculiarities" and often include such items as *to take the bull by the horns, a hot potato, bring up, get away with, a penny for your thoughts, at the drop of a hat, back to the drawing board, barking up the wrong tree, beat around the bush, best of both worlds, burn the midnight oil, cost an arm and a leg,* or *can't judge a book by its cover*. In many contexts, learners enjoy English proverbs and sayings due to their oddity and cultural flavor regardless of whether these examples are actually useful in language comprehension or production or whether they are frequent or rare.

In examinations of lexicalized phrases and sentences, it has now been established that conventionalized expressions (e.g. *can I come in?*, *need any help?*, *what's for dinner?*, *call me later*, or *do not block intersection*) are deployed to convey a possibly infinite array of meanings. Another complication is that these language stretches cannot be assembled in the process of communication (Nattinger & DeCarrico, 1992; Pawley & Syder, 1983). A defining characteristic of multiword and formulaic sentence stems is that their meanings and discourse functions cannot be predicted from the meanings of their components, such as words or parts of words (Hinkel, 2004, 2009, 2015).

More importantly, the methodological approach to analyzing language and discourse in terms of lexical sentence stems and idiomatic phrases cannot explain the structure and meanings of conventional and social formulas, idioms, and collocations (sequences of two or more words that are often used together in speech or writing), e.g. *feel free, express bus/train, give an example, give a hand, do homework, break the rules/law, take action, take a chance, take an exam, make a difference/mess/mistake/noise, make an effort, hard left/right, hard rain, heavy coat/sweater/breakfast,* or *light suitcase/meal/workload*). According to some counts, conventionalized phrases, formulaic expressions, collocations, lexical sentence stems, and multiword units number in the hundreds of thousands (Shin & Nation, 2008; Stubbs, 2004).

For second language (L2) learners, conventionalized recurrent phrases and constructions have almost always presented an area of difficulty. For instance, L2 users may misinterpret non-literal meanings of words and phrases, as well as misuse them in various contexts – often due to limitations or shortfalls in their L2 vocabulary. In addition, research has demonstrated that most L2 learners employ constructions that are error-prone and are hardly ever encountered in English spoken or written discourse (Hinkel, 2002, 2003, 2005, 2009). To be sure, in any language, there are probably different ways to say something or convey a thought, but quite often even when the meanings of phrases can be transparent, "the problem is that native speakers do not say it in that way" (Shin & Nation, 2008, p. 340), e.g. **fast wind* or **fall into sleep/love*, instead of *strong wind* or *fall asleep/in love*. In English speech and writing, phrases and expressions are typically culture-specific with implicit references to abstract or metaphorical constructs that may or may not exist in learners' natal cultures or first languages (L1s) (Hinkel, 2014).

By and large, phrases, expressions, and collocations are learned by hearing them being used frequently enough by other speakers or by reading them in various written texts. Multiword constructions are usually encountered in everyday language and acquired in the process of communication, be it oral or written. Specifically, regular, frequent, and common word combinations that occur repeatedly can help learners identify and establish linguistic patterns that can then be stored and accessed in both language reception and production (Arnon & Snider, 2010; Cowie, 1988a, 1998).

This brief preamble takes a look at a few historical perspectives and classifications of idiomatic phrases and expressions in English, as well as their uses in conversations, speaking, writing, and teaching. Because practically all idiomatic and conventionalized phrases are language and culture-specific, their instructional applications can contribute to learners' strategic fluency development. In general terms, teaching idiomatic language components can lead to improvements in learners' receptive and productive skills in various contexts.

Classifications and Definitions

As with practically all complex linguistic phenomena, various types of classifications and organizing schemes have been devised and debated to account for an extremely large body of idioms and conventionalized expressions. In the 1920s, Harold Palmer first addressed the utility of employing ubiquitous phrases and even whole sentences in learning English and developing conversational fluency (Palmer, 1925). According to Palmer's early findings, one of the fastest ways – if not the fastest way – to acquire facility in speaking was to memorize recurrent conversational expressions that could be useful repeatedly. For a beginner, Palmer stated, learning to speak in another language required the essential guiding principle: "Memorize perfectly the largest number of common and useful word groups!" (p. 187).

In his subsequent work, Palmer (1933) identified and classified an enormous number of commonly occurring lexical phases and phraseological units into content- and function-based groups that he called clusters. For the purposes of his pedagogical focus on practical language teaching and learning, Palmer also coined the term *collocation*, which, however, did not receive much notice until the 1950s. His definition of expressions and collocations for teaching (Palmer, 1933, p. 4) was later adopted in many works on idiomatic phrases and has remained foundational to this day: "successions of words [that] must or should be learnt ... as an integral whole or independent entity, rather than by the process of piecing together their component parts."

A seminal and groundbreaking work on idiom structure and meanings was further advanced by Adam Makkai (1972). Makkai divides idioms into major classes: idioms of encoding (or phrasal/lexemic idioms) when their meanings are transparent and deducible, and idioms of decoding, i.e. semantic idioms, with unpredictable meanings. In this taxonomy, poly-morphemic words are categorized as idioms only when at least two free morphemes are present, e.g. *free+way, sea+horse,* or *car+port,* thus making the meanings opaque. On the other hand, the words that consist of free and bound morphemes together are not considered to be idiomatic because they require morphological knowledge and rules to decode their meanings, thus making their meaning more or less componential and deducible. For example, the meanings of such words as *pre+view, im+possible,* or *bi+cycle* that include one free and one bound morpheme can be decoded, even if approximately, based on the meanings of their components. Therefore, these cannot be classified as idiomatic.

One of Makkai's (1972, p. 120) primary classificatory concerns is whether the compound meanings of words and/or their constituents can "potentially mislead" or "misinform" the language user. For instance, in the case of free morpheme compounds, as in *hot+dog, ball+park,* or *straw+berry,* the meanings of the entire words are not deducible. Such frequent and commonly used idioms and phrases are generally not subject to much vari-ability and are considered to be stable expressions "peculiar to a language" (p. 122). In addition, in Makkai's classification, many semantic idioms can be partial or complete sentences with a great number of social and cultural functions, e.g. requests (*would you/do you mind*), warnings (*watch your step*), invitations (*drop by any time*), promises (*I swear!*), and apologies (*so sorry, never again*). These are referred to as cultural idioms with pragmatic meanings.

The rigidity of form is a characteristic of only some, and certainly not all, idiomatic expressions. In fact, Cowie and Mackin's (1975) definition of idioms is probably one of the simplest and most comprehensive: "an idiom is a combination of two or more words which function as a unit of meaning" (pp. viii–ix). Unlike other definitions, Cowie and Mackin do not consider single-word entities idiomatic largely because individual words can be iden-tified, taught, and learned as vocabulary items. When it comes to teaching and learning idiomatic expressions, however, the first order of priority is to figure out their meanings and then to determine whether they are rigid or flexible in their forms, e.g. *take the bull by the horns* or *see you later/tomorrow/ next week/next time.* According to Cowie and Mackin, teaching and learning vocabulary extend beyond single words to longer units of language, from short phrases to complete sentences. To date, dozens of corpus analyses have largely established that, in fact, most idiomatic expressions and multiword units are variable in their forms and, to some extent, in their meanings.

In idiom classifications, phrasal verbs have a prominent place and have deservedly gained much attention. First of all, their numbers are so large that their exact or even proximate counts are unknown. The protracted debates of whether these units should be considered idioms, phrases, or merely extended vocabulary entities have not been resolved, and possibly, will never be (Fernando, 1996; Makkai, 1972, Nation & Webb, 2011). An excellent case in point is that two highly regarded and classic dictionaries published by Cambridge University Press and Oxford University Press, since the 1980s and to this day, have chosen to release dictionary compendia of phrasal verbs as separate volumes to supplement their main dictionaries of English. A key feature of phrasal verb examinations and categorizations is that they have traditionally presented a great deal of difficulty for language learners and, by extension, for teachers and material writers (Boers, 2000; Boers & Lindstromberg, 2008, 2009).

In their pioneering research in the uses of idiomatic phrases, Pawley and Syder (1983) were among the first to draw on large computerized databases of real-life language uses. The goal of the Pawley and Syder study is to solve what they call the "puzzle of native-speaker fluency" (p. 191). The puzzle is that native-speakers can produce and understand language with remarkable fluency and speed in a vast number of contexts and settings without pausing or slowing down. According to these researchers, proficient language users thus demonstrate their "ability to produce fluent stretches of spontaneous connected discourse; there is a puzzle here in that human capacities for encoding novel speech in advance or while speaking appear to be severely limited, yet speakers commonly produce fluent multi-clause utterances which exceed these limits." Based on the findings of their studies, Pawley and Syder conclude that "fluent and idiomatic control of language rests to a considerable extent on knowledge of a body of 'sentence stems' which are 'institutionalized' or 'lexicalized.'" Sentence stems are idiomatic and phraseological units of language in which grammatical form and meaning are largely fixed. The fixed elements in fact represent culturally or pragmatically recognized idiomatic expressions, concepts, and phrases.

Investigative reports on the uses of recurrent and frequent idiomatic phrases and units emerged in force in the 1990s and 2000s. In this body of research, such units are variously called chunks, clusters, clichés, collocations, extended lexical units, formulas, formulaic expressions/strings/language, idioms, idiomatic expressions, fixed phrases/strings, lexicalized sentence stems, phrasemes, phraseologisms, phraseological units, phrasal lexical items, phrasal lexemes, or prefabricated (or prefab) chunks/constructions (Cowie, 1988, 1992; Coxhead, 2008; Howarth, 1996, 1998). The main reason for the increased attention to these phrases and expressions has to do primarily with the proliferations of electronic language corpora that have allowed for identifying and quantifying recurrent combinations of words and phrases that occur in real language production.

Although there is probably no single encompassing definition of idioms, idiomatic expressions, collocations, phrases, and lexicalized stems typically include:

- Frequently recurring and culture-specific expressions with opaque meanings (e.g. *cost an arm and a leg, call it a day, better late than never,* or *in this light*)
- Collocations, i.e. words that often occur together but with flexible and variable components (e.g. *take place/part/a test/a break, ready to go/start/ close* [verb], *easy to learn, give advice/suggestion(s), at a discount/receive a discount, hard-earned money/hard-won success/victory*)
- Fixed phrases with specific and well-defined meanings, as well as phrasal verbs (e.g. *break in/out/down/up/into, in the lurch, out of place, back door, price increase/decrease, high/low price, a full plate*)
- Figurative expressions (such as metaphors) (e.g. *the world is my oyster, couch potato, heart of gold, heart of stone, melting pot, you are my sunshine, the more the merrier, not on your life, stand out like a sore thumb*)
- Conversational routines and pre-patterned speech
  (e.g. – *Excuse me, could you tell me where xxx is?*
  – *Up the stairs on your left.*
  – *I am sorry I am late.* – *No problem/No worries.*
  – *What a beautiful day!* – *Finally, some sunshine.*
  We've had a lot of rain lately.

- Set and rigidly ordered phrases (in which components are fixed in a certain <u>order</u>) (e.g. *here we go, will that be all?, is there something else?, by car/train/bus, by mail, washing machine, table cloth, silver spoon, stay/be out of sight, be at one's wits' end, ahead of time, what in the world*)

- Proverbs (e.g. *two wrongs don't make a right, the squeaky wheel gets the grease, better late than never, no man is an island*)
- Culturally-bound sayings (e.g. *a fish out of water, right as rain, count chickens before they hatch, not my cup of tea, the pen is mightier than the sword, Rome wasn't built in a day*)

Without question, the definitions of idioms, collocations, and phrasal expressions vary in different schools of thought. However, the accepted basic concept is that they are multiword units of language – words that are connected to other words – that are remembered and used as single lexical (vocabulary) items (Nation, 2013; Peters, 1983).

Idiomatic Expressions in Speaking and Conversations

Learning to understand and produce spoken language means being able to understand how language components combine and interact to produce meaning and discourse (Nattinger & DeCarrico, 1992). L2 learners need to become skilled users of vocabulary, phrases, and syntactic constructions. They need to build their spoken discourse repertoire in order to participate in conversations, formal and casual alike.

Participating in conversations requires engaging in a range of complex cognitive and linguistic tasks. In social settings, uses of language convey personal views and attitudes, as well as social values and relationships, and communicative goals (Carbaugh, 2007; Hinkel, 2014; Nation, 2008, 2009). Conversations are highly structured exchanges that progress along predictable and routine patterns, with participants adapting, adjusting and readjusting, and tailoring what they are saying – or going to say – depending on the social setting and flow of discourse. In the course of a conversation, participants' speech has to remain reasonably grammatically and phonetically intelligible, culturally structured and organized (e.g. turn-taking), cohesive, well-paced (e.g. openings, pauses, and closings), socially and contextually pertinent, and appropriately worded, e.g. politeness (Carbaugh, 2005; Carter & McCarthy, 1995, 2006; Durrant, 2014).

In idiom classifications going as far back as back the 1920s, various sets of recurrent and conventionalized phrases are typically classified by their communicative functions, such as greetings, requests, apologies, or invitations. Most proficient and fluent language users know that conversational exchanges are conventionalized and routinized, and they are able to employ idiomatic expressions at particular junctures in the speech flow to achieve their communicative goals (Coulmas, 1981). Spoken routines and idiomatic sequences can be utilized in an extraordinary range of functional contexts and for a practically unlimited variety of communicative and social purposes (Swan, 2006; Ur, 2014). However, in addition to being able to deploy conversational expressions appropriately and in context, language users need to be able to grasp the speaker's purpose. If the conversational function is not identified correctly, then the communicative goal may not be achieved (Cowie, 1992; Fernando, 1996).

Based on extensive analyses of social interactions, many analysts have definitively concluded that it is not just conversational idioms, expressions, and responses to them that are highly conventionalized, but also, by their very nature, social interactions "employ a number of standardized and stereotyped procedures" that mark and characterize them (Nattinger & DeCarrico, 1992, p. 114).

A vast body of research on interactional language uses has demonstrated unambiguously that conversational language and discourse are highly routinized and formulaic. Some studies have found, for example, that in casual conversations most exchanges are prefabricated and extremely stereotyped (Aijmer, 1996; Coulmas, 1981; Levinson, 1983). For example, in their investigation of spoken and conversational interactions, Carter and McCarthy (1995, 2006) identified an enormous array of conversational and pragmatic formulas and phrases that are continually adjusted to suit specific discourse and social contexts.

Numerous research reports have determined that much language acquisition, be it first or second, entails the acquisition of conventionalized expressions and repeated routines. In the short-term, repetition and rehearsal serve to promote the development of longer-term sequence retention and eventual language acquisition (Milton, 1998, 1999; Yorio, 1989). Teaching and learning spoken and conversational sequences and idiomatic formula requires frequent opportunities for repeated practice. This is especially true with regard to most phrases and combinations that tend to present areas of difficulty for learners (e.g. phrasal verbs, *make*-collocations and *get*-passives, as in *get married/it done*).

Idiomatic and Conventionalized Expressions in Writing

In English, what is appropriate and inappropriate in writing and written discourse is similarly highly conventionalized. In much language teaching, a great deal of attention, time, and resources are devoted to fostering learners' facility with various types of writing, and particularly so academic writing. Typically, academic writing instruction focuses on such fundamental features of written academic discourse as the idea organization and information flow (e.g., introduction, body, and conclusion), the presence and the placement of the thesis statement, and the structure of the paragraph (e.g., the topic sentence). In research on academic writing, many conventional and highly predictable phrases that mark discourse junctures are called "institutionalized" because they occur more frequently in certain types of texts than in others (Howarth, 1998; Pawley & Syder, 1983; Swales, 1990).

In the production of written academic prose, using conventionalized expressions and portions of sentences, is not a language skill that is innate in L1 users and writers. Nor is academic writing a universal ability that most (or even many) L1 writers come by in the course of their daily life. Learning to write academic texts comes about in the process of schooling and education. Both L1 and L2 academic writers have to acquire an extensive repertoire of language skills, such as idea structuring, grammar, and vocabulary. It is widely recognized in language research and pedagogy that developing academic writing abilities takes many years – and sometimes longer than a decade (Cowie, 1988; Hinkel, 2002, 2003, 2009, 2011; James, 1998). A vast amount of evidence has shown that L2 academic writers have a great deal of difficulty becoming proficient users of idioms and institutionalized phrases, without which formal written prose probably cannot be produced (Coxhead, 2008).

At present, much is known about idiomatic constructions essential in L1 and L2 academic writing, such as noun phrases (e.g. *recent discussions/debates/reports/publications ..., an important fact/issue/consideration is ..., a close/detailed examination/study ...*), or impersonal *it*-constructions (e.g. *it is well-known/likely/possible/unclear*). Additionally, considerable experience has been accumulated in how to teach various idiomatic sentence stems, conventionalized expressions, "long chunks" of text (Swales, 1990; Swales & Feak, 2012). These attributes of academic writing need to be explicitly and persistently taught because they represent requisite (and prescribed) characteristics of the Anglo–American academic genre (Fernando, 1996; Milton, 1999). For example, even educated L2 learners who do not have many opportunities to produce formal English prose may not be aware of formulaic expressions that usually mark explicit thesis statements, such as *this paper addresses/examines/focuses on ...* or *the main points/questions/issues are ...*).

In writing instruction, working with conventionalized written expressions can take the form of text and paragraph models and examples of paragraphs and essays to demonstrate their idiomatic elements. For instance, academic phrases can be useful in instruction on such discourse functions as to express a point of view, support a position, develop an argument, or present a research finding. The stereotypical language of academic and other types of writing represents a relatively well-covered set of discourse moves and their attendant phrasing (Hinkel, 2013; Swales, 1990; Ur, 2011, 2014; Widdowson, 2003).

Idiomatic Expressions and Language Teaching

Despite the attention that idiomatic expressions and phrases have received in research, in teaching materials these units of language are still relatively less commonplace than, say, vocabulary and grammar. Due to their frequency in both spoken and written language, idiomatic formulas and repeated word-combinations can be of great value to learners at practically any level of proficiency (Aijmer, 1996; Nation & Webb, 2011). One essential feature of expressions and phrases is that they include more than one word or a mean-ingful unit, and for this reason alone, they require more work and practice. Over time, however, explicit teaching can help learners to address matters of lexical retention and to expand their language repertoire. As Nattinger and Decarrico (1992, p. 32) state, "it is our ability to use lexical phrases that helps us to speak with fluency. This prefabricated speech has both the advantages of more efficient retrieval and of permitting speakers (and learners) to direct their attention to the larger structure of the discourse, rather than keeping it narrowly focused on individual words as they are produced."

Numerous idiomatic phrases can be accessible to beginning or inter-mediate learners. As has been mentioned, most idioms and conventionalized phrases have non-compositional meanings that cannot be derived from those of their constituent parts. However, frequent and common expressions can be somewhat transparent. When it comes to formulas and collocations, a reliable rule of thumb is that the shorter the phrase is, the more likely it is to be easy to remember and use (Boers, 2000; Boers & Lindstromberg, 2008, 2009; Nation, Shin, & Grant, 2016). The best examples of transparent and memorable units are those that consist of two words. This principle applies to formulaic phrases of practically any kind, including those that consist of a function word and a content word or two content words.

Another important consideration for teaching is that short collocations and phrases are encountered far more frequently than longer ones, and thus can be easier to practice. Examples of frequent phrases and expressions can be located anywhere:

> *go fishing/shopping/hiking, take turns, have breakfast/lunch/dinner, pay attention, good day, make/spend money, catch a bus/train/flight, once a week, once in a while, day and night, all day long, every time, well said, right on the mark, hard work, (right) on time, make a mistake, find/take a seat, do a favor, help out, a little help, do you mind, good luck, bar of soap/chocolate, candy bar,* and *hit or miss.*

Another useful type of practice can take the form of identifying suitable responses to conventionalized conversational expressions with other appropriate conventionalized expressions. For instance, a teacher can create a worksheet – or several worksheets – with practical and common suitable responses. Learners can practice matching routine questions or statements to possible responses, e.g. – *Your sweater is beautiful,* and possible responses: (a) – *Thank you, I like it too,* (b) – *It was on sale, and it wasn't expensive,* or (c) – *You can have it, so please accept it as a gift.*

A Final Note

A fundamental fact in regard to chunks, collocations, phrases, expressions, multiword units, formulas, formulaic language, sentence stems, lexicalized constructions, chunks, lexical bundles, idioms, prefabricated routines, or clusters by any other name is that they are ubiquitous, pervasive, and astoundingly frequent. In language teaching and learning, they are essential. For most learners, the meanings of these constructions are usually impossible to figure out from the meanings of their component parts. The grammar features of most idiomatic phrases are irregular and un-derivable, and their logical analyses defy linguistic reason. Without learning, using, and being able to understand these language units, neither spoken nor written communication can be effective or even successful in accomplishing its goals.

Currently, a relatively large number of spoken and written conventionalized expressions have been collected, catalogued, and systematized. In language pedagogy, a clear implication is that teaching grammar and vocabulary is likely to be more complicated than working with syntactic rules and single-word items. Old and new insights associated with the sheer ubiquity of idiomatic constructions can present both challenges and opportunities, but it seems vital for teachers to be aware of and become familiar with these language units.

Note

1 An earlier version of this paper appeared in 2017 in the *Iranian Journal of Language Teaching Research*, 5/3, 45–59.

References

Aijmer, K. (1996). *Conversational routines in English: Conversation and creativity*. London: Longman.

Arnon, I., & Snider, N. (2010). More than words: Frequency effects for multi-word phrases. *Journal of Memory and Language, 62*, 67–82.

Boers, F., & Lindstromberg, S. (2008). From empirical findings to pedagogical practice. In F. Boers, & S. Lindstromberg (Eds.), *Cognitive linguistic approaches to teaching vocabulary and phraseology* (pp. 375–393). The Hague: Mouton.

Boers, F., & Lindstromberg, S. (2009). *Optimizing a lexical approach to instructed second language acquisition*. Basingstoke, UK: Palgrave Macmillan.

Boers, F. (2000). Metaphor awareness and vocabulary retention. *Applied Linguistics, 21*, 553–571.

Carbaugh, D. (2005). *Cultures in conversation*. New York, NY: Routledge.

Carbaugh, D. (2007). Cultural discourse analysis: Communication practices and intercultural encounters. *Journal of Intercultural Communication Research, 36*, 167–182.

Carter, R., & McCarthy, M. (1995). Grammar and the spoken language. *Applied Linguistics, 16*, 141–158.

Carter, R., & McCarthy, M. (2006). *Cambridge grammar of English*. Cambridge: Cambridge University Press.

Coulmas, F. (1981). *Conversational routines*. The Hague: Mouton.

Cowie, A. (1998). *Phraseology: Theory, analysis, and applications*. Oxford: Oxford University Press.

Cowie, A., & Mackin, R. (1975). *Oxford dictionary of current idiomatic English, Vol. 1*. Oxford: Oxford University Press.

Cowie, A. (1988). Stable and creative aspects of vocabulary use. In R. Carter, & M. McCarthy (Eds.), *Vocabulary and language teaching* (pp. 126–137). Harlow: Longman.

Cowie, A. (1992). Multiword lexical units and communicative language teaching. In P. Arnaud, & H. Bejoint (Eds.), *Vocabulary and applied linguistics* (pp. 1–12). London: Macmillan.

Coxhead, A. (2008). Phraseology and English for academic purposes. In F. Meunier, & S. Granger (Eds.), *Phraseology in language learning and teaching* (pp. 149–161). Amsterdam: John Benjamins.

Durrant, P. (2014). Corpus frequency and second language learners' knowledge of collocations: A meta–analysis. *International Journal of Corpus Linguistics,* 19, 443–477.

Fernando, C. (1996). *Idioms and idiomaticity.* Oxford: Oxford University Press.

Fillmore, C., Kay, P., & O'Connor, M. (1988). Regularity and idiomaticity in grammatical constructions: The case of let alone. *Language,* 64, 501–538.

Hinkel, E. (2002). *Second language writers' text.* New York, NY: Routledge.

Hinkel, E. (2003). Simplicity without elegance: Features of sentences in L2 and L1 academic texts. *TESOL Quarterly,* 37, 275–301.

Hinkel, E. (2004). *Teaching academic ESL writing: Practical techniques in vocabulary and grammar.* New York, NY: Routledge.

Hinkel, E. (2005). Analyses of L2 text and what can be learned from them. In E. Hinkel (Ed.), *Handbook of research in second language teaching and learning* (pp. 615–628). New York, NY: Routledge.

Hinkel, E. (2009). The effect of essay prompts and topics on the uses of modal verbs in L1 and L2 academic writing. *Journal of Pragmatics,* 41(4), 667–683.

Hinkel, E. (2011). What research on second language writing tells us and what it doesn't. In E. Hinkel (Ed.), *Handbook of research in second language teaching and learning,* vol. 2 (pp. 523–538). New York, NY: Routledge.

Hinkel, E. (2015). *Effective curriculum for teaching L2 writing: Principles and techniques.* New York, NY: Routledge.

Hinkel, E. (2013). Cultures of learning and writing in the US academy. In L. Jin, & M. Cortazzi (Eds.), *Researching intercultural learning: Investigations in language and education* (pp. 21–35). New York, NY: Palgrave Macmillan.

Hinkel, E. (2014). Culture and pragmatics in second language teaching and learning. In M. Celce-Murcia, D. Brinton, & M. Snow (Eds.), *Teaching English as a second or foreign language* (4th ed., pp. 394–408). Boston, MA: National Geographic Learning.

Howarth, P. (1996). *Phraseology in English academic writing: Some implications for language learning and dictionary making.* Tübingen: Max Niemeyer.

Howarth, P. (1998). Phraseology and second language proficiency. *Applied Linguistics,* 19(1), 24–44.

James, C. (1998). *Errors in language learning and use.* London: Longman.

Kay, P., & Fillmore, C. (1999). Grammatical constructions and linguistic generalizations: The "what's X doing Y?" construction. *Language,* 75, 1–33.

Levinson, S. (1983). *Pragmatics.* Cambridge: Cambridge University Press.

Makkai, A. (1972). *Idiom structure in English.* The Hague: Mouton.

Milton, J. (1998). Exploiting L1 and interlanguage corpora in the design of an electronic language learning and production environment. In S. Granger (Ed.), *Learner English on computer* (pp. 186–198). London; New York, NY: Longman.

Milton, J. (1999). Lexical thickets and electronic gateways: making text accessible by novice writers. In C. Candlin, & K. Hyland (Eds.), *Writing: texts, processes and practices* (pp. 221–243). London; New York, NY: Longman.

Nation, P., & Webb, S. (2011). Content-based instruction and vocabulary learning. In E. Hinkel (Ed.), *Handbook of research in second language teaching and learning, Vol. 2* (pp. 631–644). New York, NY: Routledge.

Nation, P. (2008). *Teaching vocabulary.* Boston, MA: Heinle & Heinle.

Nation, P. (2009). *Teaching ESL/EFL reading and writing.* New York, NY: Routledge.

Nation, P. (2013). *Learning vocabulary in another language* (2nd ed.). Cambridge: Cambridge University Press.

Nation, P., Shin, D., & Grant, L. (2016). Multiword units. In P. Nation (Ed.), *Making and using word lists for language learning and testing* (pp. 71–79). Amsterdam: John Benjamins.

Nattinger, J., & DeCarrico, J. (1992). *Lexical phrases and language teaching.* Oxford: Oxford University Press.

Palmer, H. (1925). Conversation. In R. C. Smith (Ed.), (1999) *The writings of Harold E. Palmer: An overview* (pp. 185–191). Tokyo: Hon-no-Tomosha.

Palmer, H. (1933). *Second interim report on English collocations.* Tokyo: Kaitakusha.

Pawley, A., & Syder, F. (1983). Two puzzles for linguistic theory: Nativelike selection and nativelike fluency. In J. Richards and R. Schmidt (Eds.), *Language and communication* (pp. 191–225). London: Longman.

Peters, A. (1983). *The units of language acquisition.* Cambridge: Cambridge University Press.

Shin, D., & Nation, P. (2008). Beyond single words: The most frequent collocations in spoken English. *English Language Teaching Journal,* 62 (4), 339–348.

Stubbs, M. (2004). Corpus-assisted text and corpus analysis: Lexical cohesion and communicative competence. In D. Schiffrin, D. Tannen, & H. E. Hamilton (Eds.), *The handbook of discourse analysis* (pp. 304–320). Oxford: Blackwell.

Swales, J., & Feak, C. (2012). *Academic writing for graduate students* (3rd ed.). Ann Arbor: The University of Michigan Press.

Swales, J. (1990). *Genre analysis.* Cambridge: Cambridge University Press.

Swan M. (2006). Chunks in the classroom: Let's not go overboard. *Teacher Trainer,* 20, 5–6.

Ur, P. (2011). Grammar teaching: Research, theory and practice. In E. Hinkel (Ed.), *Handbook of research in second language teaching and learning,* vol. 2 (pp. 507–522). New York, NY: Routledge.

Ur, P. (2014). Practice and research-based theory in English teacher development. *The European Journal of Applied Linguistics and TEFL,* 3(2), 143–155.

Widdowson, H. (2003). *Defining issues in English language teaching.* Oxford: Oxford University Press.

Wilkins, D. (1972). *Linguistics in language teaching.* London: Edward Arnold.

Yorio, C. (1989). Idiomaticity as an indicator of second language proficiency. In K. Hyltenstam, & L. Obler (Eds.), *Bilingualism across the lifespan* (pp. 55–72). Cambridge: Cambridge University Press.

Part I
KEY CONSIDERATIONS

Chapter 1

Teaching Multiword Units
A Teacher's Perspective

Penny Ur

Multiword Units: Definitions and Distinctions

The term *multiword unit* refers to a sequence of words that is retrieved from memory and perceived or produced as a single chunk. Such a unit may consist of only two words (e.g. *take care*), or several (e.g. *on the other hand*); it may form an entire sentence (e.g. *all roads lead to Rome.*). For the purposes of this chapter, the term includes not only units that function as lexical items, but also phrases or sentences that occur very frequently in spoken or written communication and therefore are commonly perceived or produced as a single unit (e.g. *I don't know*). It also includes units that may appear in variant grammatical forms (e.g. *take into account, took into account, haven't taken into account* etc.)

An associated concept is *collocation*: the tendency of certain words to associate with certain other words in discourse, but not necessarily next to one another: for example, the adjective *rapid* with the noun *change* in a sentence like *The changes were rapid and dramatic* (compare: *the changes were speedy/ quick/fast and dramatic*). When a particular collocation frequently appears as a sequence of adjacent words (e.g. *rapid change*, see later in this chapter), it may be identified as a multiword unit.

Multiword units have been classified in various ways. One distinction is between "transparent" and "opaque" units, sometimes called "compositional" and "non-compositional": the first relating to those which could be understood from knowing the component words (like *at all times*), and the second those which could not (like *at all*) (Martinez & Schmitt, 2012). They have also been categorized in terms of what function they fulfill in a sentence or utterance: for example, whether they simply convey referential meaning (e.g. *wage war on, try out*), whether they have a discourse function (*to cut a long story short*), or convey the speaker's attitude (*I'm afraid, if I may*). Sometimes certain types of units are grouped according to their structural features: phrasal verbs like *give up*, for example, or binomials like *more or less*. All these types of multiword units need to be learned. They are not normally to be presented for the first time as sets within any of the categories described above (see further discussion of this point below, at the end of the section **In the Classroom 1**), but rather as they come up in context and are perceived to be useful to teach. The distinctions and categories, however, are useful to the teacher, and may help to support teaching decisions. For example, the non-compositional ones (whose meaning could not be guessed from their component words) will need more careful explanation than the compositional.

The Importance of Teaching Multiword Units

Vocabulary

The learning of multiword units is important for the language learner primarily because most of them function as lexical items in their own right, in the same way as single words do; few today would dispute the place of vocabulary as the crucial factor in language acquisition.

The number of single-word lexical items that a student needs in order to understand natural oral discourse has been estimated at between 5,000 and 7,000 word families; and even more (8,000 to 9,000) for unsimplified written text (Schmitt, 2008). If we assume that multiword items account for between a half and a third of natural discourse (Conklin & Schmitt, 2012), then the number of these that need to be mastered is also formidable, even taking into account the fact that many of them are compositional, and will be understood – though not necessarily produced – through knowledge of the component words. Moreover, research has shown fairly conclusively that learners within an instructional setting of three to four hours a week where English is not normally encountered outside the classroom cannot acquire even the smaller numbers of items indicated above through incidental encounter during extensive reading or listening (Huckin & Coady, 1999; Laufer, 2005; Brown & Waring, 2008). It is necessary, therefore, to supplement such incidental learning through a substantial amount of deliberate classroom teaching of both single- and multiword items.

Basic multiword units such as *of course, look for* are common and convey meanings that could not be guessed through knowledge of the component words, so should be taught in the same way as single words. Unfortunately, vocabulary lists in coursebooks still tend to focus on single words, as do traditional frequency lists of lexical items such as the General Service List (West & West, 1953), or even more modern corpus-based ones such as the Academic Word List (Coxhead, 2000), or the Academic Vocabulary List (Gardner & Davies, 2013). In most cases today, the identification and teaching of multiword units are the responsibility of the teacher.

There are, however, more reasons, besides general vocabulary acquisition, why it is important to teach these items.

Fluency

In a seminal article, Pawley and Syder (1983) suggested the idea, now widely accepted, that the use of memorized sequences is the basis of native-like fluency in a language. They included in their definition of "memorized sequences" not only lexical items such as those suggested above, but also – and mainly – common lexicalized sentences or stems such as *Will you marry me? (be) sorry to …, I don't think …* Clearly, such sequences could be composed by a learner by fitting single words into a grammatical structure according to rules, but there are two reasons why this would lower fluency. First, it takes a lot longer to formulate a sentence by choosing single words and then working out what the correct grammatical form and sequence should be than it does to retrieve a single memorized sequence. Second, the ready-made sequence is likely to be idiomatic and commonly used, and therefore more easily processed by the listener or reader. To take a simple example: the conventional question "What's the time?" could also be expressed as "What's the hour?", "Which is the hour?", "How late is it?" and so on, as it is in other languages; but the learner needs to know how it is conventionally expressed in English in order to function fluently in conversation.

Grammatical Accuracy

Many multiword units display grammatical features, and could be analyzed according to a grammatical rule: *I don't know*, for example, or *if I were you*. The first is the negative form of the present simple, using the auxiliary *do*; the second is a "second conditional" with a subjunctive form of the verb *be*. But why bother working it out? The first is the conventional way of conveying that you are ignorant of something, the second a preface to a suggestion: and these are the meanings we need to explain as we teach them. However, the fact that they are exemplars of regular grammatical features of the language is a bonus: it means that they provide the learner with reliable models of that feature which they can later use, by analogy, as a basis to build similar utterances themselves. The sentence *I don't know*, for example, can help the learner perceive and formulate other correct combinations like *I don't eat, I don't go, I don't mean* …, without needing to ponder over the use of the auxiliary *do* in a negative present simple: they simply "sound right". There is some evidence that young learners of their first language process memorized sequences in this way: they learn them first as global "chunks", and only later are able to understand that these actually have a regular structure which can be used in composing further similar utterances (Tomasello, 2003).

This is not to imply that grammatical rules as such do not need to be taught and practiced. Learners who are taught English through a limited number of hours' instruction a week in a country where English is little used outside the classroom do not have the exposure time necessary in order to encounter the huge number of exemplars that would enable them to acquire an intuitive knowledge of grammatical forms through communicative input only. They need the short cut that is provided by conscious knowledge and application of explicit rules. The learning of multiword sequences that exemplify a grammatical feature complements the intellectual grasp of the rule, and helps move the learner faster towards an intuitive feel for what is acceptable.

Motivation

Beginner learners do not have to wait to express themselves in English until after they have acquired a basic vocabulary of single words and the rules that enable them to put these together to make meanings. If they master a repertoire of basic interactional expressions early on, they will be quickly enabled to express ideas fluently and accurately in English: a huge boost to motivation ("Hey, look at me, I'm already speaking English!"). Some of the ways students can be helped to acquire such a repertoire are presented below under **Simple Oral Repetition.**

Classroom Management

This is perhaps a minor issue compared to the ones discussed above, but nevertheless worth noting, particularly in the context of beginner classes. Multiword units used for classroom management include both teacher commands, comments or questions such as "Open your books at page …", "Well done!", "Do you understand?", or "Are you ready?" and common student utterances such as "I don't understand", "How do you say … in English?", or "Please say it again". Such items need to be taught from the very early stages, particularly for multilingual classes. Many teachers teaching in monolingual classes where they share their students' mother tongue use the L1 for such classroom-management language, and in some situations this may be inevitable. But in general, teaching and thereafter using regularly such phrases in any class will enable the teacher to run the lesson in English and is likely to lead to learning of some useful interactive language.

Selection

A crucial consideration for the classroom teacher is time use: what has been called *academic learning time* (Gettinger & Seibert, 2002). In a situation where students have limited opportunities to encounter English outside the class-room, we need to use the limited lesson periods – usually no more than four hours a week, often less – as productively as possible, to produce optimal language learning outcomes. Even if students spend a similar amount of time studying out of class, there is no way, within these constraints, that we can teach them all the items we would like them to learn: we need to select the ones that are most important.

Frequency

The obvious first criterion for selection of which multiword units to teach is how frequently they occur in natural written and spoken communication:

in principle, the more common the item, the more important it is for learners to master it. Coursebooks that include multiword units in their lists of items to be learnt do not, on the whole, select these on the basis of frequency (Koprowski, 2005). However, some work has been done in recent years which can help the teacher select: for example, the corpus-based lists published by Martinez and Schmitt (2012), Liu (2003, 2012), Hsu (2014), and Garnier and Schmitt (2015). There are also useful websites, such as the *English Vocabulary Profile*, based on the Cambridge English Corpus (http://vocabulary.englishprofile.org/staticfiles/about.html). If you enter a key headword, the website will give you common multiword units that include it, classified according to the Common European Framework of Reference for Languages (CEFR) levels (A1, A2 etc.). *Just the Word*, based on the British National Corpus (www.just-the-word.com/), fulfills a similar function, but classifies the multiword units by frequency rather than by CEFR levels.

However, some of these are far from comprehensive: Martinez and Schmitt, for example, target mainly non-compositional items, and Liu's lists are based on specific types of discourse. In any case, no general frequency list can be entirely appropriate for a specific student population. The information derived from sources can be very helpful, but will need to be supplemented by the teacher's own professional judgement and familiarity with the student population and culture.

Simplicity

It makes sense to choose the simpler and shorter items for teaching before the more complex, longer ones. Basically, the easier the item the quicker it is learnt, and therefore the more we can manage to teach. So the shorter, more easily pronounced and spelt items, with meanings that correspond to those of lexical items in the students' first language (Chen & Truscott, 2010), are likely to be better and more quickly learned than the longer and more complex ones.

Relevance

Another criterion is the relevance of the item for the particular group of students. For example, expressions like *play a game, what's your favorite ..., it's my turn* may be useful for a group of younger learners, less so for older ones. A teacher of a class of students learning English for academic purposes, in contrast, may want to prioritize phrases they can use in academic papers such as *in conclusion, as a consequence (of)*; whereas in a course of English for specific purposes – for example, business English, or English for tourism – he or she will include those that are specific and relevant to the field. A particular type of relevance is that which relates to the instructional environment, as mentioned above under **Classroom Management.** It makes sense to teach multiword items that are useful aids to communication during a lesson, such as *get into groups*, even though in general discourse these may not be particularly common.

The above criteria, taken together, provide a useful set of "default" guidelines for selection, but are not to be applied too strictly. There will inevitably be situations where the teacher may find he or she wishes to teach an infrequent, less relevant or more difficult item: because it is essential for understanding a text, for example, or because a student has encountered it by chance and wants to know what it means.

In the Classroom 1: Introducing New Items

In Context

Most of the multiword units taught in the classroom will be derived from reading texts. Coursebooks may provide recommended vocabulary lists following, or preceding, a reading text, but, as mentioned above, multiword units may not appear in them. Even if they do – and modern materials designers are increasingly aware of the need to include them – there may well be ones that an individual teacher would like students to learn that are omitted. It is important, therefore, for the teacher to go through the text looking for these items and noting ones that it might be useful to teach.

As an example, here is an extract from a textbook for intermediate students:

> Journalism is rapidly changing in the digital age. Not so long ago, printed newspapers were the biggest source of daily news. But the Internet has changed all that. Nowadays, the majority of people read the news online – anywhere, at any time of the day or night, and often for free.

However, this relatively new development is not good news for every-body. In fact, many people in the newspaper industry are extremely worried about their future employment. Because of decreased sales, newspapers are cutting back on staff. 'We cannot compete with online newspapers.'

(Ben Zion & Saferstein, 2017, p. 119)

Which multiword units would you identify here for teaching to a class of intermediate-level students?

Certainly you would include ones that are clearly lexical items like *long ago, the majority of, for free, cut back (on), in fact*. Less obvious, but arguably equally useful to identify and teach are phrases such as *rapidly changing* (and its more common form *rapid change*), *daily news, all that, relatively new, worried about, cannot compete with*.

Less commonly, we may encounter useful new multiword units that come up in the context of a communicative task, or that we use in inter-action with the class. It is more difficult to catch and notice such items as they fly past in the stream of speech than it is to locate them in a written text – but often useful to do so, and may result in memorable learning. For example, when giving student teachers some tips on classroom management and discipline recently, I heard myself say "Make them an offer they can't refuse". Clearly this is a quote from *The Godfather* (Puzo, 1969), but one that has passed into popular usage and is arguably worth learning.

Out of Context

Not all new language taught in a formal course of study is necessarily first encountered in a spoken or written context. There is value to introducing multiword units on their own, just as there is value to teaching single words on their own, to be practiced later in appropriate contexts.

One useful procedure is "Word of the day": a new word taught for a minute or two, perhaps at the beginning of the lesson, or in a natural break between activities, for the students to note down and think of ways of using. This can be expanded to include multiword items: an excellent way to help students accumulate a vocabulary of common proverbs, for example, or useful idioms. Similarly, students can be asked to find useful new phrases and share them with the class.

Another procedure which can be used for individual assignments rather than in-class work is to invite learners to look up a known word in the dictionary, and find out what multiword units are associated with it. These can then be listed and shared with the rest of the class. A thesaurus can be used the same way: a word can be looked up to find which multiword units express similar, or opposite, concepts.

Note that when teaching new multiword units out of context it is tempting to teach whole lists of similar items at the same time, such as a set of phrasal verbs based on the same root verb (e.g. *get up, get off, get into, get around, get down, get at, get in, get away with*). This may not, however, facilitate learning. Research has shown that teaching lexical sets for the first time is counterproductive (Erten & Tekin, 2008; Papathanasiou, 2009; Tinkham, 1993; Waring, 1998; Wilcoz & Mednab, 2013); and the same underlying rationale (interference theory) probably applies to the teaching of any group of new items simultaneously that might be confused with one another. Grouping by general theme, however – items that would co-occur in a natural context of communication – may be helpful (Tinkham, 1993). It would seem a good idea, therefore, to select multiword units together with single-word items that all would appear in a given situation or connected with a given theme – as naturally occurs when we teach items from a text.

In the Classroom 2: Consolidation

Much research, as well as teaching common sense, supports the claim that just teaching a new item once in an English course does not ensure its mastery by the learners: it needs to be encountered a number of times (Webb, 2007). Quite how many times will depend on the difficulty of the form and/or meaning of the item, the level and ability of the learner and, perhaps most significantly, on the quality of the encounters (Laufer & Roitblat, 2015). So what we are looking at here is classroom techniques that encourage students to engage repeatedly with the target items, preferably within different contexts, using activities that will engage their attention and lead to optimal learning.

Simple Oral Repetition

As mentioned above, it is important for beginner learners to accumulate a vocabulary of multiword units to help them express themselves fluently in basic conversations as soon as possible. They need to start learning *dialogues*.

One way to facilitate this is simply to require them to learn by heart common interactive expressions like *Hello, I'm sorry, thank you, you're welcome, see you later,* as well as common exchanges such as *How are you? + Fine, thank you, What's the time? + It's … o'clock, Would you like …? Yes, please / No, thank you,* … and so on.

Performing dialogues such as these may be boring, but it is important for students to master them and "own" them so that they will be able to produce them fluently when needed. Repetition is necessary, and it is up to the teacher to find ways of making it interesting. For example, students may be invited to perform a "chain" of asking and answering round the class, and then challenged to perform the same chain as fast as possible, while the teacher times them and later announces the result.

The next stage is to teach less conventional dialogues that imply some kind of humorous or dramatic interaction but include useful multiword units. Here is a favorite of my own, adapted from Raz (1968):

A: Come here at once!
B: Who, me?
A: Yes, you. Come here at once!
B: What's the matter?
A: Be quiet!

The teacher needs, of course, to make sure the language is understood and performed with meaningful emphasis and expression, not just parroted.

Clearly, such dialogues are most appropriate for younger learners, but can be used also with older ones. Humor can be added by requiring students to perform the dialogue very fast, or very slowly; or sadly, angrily, happily, fearfully, etc. Amusing variations like this do not just add motivation: they provide a reason to repeat, consolidate, and make the language memorable. Unfortunately, many dialogues presented as models of useful language in learning materials tend to be somewhat bland, lacking in either humor or drama; in many cases the teacher of elementary classes will need to make up his or her own, or to give the conventional dialogues a "twist" to make them more interesting.

An alternative to the dialogue is the *chant*: a rhythmic recitation of multiword units that come together to make a pleasing monologue or dialogue. Again, this is used mostly with younger classes, but not only. The following is an extract from a chant used with younger classes (upper-case shows stress):

> CAN you COME, CAN you COME?
> NO, i CAN'T, i'm BUSy

The technique has become popular largely through Carolyn Graham's work on jazz chants (see www.youtube.com/watch?v=sotUp32mpOI, and Graham, 2006).

Poems and *songs* can also be learnt by heart and recited or sung. These are enjoyable, but on the whole less effective than dialogues or chants for the purpose of consolidating language knowledge. The text may be less natural, since in songs and most poems the wording may be constrained by the need to conform to a particular metre or rhyme-scheme, and authentic songs or poems of literary value are likely to be too difficult for pre-advanced classes. I have also found that although students enjoy learning and singing songs, this is largely because they just enjoy singing a good tune, and their attention is often not focused on the meaning of the words.

Meaningful repetition of multiword units, however, does not necessarily have to be based on text that has been learnt by heart: it can be done based on reading. In the technique known as *reader's theater*, students rehearse and then read aloud their "parts" from plays or scenes. This is normally seen as a means of promoting reading fluency and, indirectly, spoken fluency as well. However, the same technique can in fact be used with any text, and has the effect of familiarizing students with both the form and meaning of the given passage. A passage is selected: it could be from a regular reading text from the coursebook which includes multiword units; it could be taken from a story, advertisement, or political speech, or any other genre. Students are put into groups and told to prepare an artistic reading of the passage that is to convey its meaning to the hearers and make as dramatic an impact as possible. They should decide who should read which sections (choral reading of some of it is also an option), where they are going to put emphasis or leave pauses, at what speed and volume each bit should be read, and whether they want also to introduce sound effects or movement. They then perform the passage to the class, reading the text from the page. In my experience, even when all the groups have received the same passage, they produce widely differing, and often entertaining, interpretations. Most important: much of the language used in the passages they have worked on – including the multiword units – is likely to be imprinted on their memory.

Retrieval

Students consolidate the learning of newly-learnt items best when they review them by actively retrieving either form or meaning from memory, rather than simply being exposed to them again or looking them up in a dictionary (Barcroft, 2007; Kang et al., 2013; Karpicke & Roediger, 2008; Laufer & Roitblat, 2015). At this stage, activities typically engage written as well as oral skills.

There are a number of simple techniques that use this principle for vocabulary teaching and which can be used also for multiword units.

Dictation is one of these. In its classic form, the teacher dictates a passage, or a set of individual items, and the students write it or them down; in other words, they retrieve and produce the written form in response to the spoken. There are variations to this: for example, the students are given a page with a set of written multiword units which they have been taught, with one word missing each time. They fill in as many as they can from memory, and then complete the rest following the teacher's dictation. The same can be done, of course, with the multiword units contextualized in a set of sentences, or an entire passage. These dictations sound as if they are encouraging meaningless production; but in fact it is very difficult to write down something from dictation if you do not know what it means. Doing dictations is likely, therefore, to remind students of both form and meaning. There are also variations on the dictation technique which focus more explicitly on meaning: translation-dictation, for example, where the teacher dictates the mother-tongue item, and students write down the translation into English; or vice versa.

Another simple basic procedure which encourages retrieval is *recall*. In its simplest version, students are taught a number of multiword units, which are written on the board. These are then erased, or hidden, and students try to recall and write down as many as they can: first individually, then in pairs or small groups. Another variation is to challenge students to remember all the multiword units they have been taught in the last week or two, and write them down: they then share results in groups or pool them on the board.

Dicto-gloss combines recall with dictation. The teacher reads aloud a passage that contextualizes a number of multiword units, at normal speaking speed. The students then try, in groups, to reconstruct from memory as much as they can. After a few minutes, the passage is read aloud again. Finally, the passage is displayed, and students compare their versions with the one they can see.

Finally, *Make a sentence* is a simple traditional exercise, where students are given a number of multiword units, and asked for each to create a sentence that provides an appropriate context. As it stands, it is a fairly boring exercise; however, it has a number of more interesting variations:

- Make a sentence contextualizing at least two of the items
- Make a sentence that is true about yourself
- Make a false sentence (grammatically correct, but expressing an untruth)
- Create a story that includes them all

Awareness Raising

With older or more academic groups it is useful to do activities that not only consolidate basic knowledge of the items, but also require students to probe further into meaning and use, to analyze, compare, contrast, and so on. Such exercises take more time than the ones described above, but deepen knowledge of the target items and increase language awareness in general.

One interesting exercise is *contrastive analysis*, where students are challenged to compare the target item(s) with equivalents in the students' mother tongue. Is the mother-tongue equivalent also a multiword unit, or is it a single word? If the multiword unit in English is couched in figurative language (e.g. *on the one hand, get in the way, call it a day*) – does the mother tongue use the same metaphor or a different one to convey a similar meaning? It is particularly interesting to compare proverbs. If there is a parallel in the mother tongue, then it may express the same meaning using a different metaphor. For example: "Don't judge a book by its cover" in English translates into "Don't look at the jar (but at what is in it)" in Hebrew. Occasionally you find that the same proverb actually exists in word-for-word translation in both languages, showing that it has probably been borrowed one way or the other.

Another idea is to use *synonyms*, where students are given a list of multiword units, each paired with a word or expression that means something similar: for example, *look for/search, to and fro/back and forth, in public/publicly, chances are/it's likely that, do one's best to/make an effort to*. They then discuss what the differences are between the two items, or if they are always interchangeable. Very often, the difference is mainly in formality level, but other differences in denotation, connotation, or collocational links may be discovered. Alternatively, students may be invited to focus on a single unit such as *by and large*, and using internet dictionaries or thesauri or synonym websites to find other expressions or single words that mean the same sort of thing, but checking carefully to detect subtle differences. A more specific variation is based on phrasal verbs, using the general phenomenon that most phrasal verbs in English are used in more informal language contexts than are their single-word synonyms. Students can be challenged to find the formal one-word equivalents of common phrasal verbs such as *throw away, go up, take care of* (very often provided by the dictionary definition of these items). Alternatively, this can be done the other way round: students are given single verbs and challenged to find a phrasal verb equivalent (for this it is best to use a thesaurus).

A third type of procedure is to consider the *communicative context* or domain in which a particular multiword unit is used. Many items are neutral, not particularly marked for specific contexts (e.g. *as soon as, in favor of*). Some are so marked as to be confined to one particular domain of use (e.g. *male issue, fitness to plead* in legal language); some are very colloquial (*she's like*, for example, meaning *she says*), some clearly formal (*provided that* for *if*). It is useful to invite students to look at a text belonging to a very specific type of communication and identify some typical multiword expressions used in it. Here, for example, is an extract from a business letter:

> We are grateful for the business you have seen fit to give our firm and are proud to have you as one of our customers. We cannot, however, authorize the return of our merchandise as you have requested, inasmuch as you took delivery over 14 days ago. We regret that we cannot accommodate you in this matter and hope you will understand why we must take this position.
>
> (Ur, 2012, p. 180)

Students might consider phrases like *see fit to, inasmuch as, take delivery, in this matter*: what do they mean, and how might they be expressed in an informal context?

Conclusion

The topic of multiword units in language learning has received increasing attention in applied linguistics research literature in recent years. Most of the research focuses on two major areas: the identification and study through corpus-based surveys of frequency and various other aspects of such units; and exploration into their place and function within first and second language learning processes.

Much of this research is of interest to the teacher, and, as suggested in earlier sections of this chapter, can help to inform teaching decisions as to selection and quantity. When designing classroom procedures, however, optimal results depend not solely on the research, but rather on a combination of research-based insights with those derived from professional experience and the literature on general pedagogical issues such as academic learning time, motivation, classroom management, and more. The language teacher stands at the intersection, as it were, between applied linguistics and general pedagogy.

The aim of the present chapter has been to draw on both these fields in order to provide some ideas that may help teachers – and also, hopefully, materials writers – become more aware not only of the importance of getting learners to acquire an extensive repertoire of multiword units, but also of some practical strategies and procedures that can help them to do so effectively.

Websites

English Vocabulary Profile. http://vocabulary.englishprofile.org/staticfiles/about.html
Just the Word. www.just-the-word.com
Carolyn Graham: Jazz Chants. www.youtube.com/watch?v=sotUp32mpOI

References

Barcroft, J. (2007). Effects of opportunities for word retrieval during second language vocabulary learning. *Language Learning,* 57(1), 35–56.

Ben Zion, M., & Saferstein, L. (2017). *Revised mastering modules.* Raanana, Israel: Eric Cohen Books.

Brown, R., Waring, R., & Donkaewbua, S. (2008). Incidental vocabulary acquisition from reading, reading-while-listening, and listening to stories. *Reading in a Foreign Language,* 20(2), 136.

Chen, C., & Truscott, J. (2010). The effects of repetition and L1 lexicalization on incidental vocabulary acquisition. *Applied Linguistics,* 31(5), 693–713.

Conklin, K., & Schmitt, N. (2012). The processing of formulaic language. *Annual Review of Applied Linguistics, 32*, 45–61.

Coxhead, A. (2000). A new academic word list. *TESOL Quarterly, 34*(2), 213–238.

Erten, I. H., & Tekin, M. (2008). Effects on vocabulary acquisition of presenting new words in semantic sets versus semantically unrelated sets. *System, 36*(3), 407–422.

Gardner, D., & Davies, M. (2013). A new academic vocabulary list. *Applied Linguistics, 35*(3), 305–327.

Garnier, M., & Schmitt, N. (2015). The PHaVE list: A pedagogical list of phrasal verbs and their most frequent meaning senses. *Language Teaching Research, 19*(6), 645–666.

Gettinger, M., & Seibert, J. K. (2002). Best practices in increasing academic learning time. In A. Thomas and J. Grimes (Eds.), *Best practices in school psychology IV* (pp. 773–787). Bethesda, MD: National Association of School Psychologists.

Graham, C. (2006). *Creating chants and songs.* Oxford: Oxford University Press.

Hsu, W. (2014). The most frequent opaque formulaic sequences in English-medium college textbooks. *System, 47*, 146–161.

Huckin, T., & Coady, J. (1999). Incidental vocabulary acquisition in a second language: A review. *Studies in Second Language Acquisition, 21*(2), 181–193.

Kang, S. H., Gollan, T. H., & Pashler, H. (2013). Don't just repeat after me: Retrieval practice is better than imitation for foreign vocabulary learning. *Psychonomic Bulletin & Review, 20*(6), 1259–1265.

Karpicke, J. D., & Roediger, H. L. (2008). The critical importance of retrieval for learning. *Science, 319*(5865), 966–968.

Koprowski, M. (2005). Investigating the usefulness of lexical phrases in contemporary coursebooks. *ELT Journal, 59*(4), 322–331.

Laufer, B. (2005). Focus on form in second language vocabulary learning. *Eurosla Yearbook, 5*(1), 223–250.

Laufer, B., & Rozovski-Roitblat, B. (2015). Retention of new words: Quantity of encounters, quality of task, and degree of knowledge. *Language Teaching Research, 19*(6), 687–711.

Liu, D. (2003). The most frequently used spoken American English idioms: A corpus analysis and its implications. *Tesol Quarterly, 37*(4), 671–700.

Liu, D. (2012). The most frequently-used multi-word constructions in academic written English: A multi-corpus study. *English for Specific Purposes, 31*(1), 25–35.

Martinez, R., & Schmitt, N. (2012). A phrasal expressions list. *Applied Linguistics, 33*(3), 299–320.

Papathanasiou, E. (2009). An investigation of two ways of presenting vocabulary. *ELT Journal, 63*(4), 313–322.

Pawley, A., & Syder, F. H. (1983). Two puzzles for linguistic theory: Nativelike selection and nativelike fluency. *Language and Communication,* 191, 225.

Puzo, M. (1969). *The godfather.* New York, NY: G. P. Putnam's Sons.

Raz, H. (1968). *Dramatic dialogues.* Tel Aviv: Otsar Hamoreh.

Schmitt, N. (2008). Instructed second language vocabulary learning. *Language Teaching Research,* 12(3), 329–363.

Tinkham, T. (1993). The effects of semantic and thematic clustering in the learning of second language vocabulary. *Second Language Research* 13(2), 138–163.

Tomasello, M. (2003). *Constructing a language: A usage-based theory of language acquisition.* Cambridge, MA: Harvard University Press.

Ur, P. (2012). *Vocabulary activities.* Cambridge: Cambridge University Press.

Waring, R. (1998). The negative effect of learning words in semantic sets: A replication. *System,* 25(2), 261–274.

Webb, S. (2007). The effects of repetition on vocabulary knowledge. *Applied Linguistics,* 28, 46–65.

West, M., & West, M. P. (Eds.). (1953). *A general service list of English words: with semantic frequencies and a supplementary word-list for the writing of popular science and technology.* London: Longman Green & Co.

Wilcox, A., & Mednab, A. (2013). Effects of semantic and phonological clustering on L2 vocabulary acquisition among novice learners. *System,* 42(4), 1056–1069.

Wray, A. (2012). What do we (think we) know about formulaic language? An evaluation of the current state of play. *Annual Review of Applied Linguistics,* 32, 231–254.

Chapter 2

Working with Multiword Units in ESP/EAP

Averil Coxhead

It is important to note that there are many different terms for multiword units, and many kinds of units, just as there are different ways to go about analyzing texts to identify them (Flowerdew, 2014). In this chapter, *multiword unit* is used as an umbrella term throughout. The main kinds of multiword units which are addressed here are *collocations* (two words that co–occur) and *lexical bundles* (groups of three or more words) (see Biber, Johansson, Leech, Conrad & Finegan, 1999). Note that most of this chapter focuses on multiword units based on written and spoken corpora, rather than student writing (see Ädel & Erman, 2012, for example, for more on this kind of research).

Why Focus on Multiword Units in English for Specific Purposes and English for Academic Purposes?

A key reason for focusing on multiword units is that they can make up quite a large proportion of general English texts (Altenberg, 1998; Erman

& Warren, 2000), and this is also true of multiword units in academic and in technical or specialized texts. A striking example of how prevalent they can be in technical texts comes from a study on the vocabulary in the trades (for more on this project, see Parkinson, Coxhead, Demecheleer, Mackay, Matautia, McLaughlin & Tu'amoheloa, 2017). Over 1,000 multiword units were identified in an a written corpus of around 560,000 running words on Automotive Engineering. Most of these multiword units were made up of two or three words, and some of them were repeated fairly often in the text. That said, many of these items occurred only once. If a teacher wanted to find out how many and what kinds of multiword units are in a classroom text, there are online tools which are freely available to help with this task, including Lex Tutor's collocation site (Cobb, n.d.) or AntConc's collocation tool (Anthony, n.d.).

Secondly, identifying and working with the multiword units that learners need in their academic and professional/occupational areas of study can draw the attention of learners to "... productive patterns which are tied to specific lexis in a way that can lead them to be overlooked by traditional grammars" (Durrant, 2009, p. 163). In single-word studies in EAP, for example, there has been research into identifying academic vocabulary to help develop learners' awareness of, and ability to use, the vocabulary they will meet in their university reading (Coxhead, 2000; Gardner & Davies, 2014; Malmström, Pecorari & Shaw, 2018), listening (Dang, Coxhead & Webb, 2017) or both (e.g. see Biber, 2006) and writing (Malmström et at., 2018). Multiword unit research is extending this research from single words to multiword units.

Thirdly, the technical or academic vocabulary of a field or domain is related quite closely to its content (Woodward-Kron, 2008). We can see examples of this point in professional and academic texts, such as in Dentistry (Pinna, 2007): *bone graft* and *cortical bone*. This means that focusing on multiword units that are closely related to the subject goes hand in hand with developing an understanding of the subject. The more of these technical patterns our learners recognize and understand, the better they might understand what they are reading and be able to read more texts in their field.

Fourthly, there is evidence that multiword unit use by second or foreign language learners has benefits for fluency (Pawley & Syder, 1983), with such users being judged as having higher levels proficiency in English than others who do not use as many multiword units (Boers, Eyckmans, Kappel, Stengers & Demecheleer, 2006; Stengers, Boers, Housen & Eyckmans, 2010), and in processing texts (Conklin & Schmitt, 2012). Learners who are able to use formulaic language also find benefits in interacting with others in particular groups and identifying themselves as part of those groups (Wray, 2002).

Last, but by no means least, EAP and ESP learners need support with multiword units. Unfortunately, language learners tend to process texts one word at a time (Conklin & Schmitt, 2012), and learning to use academic multiword units is a slow process (see Li & Schmitt, 2010). Jones and Haywood (2004) found that EAP learners tended not to use lexical bundles in their writing, even after classroom-based exposure to them during an intensive pre-university EAP course. Learners might not necessarily know much about multiword units in English overall or understand why they are an important part of the language they need in EAP/ESP. It could be that learners do not encounter multiword units in their textbooks, dictionaries or previous learning, even though there is a growing awareness of multiword units in materials and dictionaries (for example, the *Longman Collocations Dictionary and Thesaurus*, the *Oxford Dictionary of Collocations*, and the *Macmillan Collocations Dictionary*). But it is important to note that even learners who know about multiword units might make conscious decisions about whether or not to learn them, based on their own beliefs about vocabulary learning (Coxhead, 2008). The more we know about the decisions our learners make about their vocabulary learning, the better, in general, whether we are teaching English for general, academic, or specific purposes.

What Are Some Key Features of Multiword Units in EAP/ESP?

The concept of frequency is important in general English vocabulary and multiword units in English (see Nation, 2013): some words and multiword units occur more often than others. Learners will encounter some multiword units more often than others in their reading and writing. For example, the lexical bundle *on the one hand* is less frequent in spoken and academic written English than *on the other hand* (Pickering & Byrd, 2008). Word lists based on multiword units often use frequency as one of the criteria to decide on the usefulness of a word pattern for language learners. As an example of frequency and multiword units in ESP, Table 2.1 shows examples of multiword units which occur 100 times or more from

Table 2.1 Multiword units occurring more than 100 times in the Automotive Engineering written corpus (Coxhead, 2017)

Multiword unit	Frequency in the written Automotive Engineering corpus
cooling system	327
control valve	240
fuel system	207
cylinder head	192
ignition system	169
high pressure	165
fuel filter	158
low pressure	158
idle speed	139
battery voltage	126
electronic control	104
engine speed	103
fuel injector	103
electronic fuel injection	102
fuel pressure	101
drive shaft	100

a written Automotive Engineering corpus (containing approximately 560,000 running words) (Coxhead, 2017). Note how the frequency of the technical multiword units drops quite quickly from *cooling system* with 327 occurrences to *drive shaft* at 100 occurrences. The same kind of drop in frequency can be found in general English (see Nation, 2013).

A key element of technical vocabulary is that it tends to be limited to a particular field (see Chung & Nation, 2003; Nation, 2013). For example, *cooling system* and *cylinder head* are not usually found in everyday or medical texts. This means that learners will not encounter multiword units in their field unless they are actively engaged in reading or listening to texts from that field.

Multiword units in EAP and ESP might include high frequency words, such as *high pressure* and *low pressure* from Table 2.1. Ward's (2007) research into engineering illustrates how high frequency words like *time* combine with other words to make up a technical multiword unit, as in *settling time* and *reaction time*. Learners need to know that these words together make up a new unit of meaning in a specialized area of study, and sometimes the meaning might be fairly easy to guess, but other times not so easy to guess. *Idle speed*, for example, might take some work and examples to understand fully.

Research in EAP by Hyland (2008) suggests that the amount of multiword units can differ across disciplines, which is an important point for learners and teachers. Hyland (2008) focused on four-word lexical bundles in fields such as Electrical Engineering, Business Studies and Biology. He found that Electrical Engineering contained the highest percentage of lexical bundles, at around 3.5 percent, followed by Business Studies (2.2 percent) and Biology at 1.7 percent. Byrd & Coxhead (2010) also found lower amounts of lexical bundles in Arts and Sciences in a written academic corpus, but higher proportions in Law (almost 5.5 percent) and Commerce (2.65 percent).

Multiword units may have different roles, or functions, in texts. In a study of university classroom teaching and university textbooks, Biber, Conrad, and Cortes (2004) found three main functions of the lexical bundles used by the writers: organizing content (discourse organizers); expressing the attitude of the writer; and presenting or discussing content. This framework has been used in subsequent studies such as by Nesi and Basturkmen (2006), who investigated lexical bundles in spoken academic texts (lectures) and found some overlap with Biber et al. (2004). This kind of information is useful for EAP teachers and learners, because it can help with understanding not only the content of texts, but how they are organized and what the point of view of a writer might be.

This section has looked at several key aspects of multiword units in EAP and ESP. Let's move on to these units in textbooks.

Multiword Units in EAP and ESP Textbooks

In many teaching and learning contexts, textbooks play a major role in language classrooms, which is why researchers such as Biber et al. (2004; see also Biber, 2006) have focused on them. Some researchers have looked at multiword units in EAP and ESP textbooks to determine the extent to which published materials focus on this element of language. Several key findings are important for teachers to keep in mind from these studies. Firstly, studies focusing on EAP textbooks and university textbooks on lexical bundles by Chen (2010) and multiword constructions by Wood and Appel (2014) suggest that these two kinds of texts contain quite different proportions and amounts of multiword units. Wood (2010) found that multiword units in EAP textbooks tended to be less oriented towards academic structures and more focused on classroom instruction.

Coxhead, Dang and Mukai (2017) investigated lexical bundles in spoken tutorials and laboratory corpora at university and in 15 series of EAP speaking and listening textbooks and a set of ESP textbooks. There was no focus on multiword units in laboratories in the textbooks, but three of the EAP textbooks did present a total of 176 expressions which the textbook authors suggest learners might find useful in tutorials, such as ways to ask for confirmation or more information (for example, *could you clarify …*) or paraphrase (e.g. *in other words*). Unfortunately, many of the 176 expressions were either not found or were not very high frequency in the tutorial and laboratory corpora in the Coxhead et al. (2017) study.

One reason why there might be some differences between EAP texts and university-level spoken and written texts could be that textbooks could be focusing on other elements of language which are essential for EAP students, rather than multiword units. It could also be that there is so much to cover in EAP that there is little space left in a textbook for multiword units. But if textbooks are not yet a major source for multiword units in EAP or ESP, then what other resources are available for teachers to work with them? The next section looks at lists of multiword units in EAP and ESP.

Published Lists of Multiword Units in EAP or ESP

One way to identify multiword units is to look to research in EAP and ESP that uses corpus-based approaches to identify patterns and then produces a list of items which have been selected because of their frequency or range of occurrence in the corpora, for example, or because they met some selection criteria put in place by the researchers. This section contains examples of studies which teachers might find useful, starting with investigations of collocations, particularly in EAP.

Durrant (2009) investigated academic collocations in a large written corpus of five academic disciplines: Arts and Humanities; Engineering; Law and Education; Medicine and Health Sciences; Science; and Social Sciences. He identified and further investigated 1,000 collocations and found that their frequencies varied according to the disciplines. Durrant (2009) points out that the collocations in his study have grammatical patterns, which is useful for teachers and learners in EAP. For example, he finds many examples of collocations that have the pattern *verb + that*, as in *assume, demonstrate, reveal, note, hypothesize* and *indicate*.

Ackermann & Chen (2013) also carried out a large-scale study of academic collocations and it resulted in a large list of 2,469 items, carefully checked by computers and researchers. Ackermann & Chen (2013) also focused on grammatical patterns in their collocation study, finding that a great majority of these multiword units contained combinations of nouns, such as *noun + noun* (e.g. *target audience*) or *adjective + noun* (*causal link*). Both these studies highlight the sheer amount of collocations in EAP written texts, and are particularly useful for focusing on the grammatical nature of these multiword units. The full Academic Collocation List is available for downloading from the Pearson (n.d.) website.

Also in the field of EAP but looking more widely than collocations, Liu (2012) also used corpora to investigate a range of multiword units in two large academic corpora, including phrasal/prepositional verbs, idioms, and lexical bundles. Liu (2012) lists 228 multiword units by frequency from his research, including high frequency items such as *such as, for example*, and *as well as*. Another study which included idioms in academic texts was carried out by Simpson and Mendis (2003), who developed a list of idioms in academic spoken English (e.g. *the bottom line, the big picture*) and categorized them according to functions, including description (*a dime a dozen*) and metalanguage (e.g. *cut to the chase*).

Research into lexical bundles has resulted in a number of lists in EAP, such as the work by Biber et al. (2004) mentioned above. Simpson-Vlach and Ellis (2010) carried out a corpus-based study of academic formulas using two academic corpora (written and spoken) and two general corpora (written and spoken), so as to select multiword units that occurred more often in academic than general English. Having identified academic formulas in these corpora, Simpson-Vlach and Ellis (2010) asked language teachers and language testers to rate the formulaic nature of the academic formulas, their cohesive meaning, and the extent to which they would be worth teaching. The final lists from this study are: 200 spoken academic formulas (e.g. *be able to, you know what I mean*), 200 written academic formulas (*is consistent with; as a consequence*), and a "core" list of 207 items which are both written and spoken (e.g. *in terms of; at the same time*). Simpson-Vlach and Ellis (2010) also categorized the formulas into functions such as stance, discourse organization, and referential formulas. The three list of formulas are available for downloading from Smith (n.d. a).

Some ESP-oriented studies have looked into multiword units in particular areas of study, such as Finance (see Cheng, 2012), in professional fields such as Aviation (e.g. *sniffer dog, black box, base leg, crosswind leg*) (Aiguo, 2007), and medical communication, such as *shooting pains* and *be under the weather* (Basturkmen, 2010). Fox and Tigchelaar (2015) carried out a semi-replication of the academic formulas research by Simpson-Vlach and Ellis (2010) but with a focus on formulas in Engineering. Fox and Tigchelaar (2015) identified 99 formulas and categorized them into referential formulas (e.g. *a positive effect on, a reduction in*), stance expressions (e.g. *assumed to be, an important role*), and discourse organizers (e.g. *are shown in table; as discussed in*). Note that these multiword units are less directly Engineering-focused. Rather, they serve particular functions in the corpora that they came from. Again one of the selection criteria was that these multiword units were "teachable". Ward's (2007) study on collocations in Engineering focused on more technical multiword units and combinations from corpora with key technical words, such as *reactor*, and found collocates with *flow, tubular, batch,* and *catalytic*. Ward (2007) found that around two thirds of the uses of the words *gas* and *heat* occur in collocations made up of two, three, or four words.

A clear advantage of working with a published list of multiword units is that, if they have been well-made and are closely connected to the focus of EAP/ESP learners, then teachers can focus on how to use the list well, rather than putting energies into developing their own lists. Some multiword unit lists are freely available from the internet, which is another advantage for teachers and learners. That said, developing and evaluating word lists is a time-consuming, and at times, technically difficult, process. There are drawbacks when working with published lists of multiword units. Large lists can be daunting for language teachers and learners and cause problems with deciding which units can be usefully integrated into a course of learning. Further, lists that focus on frequency and range in EAP texts, for example, tend to throw up multiword units that might not seem particularly academic to learners (Byrd & Coxhead, 2010), such as *the thing that* and *if you look at*. This is not to say that these multiword units are not useful, rather, that expectations of what might be technical or academic vocabulary might not be the same as what is in a list of multiword units.

Some items in lists of multiword units might not be complete, such as *in the form of, in the absence of, at the time of,* and *as well as the* (Biber et al., 2004; Hyland, 2008; Byrd & Coxhead, 2010). Learners need to notice these multiword units, and these units could be buried in long passages of text. For example, *on the basis of* occurred only 308 times in an academic written corpus containing around 3.5 million words, which translates to roughly two occurrences per 15,000 words (Byrd & Coxhead, 2010). Along with information about frequency, learners also need to know about the actual use of a multiword unit in context (Byrd & Coxhead, 2010).

These multiword word list studies in EAP and ESP all reflect a great deal of work and careful research, but they also present possible problems for teachers and learners in terms of deciding which multiword list might be the most useful, if any. Let's now turn to that particular issue.

How Can Teachers Evaluate Lists of Multiword Units?

Byrd and Coxhead (2010) point out that it is important that teachers and learners find out about the development and evaluation of a word list. They recommend establishing, for example, whether the list was developed using a written or a spoken corpus or both, about the texts which were gathered for the corpus (if one was used), who the list was made for and why, what principles were used to guide the selection of items for inclusion in the list, and whether and how a list was evaluated. Nation (2016, p. 78) provides a useful list of questions to help teachers evaluate a word list (Table 2.2).

Working with Multiword Units in Planning, Testing, and Teaching

This section looks more closely at principles to consider when planning for specialized vocabulary in EAP and ESP courses, as well as testing these units. Pedagogical principles to think about are the focus of the final part of this section.

Table 2.2 Questions for teachers to evaluate a multiword list, adapted from Nation (2016, p. 78)

Aspect of the list	Question
Definition	Is the definition of what is counted as a multiword unit clear?
Learner needs	Does the definition match the needs of the list users?
Consistency	Is the definition applied consistently when developing the list?
Frequency data	Does the list provide frequency data?
Corpus content	Does the content of the corpus which was used to develop the list match the kinds of texts that users need or use?
Non-adjacent items	Are non-adjacent items included in the list, and if they are, have they been checked to ensure that they are actually part of the multiword unit?
Counting	Are variants of multiword items being counted in one group?
Grammatical formation	Are the multiword units grammatically well-formed?
Lexical substitution	Are substitutes being counted or are the items not replaceable?

Planning

There are some key concepts to keep in mind when planning for multiword units for ESP and EAP courses. As we have already seen above, frequency is a core element to consider. Learners and teachers need to focus on the most frequent multiword units first because they will encounter these items most often. They can also then use that knowledge of the more frequent multiword units to build on learning other multiword units (see Nation, 2013 for more on frequency). Items that are closely related to a topic are likely to be repeated in a text, and therefore more frequent, which is a good indication that they need some attention from teachers and learners. Conversely, quite a few multiword units will only occur once in a text, and are less likely to require much attention from learners and teachers. Nation (2013) calls these items *low frequency* vocabulary. A basic guiding principle is that the longer the multiword unit (or the more words it contains), the less frequent it will be in a text.

Teachers need to think about the choice of texts for reading and writing in EAP and ESP, particularly if we want to encourage students to notice, learn, and use multiword units. For example, the multiword unit *full throttle* is connected to Automotive Engineering and is unlikely to occur in general English texts. Learners, overall, know more words in English than they can actually produce (see Malmström et al., 2018), and this is likely to be true of multiword units also. If writing tasks are not academic or technical in nature, it will possibly be quite difficult for learners to try to use technical or academic multiword units, and therefore gain feedback on the appropriateness and accuracy of their use of those word patterns.

Now, it may sound a little strange, but one of the most important points to bear in mind about multiword units is that they are *units*. That is, these items belong together. They have a bond that is statistically-based and/or frequency-based. This point is important, because as Wray (2000) states, multiword units tend to get pulled apart by language teachers in classrooms, and each part of the unit gets examined. But formulaic language is not pulled apart in writing and speaking, rather it is used as a whole. There can be unintended consequences when pulling multiword units apart. Learners can fail to put them back together again correctly, or get confused about what the original and correct construction might be (as we found in a study by Boers, Demecheleer, Coxhead & Webb, 2014). Keeping multiword units together, as much as is practically possible, may help learners to look beyond single words to see multiword units.

Finally, building knowledge of multiword units in EAP and ESP can take time. Jones and Haywood (2004) found that time was a major factor that counted against the learning of academic multiword units in an EAP course, particularly when it came to learners actually using these units in academic writing.

Testing

If multiword units are worth classroom time, then surely they are also worth taking the time to test. Tests do not have to be large-scale and demanding of precious classroom time. Instead, they could be regular, weekly, and low-stakes, such as File's (2014) in-class test, which effectively serves as targeted revision for learners. File (2014) suggests asking learners to write down 15 words that they have studied over the last week, but they could equally well be asked to note down 15 multiword units that they had studied over a week. Here are some of File's (2014) questions for the test, which he suggests could be put onto a series of slides for the whole class to see, and here they are adapted so as to focus on multiword units:

---

a. Which of your multiword units have a positive meaning? Put a (+) mark next to words that can have a positive meaning.
b. Which of your multiword units have a negative meaning? Put a (–) mark next to words that can have a negative meaning.
c. Can you list a synonym for five of your multiword units?
d. Choose five multiword units and write a sentence using each one that demonstrates its meaning.
e. Have you used any of multiword units this week? Tell your partner when and where.
f. Choose five multiword units you haven't used this week and think about where and when you might use them.
g. Discuss a key concept in your academic or specific purpose studies with a partner and try to use at least five of your multiword units in your discussion.

Note that learners can use these questions to quiz each other. They do not have to rely on the teacher to provide these prompts.

An interesting example of a test in English for Medical Purposes incorporates multiword units from Wette & Hawken (2016). This test focuses on elements of medical terminology, such as formal and informal written forms, and lay and technical terms. For example, test takers might be asked to match technical medical terms such as *discharge* and *light bleeding* with more everyday expressions such as *leaking* and *spotting*, or produce informal phrases in place of formal or technical equivalents (*excise the dead tissue*; *lose consciousness*). This test clearly focuses on formulaic and technical language as part of medical communication, to prepare learners for encounters in their professional lives with members of the public who might not understand medical terminology.

Teaching

There is, in general, quite a lot of uncertainty about teaching multiword units (Meunier, 2012; Coxhead, 2018a, 2018b). A useful framework to consider is Nation's (2007; Nation & Yamamoto, 2012) Four Strands, which can be adapted to think about planning for multiword units in EAP and ESP. The strands are: meaning-focused input, which involves learning from reading and listening; meaning-focused output, which involves learning from speaking and writing; language-focused learning, which involves focusing on aspects of multiword units such as spelling and pronunciation; and fluency, where learners draw on their knowledge of multiword units to produce them fluently in speaking and writing, and understand them in reading and listening. Nation (2016) outlines ways to use word lists using the Four Strands as an overarching framework. The strands are meant to be balanced, meaning that equal amounts of time should be spent on each strand, unless there is a particular need to focus on particular strands.

When preparing classroom activities which involve multiword units, it is useful to think about what strands they belong to. For example, if students are investigating multiword units in specialized corpora using the concordance program and Law Corpus (available on Tom Cobb's Lex Tutor website), or Mark Davies' (n.d.) Academic Word and Phrase website that draws on the Corpus of Contemporary American English (COCA), then these learners could be focused on language-focused learning. If they are reading textbooks to prepare for class, this is meaning-focused input, and giving a class talk on a particular subject using multiword units that relate to that subject in the talk is meaning-focused output.

A common call to multiword unit arms in language teaching is to raise learners' awareness, through activities such as text analysis and chunking (see, for example, Boers & Lindstromberg, 2012; Jones & Haywood, 2004; Boers et al., 2006). Ward (2009) has some useful examples of activities which focus on raising learners' awareness of collocations in Engineering, such as matching collocations with meanings, rearranging phrases or sentences, and working with texts to find examples and examine uses of collocations in texts. Training learners to become more aware of multiword units in context could involve identifying multiword units in texts and highlighting them in some way (see, for example, Boers, Demecheleer, He, Deconinck, Stengers & Eyckmans, 2017). Note that many such studies have focused on multiword units in English for general purposes, rather than for specific or academic purposes. Websites such as the Academic Collocations List (ACL) (Ackermann & Chen, 2010; see also Pearson, n.d.) can be used to highlight multiword items in texts (Smith, n.d. a; see also Smith, n.d. b for an Academic Collocations List Highlighter). This means teachers can upload classroom texts and find out how many and which ACL items are in these texts. The same website can also produce gap-fill exercises based on the Academic Collocations List. Any such activities need to be part of a program of learning that encourages multiple encounters with multiword units and opportunities for use. Again, considering a multiword unit as a unit is a key point to keep in mind when doing language-focused learning activities.

Training learners to look to the left and the right of a key word in multiword units (Coxhead & Byrd, 2012) might be useful for raising awareness of pattern in multiword units. Table 2.3 shows some examples of the words which co-occur with the key word *throttle* from the written Automotive Engineering corpus (Coxhead, 2017). The table shows the frequency of the multiword units, and clearly shows that items to the left are adjectives, while items to the right are often nouns.

It is vital that any such activities on identifying, highlighting, or analyzing multiword units for EAP or ESP students is part of a program that ensures that the learners have plenty of exposure to these units, opportunities to use them and gain feedback on use, and lots of repetition to increase the likelihood of remembering these word patterns. The aim is to meet and use these items as much as possible so that they become available for fluent use by learners and for easy recognition. It can be very difficult to remember something that you have only met once.

Table 2.3 Examples of multiword units with *throttle* (Coxhead, 2017)

	Multiword units with the key word throttle	Frequency in the written Automotive corpus
Collocations to the right of throttle	position	46
	valve	26
	position sensor	25
	body	20
	butterfly	9
	lever	8
	plate	7
	shaft	7
	opening	6
	pressure	6
	wide open	6
Collocations to the left of throttle	full	17
	mid	8

Because there are so many multiword combinations in EAP and ESP that require attention and learning and limited classroom time, it is particularly important to teach learners strategies for dealing with multiword units. Strategies for keeping track of multiword units, such as notebooks, require some careful setting up because learners need to know how to choose multiword units that they select for learning, how to keep good records (for example, how they will enter the multiword unit into their records), and how to revise to good effect.

Conclusion

There is much work to be done in the area of multiword units in EAP and ESP, for example, in terms of the development and evaluation of specialized word lists of such units, and their integration into programs of teaching and learning. Research into pedagogical approaches to multiword units is ongoing (see, for example, the work by Frank Boers and colleagues), particularly in relation to general English. It would be heartening to see much more research into EAP and ESP, in first and second/foreign language contexts, and at different levels of education, for example at middle school and secondary school level through to undergraduate and postgraduate studies.

References

Ackermann, K., & Chen, Y.-H. (2013). Developing the Academic Collocation List (ACL) – A corpus-driven and expert-judged approach. *Journal of English for Academic Purposes, 12*(4), 235–247.

Ädel, A., & Erman, B. (2012). Recurrent word combinations in academic writing by native and non-native speakers of English: A lexical bundles approach. *English for Specific Purposes, 31*, 81–92.

Aiguo, W. (2007). Teaching aviation English in the Chinese context: Developing ESP theory in a non-English speaking country. *English for Specific Purposes, 26*, 121–128.

Altenberg, B. (1998). On the phraseology of spoken English: The evidence of recurrent word-combinations. In A. Cowie (Ed.) *Phraseology: Theory, analysis, and application* (pp. 101–122). Oxford: Clarendon Press.

Anthony, L. (n.d.). AntConc (Version 3.5.7) [Computer Software]. Tokyo, Japan: Waseda University. Available from www.laurenceanthony.net/software

Basturkmen, H. (2010). *Developing courses in English for Specific Purposes.* Basingstoke, Hampshire, UK: Palgrave Macmillan.

Biber, D. (2006). *University language.* Amsterdam: John Benjamins.

Biber, D., Conrad, S., & Cortes, V. (2004). If you look at…: Lexical bundles in university teaching and textbooks. *Applied Linguistics,* 25(3), 371–405.

Biber, D., Johansson, S., Leech, G., Conrad, S., & Finegan, E. (1999). *The Longman grammar of spoken and written English.* Harlow, UK: Pearson Education.

Boers, F., Demecheleer, M., Coxhead, A., & Webb, S. (2014). Gauging the effectiveness of exercises on verb-noun collocations. *Language Teaching Research,* 18(1), 50–70.

Boers, F., Demecheleer, M., He, L., Deconinck, J., Stengers, H., & Eyckmans, J. (2017). Typographic enhancement of multiword units in second language text. *International Journal of Applied Linguistics,* 27(2), 448–469.

Boers, F., Eyckmans, J., Kappel, J., Stengers, H., & Demecheleer, M. (2006). Formulaic sequences and perceived oral proficiency: Putting a lexical approach to the test. *Language Teaching Research,* 10, 245–261.

Boers, F., & Lindstromberg, S. (2012). Experimental and intervention studies on formulaic sequences in a second language. *Annual Review of Applied Linguistics,* 32, 83–110.

Byrd, P., & Coxhead, A. (2010). On the other hand: Lexical bundles in academic writing and in the teaching of EAP. *University of Sydney Papers in TESOL,* 5, 31–64.

Chen, L. (2010). An investigation of lexical bundles in ESP textbooks and electrical engineering introductory textbooks. In D. Wood (Ed.), *Perspectives on formulaic language: Acquisition and communication* (pp. 107–125). London: Continuum.

Cheng, W. (2012). *Exploring corpus linguistics: Language in action.* New York, NY: Routledge.

Chung, T., & Nation, I. S. P. (2003). Technical vocabulary in specialised texts. *Reading in a Foreign Language,* 15(2), 103–116.

Cobb, T. (n.d.) *Compleat Lexical Tutor.* Available at www.lextutor.ca/vp/comp/.

Conklin, K., & Schmitt, N. (2012). The processing of formulaic language. *Annual Review of Applied Linguistics,* 32, 45–61.

Coxhead, A. (2000). A new academic word list. *TESOL Quarterly,* 34(2), 213–238.

Coxhead, A. (2008). Phraseology and English for academic purposes: Challenges and opportunities. In F. Meunier, & S. Granger (Eds.),

Phraseology in language learning and teaching (pp. 149–161). Amsterdam: John Benjamins.

Coxhead, A. (2017). Formulaic vocabulary in the trades: Applied Linguistics meets Automotive Engineering. Paper presented at AAAL 2017, March 19–22, 2017, Portland, Oregon.

Coxhead, A. (2018a). Replication research in pedagogical approaches to formulaic sequences: Jones & Haywood (2004) and Alali & Schmitt (2012). *Language Teaching,* 51(1), 113–123.

Coxhead, A. (2018b). *Vocabulary and English for Specific Purposes Research: Quantitative and qualitative perspectives.* London: Routledge.

Coxhead, A., & Byrd, P. (2012). Collocations and Academic Word List: The strong, the weak and the lonely. In I. Moskowich and B. Crespo (Eds.), *Encoding the Past, Decoding the Future: Corpora in the 21st Century* (pp. 1–20). Cambridge: Cambridge Scholars Publishing.

Coxhead, A., Dang, Y., & Mukai, S. (2017). University tutorials and laboratories: Corpora, textbooks and vocabulary. *English for Academic Purposes,* 30, 66–78.

Dang, Y., Coxhead, A., & Webb, S. (2017). The Academic Spoken Word List. *Language Learning,* 67(3), 959–997.

Davies, M. (n.d.). Academic word and phrase. Available at www.wordandphrase.info/academic/.

Durrant, P. (2009). Investigating the viability of a collocation list for students of English for academic purposes. *English for Specific Purposes,* 28, 157–169.

Erman, B., & Warren, B. (2000). The idiom principle and the open choice principle. *Text,* 20(1), 29–62.

File, K. (2014). A low-stakes vocabulary test. In A. Coxhead (Ed.), *New ways in teaching vocabulary, revised* (pp. 107–110). Alexandria, VA: TESOL.

Flowerdew, L. (2014). Which unit of linguistic analysis of ESP corpora of written text? In M. Gotti, & D. Giannoni (Eds.), *Corpus analysis for descriptive and pedagogical purposes* (pp. 25–41). Bern: Peter Lang.

Fox, J., & Tigchelaar, M. (2015). Creating an engineering academic formulas list. *Journal of Teaching English for Specific and Academic Purposes,* 3(2), 295–304.

Gardner, D., & Davies, M. (2014). A new academic vocabulary list. *Applied Linguistics,* 35(3), 305–327.

Hyland, K. (2008). As can be seen: Lexical bundles and disciplinary variation. *English for Specific Purposes,* 27(1), 4–21.

Jones, M., & Haywood, S. (2004). Facilitating the acquisition of formulaic sequences: An exploratory study in an EAP context. In N. Schmitt (Ed.), *Formulaic sequences* (pp. 269–291). Amsterdam: John Benjamins.

Li, J., & Schmitt, N. (2010). The development of collocation use in academic texts by advanced L2 learners: A multiple case study approach. In D. Wood (Ed.), *Perspectives on formulaic language: Acquisition and communication* (pp. 22–26). New York, NY: Continuum.

Liu, D. (2012). The most frequently-used multi-word constructions in academic written English: A multi-corpus study. *English for Specific Purposes, 31,* 25–35.

Malmström, H., Pecorari, D., & Shaw, P. (2018). Words for what? Contrasting university students' receptive and productive academic vocabulary needs. *English for Specific Purposes, 50,* 28–39.

Meunier, F. (2012). Formulaic language and language teaching. *Annual Review of Applied Linguistics, 32,* 111–129.

Nation, I. S. P. (2007). The four strands. *Innovation in Language Learning and Teaching, 1*(1), 2–13.

Nation, I. S. P. (2013). *Learning vocabulary in another language* (second edition). Cambridge: Cambridge University Press.

Nation, I. S. P. (2016). *Making and using word lists for language learning and testing.* Amsterdam: John Benjamins.

Nation, I. S. P., & Yamamoto, A. (2012). Applying the four strands. *International Journal of Innovation in English Language Teaching and Research, 1*(2), 167–181.

Nesi, H., & Basturkmen, H. (2006). Lexical bundles and discourse signalling in academic lectures. *International Journal of Corpus Linguistics, 11*(3), 283–304.

Parkinson, J., Coxhead, A., Demecheleer, M., Mackay, J., Matautia, L., McLaughlin, E., & Tu'amoheloa, F. (2017). *The Language in the Trades Education project.* Wellington: Ako Aotearoa.

Pawley, A., & Syder, F. (1983). Two puzzles for linguistic theory: Nativelike selection and nativelike fluency. In J. Richards, & R. Schmidt (Eds.), *Language and communication* (pp. 191–226). New York, NY: Longman.

Pearson (n.d.). The Academic Collocations List. Available at https://pearsonpte.com/organizations/researchers/academic-collocation-list.

Pickering, L., & Byrd, P. (2008). Investigating connections between spoken and written academic English: Lexical bundles in the AWL and in MICASE. In D. Belcher, & A. Hirvela (Eds.), *The oral/literate connection: Perspectives on L2 speaking, writing and other media interactions* (pp. 110–132). Ann Arbor: University of Michigan Press.

Pinna, A. (2007). Exploiting LSP corpora in the study of foreign languages. In D. Gálová (Ed.), *Languages for specific purposes: Searching for common solutions* (pp. 146–162). Newcastle, UK: Cambridge Scholars Publishing.

Simpson, R., & Mendis, D. (2003). A corpus-based study of idioms in academic speech. *TESOL Quarterly, 37(3)*, 419–441.

Simpson-Vlach, R., & Ellis, N. C. (2010). An academic formulas list: New methods in phraseology research. *Applied Linguistics, 31*(4), 487–512.

Smith, S. (n.d. a). The Academic Formulas List. Available at www.eapfoundation.com/vocab/academic/afl

Smith, S. (n.d. b). Academic Collocations List highlighter. Available at www.eapfoundation.com/vocab/academic/acl/highlighter

Stengers, H., Boers, F., Housen, A., & Eyckmans, J. (2010). Does 'chunking' foster chunk-uptake? In S. De Knop, F. Boers, & A. De Rycker (Eds.), *Fostering language teaching efficiency through Cognitive Linguistics* (pp. 99–117). Berlin: Mouton.

Ward, J. (2007). Collocation and technicality in EAP engineering. *Journal of English for Academic Purposes, 6*, 18–35.

Wette, R., & Hawken, S. 2016. Measuring gains in an EMP course and the perspectives of language and medical educators as assessors. *English for Specific Purposes, 42*, 38–49.

Wood, D. (2010). Lexical clusters in an EAP textbook corpus. In D. Wood (Ed.), *Perspectives on formulaic language: Acquisition and communication* (pp. 88–106). London: Continuum.

Wood, D. C., & Appel, R. (2014). Multiword constructions in first year business and engineering university textbooks and EAP textbooks. *Journal of English for Academic Purposes, 15*, 1–13.

Woodward-Kron, R. (2008). More than just jargon: The nature and role of specialist language in learning disciplinary knowledge, *Journal of English for Academic Purposes, 7*(4), 234–249.

Wray, A. (2000). Formulaic sequences in second language teaching: Principle and practice. *Applied Linguistics, 21*(4), 463–489.

Wray, A. (2002). *Formulaic sequences and the lexicon.* Cambridge: Cambridge University Press.

Chapter 3

Teaching Idioms and Idiomatic Expressions Across the Second Language Curriculum

John I. Liontas

Introduction

Ask anyone to define what idiomaticity is and is not, and you are likely to obtain as many answers as there are individuals willing to define the term. Ask the same question among classroom teachers, language practitioners, and curriculum developers, and the answers you are likely to obtain are at a minimum as many syllables and characters as the monolexemic cover term ID-I-O-MA-TIC-I-TY contains: seven syllables, 12 characters. Yet the answer to the question, I would argue, is as plain as the individual words comprising the term: *idiom* and *idiomatic.*

Indeed, a critical perusal of the available literature on the subject will reveal a vast nomenclature for the cover term *idiom(aticity)*. Explained semantically, the recursive morpheme -ity, applied to adjectival bases such as "formulaicity" and "authenticity," for example, enables the qualitative ascription of "constituting (an) idiom(s)" or "containing (an) idiom(s)" as well as the "quality or state of being idiomatic." Both "idiom(s)" and "idiomatic" are held as puzzling phrases that transgress either the laws of grammar or the laws of logic. Investigative efforts spanning several decades in the last century alone to uncover their characteristic patterns and rules for analyzing such linguistic structures have had mixed results at best given that nearly all fixed and semi-fixed phrases defined as "idioms" exhibit a special lexical and syntactic character, namely, "own, private, peculiar."

Against this backdrop, this chapter discusses the pragmatic efficacy of teaching *idiomaticity* or *idiomatology* – the study of idioms and idiomatic language – across the second language curriculum. Following a brief review of the nomenclature commonly associated with such language, the chapter advances specific recommendations for how best to expose second language learners to knowledge of idiomaticity in an explicit and systematic way befitting natural use. Key theoretical approaches and empirical paradigms aside, the development of such knowledge in second language learners is then highlighted, the challenges presented acknowledged, and, lastly, the various meanings and functions idioms and idiomatic language serve in diverse context-sensitive social and academic situations are explicated within communicative constructs worth pursuing in second language comprehension and production. Implications underpinning the teaching and learning of idioms and idiomatic language in effective and efficient ways are also discussed and summarized.

Much Ado About the Idiomaticity Labyrinth

Anyone attempting to examine matters of idiomaticity up close will soon come across hundreds upon hundreds of accounts spanning more than ten decades. Without exception, idiomatologists and lexicologists alike have attempted to define, describe, and explain idiomaticity from a number of theoretical perspectives and empirical paradigms. Collectively, these accounts have generated many terms and related concepts emphasizing the theoretical emphasis pursued. One common dimension underlying many of these accounts is *compositionality* (or lack thereof). Indeed, it is the exceptionality of the semantic non-compositionality of idioms that permits their long-established interpretation as non-conforming semantic entities representing a continuum of a wide range of dimensions too numerous to mention all here in detail. Suffice to underscore that to date there have been numerous English adaptations of "idiomatology" within the sociocultural (Roberts, 1944), transformational-generative (Katz & Postal, 1964; Weinreich, 1969; Fraser, 1970), naturalist (Chafe, 1968), syntactic (Newmeyer, 1972, 1974), semantic (Nunberg, 1978; Fernando & Flavell, 1981), and pragmatic (Strässler, 1982) approaches.

The problematization of idiom (and related lexicalized expressions) in early generative approaches or modern linguistics aside, the study of idiomatology also involved a great many rigorous discussions on the essential properties (Bell, 1991, p. 3: alteration of grammatical rules, conventional phrases, alteration of word order, figurativeness; Nunberg, Sag, & Wasow, 1994, pp. 492–493: conventionality, formal inflexibility, figuration, proverbiality, informality, affect) and features (Fernando, 1996, p. 3: compositeness, institutionalization, semantic opacity) deemed a necessary condition for idiom status, or the different types of linguistic characteristics (Barkema, 1996: compositionality, collocability, and flexibility) of idiomatic expressions; the storing of idioms alongside morphemes, words, and abstract grammatical frames in an extended mental lexicon (Goldberg, 2006); and the idiomaticity problem multiword expressions present for Natural Language Processing and especially for machine translation (Sag, Baldwin, Bond, Copestake, & Flickinger, 2002).

Much theoretical emphasis was also placed on deciphering the six-level frozenness hierarchy of the semantic representation of phrasal idioms (Fraser, 1970, p. 39: unrestricted, reconstitution, extraction, permutation, insertion, adjunction, completely frozen); the classes (Nunberg, 1978: normally decomposable, abnormally decomposable, semantically non-decomposable) and subclasses (Fernando, 1996: pure, semi-pure, literal) of idioms; the classification of idioms based on compositionality (Cacciari & Glucksberg, 1991: compositional-opaque, compositional-transparent, quasi-metaphorical), degrees of metaphoric transparency (Moon, 1998, pp. 22–23: transparent, semi-transparent, opaque), form–meaning relationship (Seidl & McMordie, 1988, p. 13: irregular form/clear meaning, regular form/unclear meaning, irregular form/unclear meaning), form (Makkai, Boatner, & Gates, 1995: lexemic idioms (verbal, nominal, adjectival, adverbial), tournures, well-established sayings and proverbs), structure (McCarthy

& O'Dell, 2002, p. 6: verb + object/complement, prepositional phrase, compound, simile, binomial, trinomial, whole clause or sentence), and syntax, semantics, and function (Cowie, Mackin, & McCaig, 1983, p. xi: clause and phrase idioms (syntax), pure idioms, figurative idioms, restricted collocations, and open collocations (semantics), sayings and catchphrases (function)).

In these theoretical accounts, *idiomatology* or *phraseology* (from Greek φράσις phrasis, "way of speaking" and -λογία -logia, "study of") included the study of set or fixed expressions and multiword lexical units displaying a peculiar manner or style of verbal expression. Such units are often collectively referred to in the literature as *collocations, formulaic sequences, idiomatic expressions, idioms, lexical bundles, phrasal verbs, phrasemes* (or *phraseological units*), and *prefabricated expressions,* to name but the most common nomenclature available to date. In all these lexicalized units, the sum of the usual individual meanings of their (apparent) constituents violates common compositional rules and does not mean what the bilexemic or polylexemic word group mean independently in common use. According to Sag, Baldwin, Bond, Copestake, and Flickinger (2002), multiple words units can be described as "idiosyncratic interpretations that cross word boundaries (or spaces)" (p. 2). These units – lexemes, multiword, or multimorphemic sequences/units/phrases or sentences – exhibit relative syntactic and semantic stability, are lexicalized and idiomatized, and perform diverse functions in a text, such as an emphatic or intensifying function (Gläser, 1998, p. 125).

Canonical forms aside – *idiom, idiomatic expression, figure of speech* – idiomatologists, phraseologists, and lexicographers alike have often referred to such expressions as *chunks, prefabricated patterns, prefabs,* and *routine formulae.* Because of their formulaicity, they were often characterized as *formulaic language* or *formulaic sequences.* They were also frequently seen as *lexicalized stems, lexical phrases/bundles,* or simply *phraseological units* or *phrasemes* and *phraseologisms.* More recently, a label regularly applied was that of "multiword" to such lexemes as "building blocks,""chunks,""constructions," "expressions," "sequences" or "units," not to mention "sequences/strings" to "multiunit." On occasion, the lexemes "phrases" and "strings" were also closely associated with the label "multiword" just as it also appears as "multimorphemic phrases/sentences/sequences/units." With authors listed alphabetically, Table 3.1 presents a truncated constellation of 76 terms commonly applied to lexemes of repeated structures exhibiting language peculiarities that defy the expected rules of grammar and/or logic.

Table 3.1 Common Expressions Nomenclature

Lexemes	Researchers
(cultural) allusions	Alexander (1984); McCarthy (1998)
(irreversible) binomials/ trinomials	Bolinger (1962); Gibbs (1994); Malkiel (1959); Makkai (1972); McCarthy (1998); McCarthy and O'Dell (2002); Mollin (2012); Norrick (1988)
binomial/trinomial idioms	McCarthy and O'Dell (2002)
catchphrases	Alexander (1984)
chunks	Carver (1970); Lieven (2006); Peters (1983); Swan (2006); Tomasello (2003)
clause/phrase idioms	Cowie, Mackin, and McCaig (1983)
clusters	Hyland (2008a); Kenny (2000); Palmer (1933)
(weak/open/strong/ semi-fixed/fixed/frozen/ bound/lexical/grammatical) collocations/colligations	Bartsch (2004); Cowie (1981); Cruse (1986); Firth (1957, 1968); Hoey (2005); Peters (2016); Siepmann (2005); Sinclair (1987, 1991); Walker (2011)
colloquial idioms	Ball (1968)
complex lexical units	Arnaud and Savignon (1997)
compound idioms	McCarthy and O'Dell (2002)
conventionalized language	Yorio (1989)
core idioms	Grant and Bauer (2004)
discourse markers	McCarthy (1998)
discourse-structuring devices	Alexander (1984)
figurative idioms	Boers (2001); Boers, Demecheleer, and Eyckmans (2004a, 2004b); Boers, Eyckmans, and Stengers (2007); Cowie, Mackin, and McCaig (1983); Mulhall (2010)
figurative language	Liontas (2018c)
fixed expressions and idioms	Moon (1998)
formulaic sequences	Appel and Trofimovich (2017); Bishop (2004); Boers, Eyckmans, Kappel, Stengers, and Demecheleer (2006); Conklin and Schmitt (2007); Dörnyei, Durow, and Zahran (2004); Hatami (2015); Henriksen (2013); Jiang and Nekrasova (2007); Lindstromberg, Eyckmans, and Connabeer (2016); Read and Nation (2004); Schmitt (2004); Schmitt and Carter (2004); Schmitt, Dornyei, Adolphs, and Durow (2004); Serrano, Stengers, and Housen (2014); Wray (2017)

(continued)

Table 3.1 (Cont.)

Lexemes	Researchers
formulaic speech	Girard (2004); Wong-Fillmore (1976)
formulaic language/ expressions	Biber (2009); Conklin and Schmitt (2012); N. Ellis (2012); N. Ellis, Simpson-Vlach, and Maynard (2008); Gibbs (1994); Imura and Shimizu (2012); Myles, Hooper, and Mitchell (1998); Weinert (1995); Wray (1999, 2002, 2012, 2013)
formulas	R. Ellis (1994); Raupach (1984)
frozen expressions	Alexandropoulos (2012); Vale (2003)
frozen idioms	Cutler (1982); Fraser (1970); Gibbs (1980); Gibbs and Gonzales (1985)
frozen metaphors	Moon (1997)
frozen similes	Gibbs (1994); McCarthy (1998)
gambits	McCarthy (1998); Keller (1979, 1981)
holophrases	Corder (1973)
idioms	Abel (2003); Arnaud and Savignon (1997); Bortfeld (2003); Fernando (1996); Fraser (1970); Cooper (1999); Geeraert, Newman, and Baayen (2017); Goldberg (2006); Irujo (1986, 1993); Kövecses and Szabó (1996); Laufer (2000); Liontas (1999, 2001, 2002a, 2002b, 2017a, 2018f); McCarthy and O'Dell (2002); Malt and Eiter (2004); Makkai, Boatner, and Gates (1995); Newmeyer (1972, 1974); Nunberg, Sag, and Wasow (1994); Roberts (1944); Smith (1925); Strässler (1982); Vanlancker-Sidtis (2003); Vasiljevic (2015); Weinreich (1969)
idiom blends	Cutting and Bock (1997)
idiomatic expressions	Bobrow and Bell (1973); Cacciari and Glucksberg (1991); Caillies and Butcher (2007); Cieślicka (2006); Cowie, Mackin, and McCaig (1983); Hinkel (2017); Swinney and Cutler (1979); Titone and Connine (1999)
idiomatic language	Liontas (2018e)
idiomatic phrases	Sprenger, Levelt, and Kempen (2006)
idiomatic similes	Alexander (1984)
idiomatic speech routines	McCarthy (1998)
incorporating verb idioms	Gibbs (1994)

Table 3.1 (Cont.)

Lexemes	Researchers
institutionalized/lexicalized (sentence) stems	Pawley and Syder (1983)
lexemic idioms	Makkai, Boatner, and Gates (1995)
lexical phrases	Nattinger and DeCarrico (1992)
lexical bundles (also referred to as N-grams)	Biber and Barbieri (2007); Biber, Johansson, Leech, Conrad, and Finegan (1999); Chen and Baker (2010); Cortes (2002, 2006); Hyland (2008b); Nekrasova (2009); Tremblay, Derwing, Libben, and Westbury (2011)
lexical chunks	Lewis (1993)
lexical patterns and collocational knowledge	Carter (1998); Hoey (1991); Lewis (1993); Schmitt (2000)
memorized sentences and lexicalized stems	Pawley and Syder (1983)
metaphorical/allusive idioms	Alexander (1984)
mobile expressions/idioms	Jackendoff (1997)
multi-morphemic sequences	Peters (1983)
multi-morphemic phrases/sentences	Peters (1983)
multi-morphemic units	Myles, Hooper, and Mitchell (1998)
multiword building blocks	Arnon and Christiansen (2017)
multiword chunks	McCauley and Christiansen (2017)
multiword constructions	Culicover, Jackendoff, and Audring (2017); N. Ellis and Ogden (2017); Liu (2012); Wood and Appel (2014)
multiword expressions	Hoang and Boers (2016); Omidian, Shahriari, and Ghonsooly (2017); Sag, Baldwin, Bond, Copestake, and Flickinger (2002); Schmitt (2000)
multiword items	Moon (1997)
multiword phrases	Arnon and Snider (2010)
multiword patterns	Biber (2009)
multiword sequences	Jackendoff (1997); Pawley and Syder (1983)
multiunit sequences	Theakston and Lieven (2017)
multiword strings	Mauranen (2000)

(*continued*)

Table 3.1 (Cont.)

Lexemes	Researchers
multiword (lexical) units	Arnon and Christiansen (2017); Baker and McCarthy (1988); Cowie (1992); Geeraert, Newman, and Baayen (2017); Schmitt (2010)
phrasal verbs/compounds	Alexander (1984); Gibbs (1994)
phraseological units	Gläser (1998); Pawley and Syder (1983)
phrasicon	De Cock, Granger, Leech, and McEnery (1998)
proverbs (proverbial idioms)	Alexander (1984); Gibbs (1994); Liontas (2018d); Makkai (1972)
prefabricated routines and patterns	Bolinger (1976); Granger (1998); Hakuta (1974)
pseudo idioms	Mulhall (2010)
pure idioms	Cowie (1981); Cowie, Mackin, and McCaig (1983); Mulhall (2010)
recurrent word combinations	Altenberg (1998); De Cock (1998)
restricted/open collocations	Cowie, Mackin, and McCaig (1983)
routine formulae	Coulmas (1979)
sayings/catchphrases	Cowie, Mackin, and McCaig (1983)
semi-idioms	Mulhall (2010)
situation-bound utterances	Kecskes (2000)
speech formulae	Peters (1983)
tournures	Alexander (1984); Makkai (1972); Makkai, Boatner, and Gates (1995)
vivid phrasal idioms	Liontas (1999, 2001, 2002a, 2002b)
whole clause/sentence idioms	McCarthy and O'Dell (2002)

Important to note here is that each one of the terms or labels mentioned above carries its own unique meaning, not uncommon in the literature on the subject. Regardless of lexemic choice, nearly all of these labels refer to a previously stored prefabricated sequence of (dis)continuous words or other elements, such as a multi-morphemic phrase, sentence, or unit of clause length or longer, which at the time of use is not subject to linguistic rule generation or analysis by the language grammar, and which is memorized and retrieved as a whole from the user's memory and/or extended mental lexicon. During recall, both the grammatical form and lexical content is wholly or largely fixed and not generated from the individual words comprising the prefabricated item in question.

Collectively, these single items or multiword complexes of recurrently repetitive series of words comprise essential units of language, carry unitary meanings, form a core component of natural language use, and, perhaps most importantly, are stored as prefabricated units that are pulled from memory fully formed at the time of use. Without exception, they all characterize culturally authentic proficient language use in comprehension and production. Such accounts have most certainly enriched and redefined in many respects the discussion of literal–idiomatic language or literal–figurative language. They also have added to the overall cacophony and misapplication of terms and concepts associated with them. As a result, it has become increasingly more difficult to compare findings among studies purporting to investigate the same idiomatological phenomena of natural language use during comprehension and/or production (see Myles & Cordier, 2017).

And while individual investigative efforts need not be mentioned here – they are too numerous after all – it must be said most clearly and most assertively that the field of idiomatics, as nascent as it is presently, is in desperate need of an easy-to-understand nomenclature of the very discipline it seeks to define: *idiomatology* (or *idiomaticity*), the study of idioms and idiomatic language. In no way am I suggesting that concerted effort be directed yet again to the compilation of idiomatic words and phrases. Such efforts have been undertaken for centuries by phraseologists and lexicologists alike, resulting in hundreds upon hundreds of lexica and specialized dictionaries. What I am calling for, however, is the need to offer descriptions (and terminology) that are authoritative, definitive, and comprehensive.

- *Authoritative descriptions* are those that precisely (and truthfully) define the subject of investigation in an unapologetic fashion: *idiom*, an expression whose meaning is not the regular sum of the meanings of its individual component parts. Seen as "language," as part of the language system, idiom defines language as a mode of expression, parlance, vernacular speech, jargon, usage, style, and talk. Seen as "phrase," idiom defines phrase as an expression, turn of phrase, locution, and set phrase. Each one of these attributes, in turn, could be described (and accurately analyzed) in more definitive and comprehensive ways.

- *Definitive descriptions* have the advantage of being both categorical and unambiguous. Seen as "language," "phrase," or both, expressions can be tested to see if they violate the expected rules of grammar or logic. Those that do not can be placed on one end of the meaning continuum. Those expressions can be referred to as "free combinations," as such expressions permit the substitution of every element by another item of the same class respectively. Such expressions yield a new idiosyncratic meaning each time a substitution occurs. Conversely, those that do violate the expected rules of grammar or logic can be placed on the opposite end of the continuum. Those expressions can be known as "idioms proper" or "genuine idioms," as such expressions yield a conventionalized meaning that is separate from the composite meanings of their constituents. Collectively, the constituents of such expressions express a holistic literal meaning, which has little to do with the figurative or metaphorical meaning intended in that particular setting or text. As a result, *what is said* literally is not *what is meant* figuratively. Because of its institutionalized usage, the latter figurative meaning is easily recognized among the members of a specific speech community, particular profession, or academic discipline. More often than not, loquacious explanations or paraphrases clarifying its meaning are thus unwarranted. Between those two ends of the continuum, "free combinations" and "idioms proper," the expressions commonly referred to as "collocations" can be placed. *Collocations* are the arrangement or conjoining of words (or terms) that co-occur with a frequency greater than chance. Collocations are commonly classified as *weak collocations* or *open collocations* (words are placed side by side or in relation with many other words freely), *strong collocations* or *semi-fixed collocations* (two or more words collocate with a high degree of predictability and are linked with one another in a relatively fixed and restricted word association), and fully *fixed collocations* (the habitual juxtaposition of a particular word with another word or common word combinations that fully prohibit the substitution of elements).
- *Comprehensive descriptions* provide complete and detailed accounts of all those expressions referred to in the literature as *multiword expressions* (MWEs), including *idioms*. According to the category of their elements, the distributional properties of linguistic items in actual language use, *collocations*, for example, are further sub-classified into "lexical collocations" and "grammatical collocations" (also called "colligations," Firth, 1957, 1968; Hoey, 2005). *Lexical collocations* refer to the combination of two

(or more) content words such as nouns, verbs, adjectives, and adverbs. *Grammatical collocations* denote the association of these words with a certain preposition. (For a detailed discussion of different definitions of the term "collocation," see Bartsch, 2004, pp. 26–64.) Linguistic characteristics aside, pertinent as they are, it is the compositional nature of all expressions that demands primary consideration here. While all *idioms proper* exhibit non-compositional tendencies, *collocations* are semi-compositional, and *free combinations* are compositional. In addition, the features of "conventionality," "figuration," "proverbiality," "informality," and "effect" are closely associated with idiomaticity *per se*. Each feature, in turn, conveys a more detailed description of the type of expression under investigation. In addition, lexico-syntactic and phonological variation and modification between different classes of (idiomatic) expressions used across geographic regions and dialectal differences or sociopragmatic and paralanguage constraints affecting the comprehension and production of idioms and idiomatic expressions in general further apprehends the picture of the detailed descriptions sought here.

In sum, descriptions (and terminology) that are *authoritative* (precise and truthful), *definitive* (categorical and unambiguous), and *comprehensive* (complete and detailed), of the sort explicated here, can no doubt spawn a number of fresh lexemic perspectives on idiomaticity that are as distinct as the researchers and language practitioners who toil to collect, catalogue, define, typologize, and understand the properties and proper function of idioms and idiomatic expressions in academic, social, and professional language across diverse contents and contexts displaying authentic language use. In more ways than one, such descriptions (and terminology) with well-defined criteria provide the necessary language to launch meaningful explorations where the subject under investigation, *idiomaticity*, is no longer a "puzzle to be solved" or a "riddle wrapped in mystery inside an enigma" (Liontas, 2018a). Having a well-defined "common language" allows all those involved in idiomatology, or phraseology, to systematically probe many a lexemic and idiomatic phenomena from the ground up and across multiple levels – from the earliest stages of language instruction to the highest levels in academia and the profession – before empirical and classroom-based findings can be faithfully compared, refined, accepted, and, where appropriate, reanalyzed, recast, or simply refuted.

If classroom teachers and doctoral candidates appear to be perplexed by idiomaticity and its epistemology, and second/foreign language learners or (under)graduate students enrolled in our education programs included, it is, I submit, because of the labyrinthine mosaic of terms, labels, and concepts those of us working in diverse disciplines and fields have created over the years. Seeking clear-cut boundaries with sharp demarcation lines is, and may well remain in the foreseeable future, a futile pursuit. Moon (1997) stressed this challenge more than two decades ago: "There are many different forms of multiword item, and the fields of lexicology and idiomatology have generated an unruly collection of names for them, with confusing results ... Note that there is no generally agreed set of terms, definitions and categories in use" (p. 43). Her warning is equally echoed two decades later by Hinkel (2017), who in her opening paragraph asserts that:

> What represents an idiom, a proverb, a conventionalized expression, or a grammatically irregular unit of language is **notoriously—famously—difficult to define** and hence to identify ... With the emergence of computer technology and the proliferation of large and analyzable language corpora in a range of texts and genres, broad expectations arose that **the conundrum of defining and identifying idiomatic and phrasal expressions** could potentially be accorded a measure of systematicity. However, perhaps counter-intuitively, **analyses of language corpora have further added to the typological and terminological stew:** computerized examinations of both spoken and written language data have shed light on the enormity, variability, and complexity of idiomatic and recurrent expressions.
>
> (Hinkel, 2017, p. 46, emphasis added)

And while all this "cacophony" of terms, definitions, and categories may reflect the scope of theoretical perspectives and backgrounds of the authors who have swelled the taxonomy of idiomaticity to new heights using contrasting terminologies and measures in pursuit of their studies' hypotheses, it also becomes exceedingly problematic to identify and resolve nomenclature accurately between first and second language acquisition studies and across cross-cultural, cross-linguistic, and psycho- and neurolinguistic studies, for example, chiefly because of the application of conflicting or overlapping terms and criteria to the same general notion, theory, or model (Myles & Cordier, 2017).

Unsurprisingly, extensive scholarly energy went into postulating and scrutinizing solutions for processing, comprehending, and dichotomizing expressions that, by all accounts to date, seem to defy logic and syntactic structure, resulting into numerous competing hypotheses or models focusing on the lexical representation, processing, and comprehension of idioms and of language use in first (L1) and second languages (L2), the most researched of which remain the *idiom list (literal first) hypothesis* (Bobrow & Bell, 1973), the *lexical representation (simultaneous processing) hypothesis* (Swinney & Cutler, 1979), the *figurative first hypothesis* (or *direct access model*), the *holistic hypothesis* (Jiang & Nekrasova, 2007, Wray, 2002), the *idiom decomposition model* (Gibbs, 1980, 1995; Gibbs & Nayak, 1989; Gibbs, Nayak, & Cutting, 1989), the *configuration model* (Cacciari & Tabossi, 1988), the *hybrid model* (Caillies & Butcher, 2007; Cutting & Bock, 1997; Sprenger, Levelt, & Kempen, 2006) or *constraint-based model* (Libben & Titone, 2008; Titone & Connine, 1999; Titone, Columbus, Whitford, Mercier, & Libben, 2015), and the *dual route model* (Van Lancker Sidtis, 2004, 2012; Van Lancker Sidtis, Cameron, Bridges, & Sidtis, 2015). Notable L2 hypotheses or models include the *graded salience hypothesis* (Giora, 1997), the *idiom diffusion model* (Liontas, 1999, 2002a, 2015), the *dual idiom representation model* (Abel, 2003), and the *literal salience model* (Cieślicka, 2006).

Collectively, all these L1 and L2 theoretical perspectives and empirical paradigms about the representations and mechanisms responsible for idiomatic language comprehension and productivity, not to mention the many heated debates among computer scientists, linguists, and psychologists who are employing large corpora, statistical-computational tools, and accessible experimental techniques such as frequency statistics and association indexes (see, for example, Bartsch, 2004; Biber, 2009; Ellis, Simpson-Vlach, & Maynard, 2008; Geeraert, Newman, & Baayen, 2017; Henriksen, 2013; Liu, 2012; Mauranen, 2000; McCauley & Christiansen, 2017; Moon, 1998; Walker, 2011), have placed idiomaticity at the center of scholarly debate that has been ongoing for over a century, not least because, as Weinreich (1969) put it, "idiomaticity is important for this reason, if for no other, that there is so much of it in every language" (p. 23). Making heads or tails of idiomaticity and the respective categories or classes of expressions it seemingly represents remains a formidable challenge – incorporating them across the curriculum an even greater Herculean contest. It is these concerns that we turn to next.

Exposing Second Language Learners to Knowledge of Idiomaticity

To be crystal clear, the sphere of idiomaticity needs to be omnipresent in the learning process from the beginning of language acquisition. As learners ascend to higher levels of language proficiency, their facility with, and exposure to, the scope of idiomaticity should follow suit and increase proportionally in both breadth and depth. While studying the lexicon of individual words and the grammar for combining them freely into larger lexemic units is undeniably important in attaining mastery of the target language itself, it is nonetheless the peculiar lexemic and syntactic combination of morphemes into higher units or structures too irregular to fit grammatical constructions that renders them idiomatic and natural in language use: *bend over backwards, grab the bull by the horns, hook, line and sinker, kick the bucket, pull someone's leg, put the cart before the horse, read between the lines, red flags, red herring, spill the beans, the bottom line, throw in the towel, walk on eggshells.*

Frequency of usage across various print and non-print sources and their actual use in natural language, related informal and colloquial restrictions in register and style or internal modification, passivization, and topicalization transformations notwithstanding, are key to closely examining the character and quality of idiomaticity proper across the second language curriculum. A keen understanding of the conventionalized mono- or polymorphemic lexemic meaning of such idiomatic expressions and the real-life functions they fulfill in everyday human discourse, regardless of the specific speech community, particular profession, or academic discipline in which they are purposefully employed, combined with diachronic and synchronic investigations of language creativity over time and space, will no doubt hasten their mastery even when geographical varieties and dialectal-register peculiarities and emblematic gesture influences, and there are many across the English-speaking world, punctuate and solidify their natural use in the language (Allen, 1995; Boers, Eyckmans, & Stengers, 2007; Eyckmans & Lindstromberg, 2016; Ibáñez, Manes, Escobar, Trujillo, Andreucci, & Hurtado, 2010).

Irrespective of their literal or figurative meanings, idioms and idiomatic expressions of all types and lengths should be couched within culturally appropriate constructs that epitomize proper language use application. Idiomatic performance should not result from direct transfers of meaning from one's mother tongue as such word-for-word transfers more often than not result in incongruous translations that bear little resemblance to the original lexemic meaning. If cross-cultural comparisons are deemed necessary or desirable, care should be taken not to overemphasize the "sameness" of expressions across languages overtly. And while there are common words and phrases that are *calques* ("loan translation of a foreign word or phrase", from French *calque*, literally "a copy"), especially when *idiom calquing* is involved, greater emphasis should be placed on the recurrent situation in which the use of such expressions is deemed socio-pragmatically appropriate or even necessary than on literal word-for-word translations from one language into another or *folk literalizations*, the re-creation of literal meanings for idioms.

Proper language use application also entails a close examination of the words (or terms) that habitually co-occur with a frequency greater than chance. Because all languages have a large number of words that *collocate* (derived from Latin *collocatus* (past participle of *collocare*), equivalent to *col-* (together) plus *loc(us)* (location, place, to place/locate/go together, set in place)) and *colligate* (derived from Latin *colligatus* (past participle of *colligare*), equivalent to *col-* (with, together) plus *ligare* (to tie, bind, fasten, or group together)) in a lexemic or syntactic relation to form fixed relationships, it is imperative that students become aware of, and notice, the arrangement or conjoining of words. Studying the habitual juxtaposition of a particular word with another word or common word combinations permits learners to make collocations a significant part of their vocabulary learning process. More importantly, learners gain valuable exposure to and experience with a range of sequences of lexical items which habitually co-occur, and which are lexically complex: *bear in mind, break a leg, break someone's heart, break the ice, catch a ball/chill/cold/thief, catch the flu, chair a meeting, close/make a deal, come first/second/third, come to a compromise/decision, come to an agreement/end, come to terms with, come to the point, dead/right on time, deep in thought, deeply regret the loss of someone or something, early riser, feel free, from dawn till dusk, get the sack, go bananas/berserk/dark/nuts/wild/yellow, go out of business, go to great lengths to do something, hard-earned money, have a good time, have breakfast/ brunch/lunch/dinner, keep a diary/promise/secret, keep calm/control/quiet, keep in touch, light sleeper, make a difference/loss/mess/mistake/noise/profit, make trouble, pay attention, pay by money order, pay one's respects, pay someone a compliment/ visit, pay the bill/piper/price, run out of gas/patience/time, save/spare/spend time, take a break/chance/dive/hike/leak/leap of faith, the smart money is on, throw money around/away, throw money at something/the problem, throw/pour money down the drain, throw/toss money out the window.* Concomitantly, they also learn to appreciate the semantic integrity or cohesion of a collocation, that is, each lexical constituent is a semantic constituent in that the meaning conveyed by one (or more) of its mutually selective constituent elements is highly restricted contextually, and different from its transparent meaning in more neutral contexts. Expressed differently, the immediate environment in which a collocation occurs both marks and restricts its semantic cohesion as well as the implied meaning and communicative use of said collocation, variations notwithstanding.

Coupled with idiomatic variants and the discourse settings in which they find currency, the range of such sequences of lexical items grows exponentially to create a network of expressions that is hard to dismiss as mere peripheral language not worth its salt. Depending on learners' linguistic ability and intellectual maturity, teachers are counseled to offer students structured opportunities to investigate the extensions of a preselected lexeme and copy or write sentences supporting their many senses in context. Those expressions that exhibit idiomatic or figurative/proverbial use should be given primary priority. Table 3.2 below provides 136 such expressions connected to the lexical unit "throw" (and there are many more). Collectively, these multiword *throw*-expressions represent a plethora of nuances of meaning not easily ascertained from a mere literal reading of their constituent elements (morphological form, semantic content, syntactic category). Only through attentive noticing and word-sense disambiguation in context will learners be able to narrow the possible senses (meaning and function) down to the probable ones. Most assuredly, they will become aware of how frequently used strings of linguistic elements can be and are converted into distinct chunks of prefabricated expressions. Over time, and through extensive practice and controlled repetition, requiring both attention and effort, experiencing these unit-based lexemes in supporting contextual constructs will lead to greater automatization in comprehension in general and production in particular.

To maximize learning, learners are to employ any of the print or digital resources available to them. The use of general dictionaries without clear description for the lemmatization of collocations is to be discouraged. Instead, the use of (monolingual or bilingual) specialized dictionaries (for professional translators or EAP/ESP language practitioners and students alike) of frequent collocations in a (specialized) language or domain is highly encouraged (see, for example, the 560 million word *Corpus of*

Table 3.2 Notable Expressions Containing the Lexeme "Throw"

a herring-throw
a stone's throw (across/away)
a throwaway (= junk)
an Eighties throw-back
do not throw the baby (out) with the bathwater
not a word to throw at a dog
not trust someone as far as one can throw them
people (who live) in glass houses shouldn't throw stones
throw (a dog) a bone (to)
throw a challenge
throw (someone) a curve(ball)
throw a fight/game/match
throw/have a (hissy) fit
throw a glance at
throw (someone) a googly
throw a Hail Mary (pass/route)
throw a lifeline to (or throw someone a lifeline)
throw a map
throw a (surprise) party
throw/raise a red flag
throw a scare into (someone)
throw a sheep
throw a sickie
throw/put a spanner/wrench (in the works)
throw a (temper) tantrum
throw a Technicolor yawn
throw a tub to the whale
throw a wet blanket over something
throw a wobbler

(continued)

Table 3.2 (Cont.)

throw a wobbly
throw a (monkey) wrench into something (in the works)
throw about/around
throw an eye on/over (something)
throw/pitch an idea
throw around the old pigskin
throw away
throw away an opportunity
throw away the key
throw away the scabbard
throw away your future
throw back
throw back on
throw behind
throw bodies at a problem
throw chunks
throw/pour cold water on (something)
throw/roll/shoot dice
throw dirt enough, and some will stick
throw down a challenge
throw down the gauntlet
throw dust in someone's eyes
throw enough mud at the wall, some of it will stick
throw everything at the wall to see if it sticks
throw everything but the kitchen sink
throw/knock (someone) for a loop
throw (someone) for a loss
throw good money after bad
throw in (a free ...)

Table 3.2 (Cont.)

throw in (add, insert, introduce)
throw in one's hand
throw in one's lot with
throw in the foreground/background
throw in the towel/sponge
throw in with
throw (one) into a tizz(y)
throw it all in
throw it back up
throw it over the wall
throw/cast/shed (some) light on/up on/upon something
throw money around
throw money at someone/something
throw money at the problem
throw money away (flush money down the toilet)
throw money down the drain (a rat hole)
throw money out the window (spend money like a (drunken) sailor)
throw (someone's) name around
throw/put (one's/someone's) name in the hat
throw (someone) off (balance/course/stride/track)
throw on (clothes)
throw (someone or something) on the scrap heap
throw one's arms around someone's shoulder/neck
throw one's bonnet/cap over the windmill
throw one's hands up (in the air)
throw/toss one's hat in/into the ring
throw one's hat over the wall/fence
throw one's life away
throw one's rattle/toys out of the pram

(*continued*)

Table 3.2 (Cont.)

throw one's voice
throw one's weight/influence/support behind someone/something
throw one's weight about/around
throw oneself at/on/upon/into/down
throw oneself at (someone's) feet
throw oneself at/on the mercy of the court
throw oneself away
throw oneself between
throw open
throw out
throw out of whack
throw out one's back
throw out the back
throw out the playbook
throw out the window
throw over
throw people together
throw punches
throw salt on someone's game
throw salt over one's (left) shoulder
throw shade (on/at someone)
throw (some) shapes
throw stones
throw someone a line
throw someone (or something) aside/away
throw someone in at the deep end
throw someone off the scent/trail
throw someone out into the cold
throw someone out on his or her ear

Table 3.2 (Cont.)

throw someone to the dogs/lions/wolves
throw something at someone or something
throw something in
throw something (back) in someone's face (= rub it in to someone's face)
throw (something) in(to) the pot
throw/call/bring something into (serious) question
throw/put something into (sharp/stark) relief
throw the book at someone
throw the children in the back (seat)
throw/cast the first stone
throw the kitchen sink at something
throw to the four winds
throw (caution) to the wind(s)
throw together (something)
throw (someone) under the bus
throw up
(make oneself) throw up
throw up on someone
throw up one's hands in horror/despair
throw up the sponge

Contemporary American English (COCA) at https://corpus.byu.edu/coca/, the largest freely available and most widely used corpus of English, or the free download of the *Oxford Collocations Dictionary of English*, based on the 100-million-word *British National Corpus (BNC)* and containing over 150,000 collocations for nearly 9,000 headwords with over 50,000 examples showing how collocations are used in context naturally, with notes, grammar and register information at www.freecollocation.com). Learners may even become aware of the ways words are placed or arranged together to create "blocks" or "chunks" of language without breaking the rules of natural language. Notably, they are afforded prime opportunities to analyze and discover the strength of the collocational links characterizing the *collocation* (the sequence of words or terms) as either weak or strong. When a word can collocate (be placed side by side or in relation) with many other words freely, such a collocation is referred to as a *weak collocation* or *open collocation* (*free time, make time, make time for, right on time, run out of time, save time, spare time, spend some time, take your time, tell someone the time, waste time,* etc.). In contrast, when the link between the two (or more) words is relatively fixed and restricted, it is considered a *strong collocation* or *semi-fixed collocation* (*crystal clear, prim and proper, under the weather*). In such cases, words bound together and the use of a certain word or a particular combination of words conjures (and predicts) the other word(s), with varying degrees of success. Semi-fixed and fixed expressions of two or more words are believed to have a high degree of predictability in their word associations. Through repeated context-dependent use, certain semi-fixed expressions become established and recognized as natural speech while others become fully fixed and "frozen," or as Cruse (1986, p. 41) says, "bound" collocations (*curry favor, foot the bill*). Such conventional units of expression are referred to by some as *frozen idioms* or *frozen metaphors* precisely because no further modifications are possible – they are, in a word, "frozen-in-time" (Cutler, 1982; Fraser, 1970; Gibbs 1980; Gibbs & Gonzales, 1985; Moon, 1997).

And just as someone's character becomes apparent when one considers the type of persons that he or she associates with ("Show me your friends and I'll tell you who you are"), or so it is widely claimed by the Spanish proverb ("Dime con quién andas, y te diré quién eres"/"Tell me who you walk with, and I'll tell you who you are"), similarly, learners can learn much about words and their use in natural language by studying the company words keep. As the English saying goes, *birds of a feather flock together.* By extension, because collocations may be strong or weak, learners are similarly urged to discover the patterns of collocation advanced by the various types of collocation and take note of the most common types: (subject-) noun + verb (*the companies merged, the economy boomed, the wind howled*), adjective + noun (*bright light, excruciating pain, fine weather, heavy drinker/drug-user/smoker, high winds, key issue, maiden voyage, major problem, torrential rain*), noun + noun (*ecstasy and agony, pride and prejudice, round of applause, sense of pride*), adverb + adjective (*bitterly disappointed, blissfully unaware, completely satisfied, deeply concerned, fully aware, happily married, seriously injured*), verb + (object-)noun (*break the rules, commit suicide, commit murder, make mistakes, pose a problem, run the risk*), verb + expression with preposition or phrasal verb (*burst into tears, look at, run out of money*), verb + adverb (*fail miserably, handle carefully, it is raining heavily, wave frantically, whisper softly*), adverb + verb (*simply vanished, softly whispered, vaguely remembered*), noun + preposition (*interest in*), preposition + noun (*by accident*), and adjective + preposition (*angry at*).

What is critical to note here is not so much the type of collocation under investigation or the pre-established syntactic-lexical relation among various collocations but, more importantly, the manner in which collocations – serving as "semi-preconstructed phrases" that enjoy wide institutionalized currency – allow language users to express their ideas naturally and with maximum clarity and economy. But to do so, language learners must cognize which combination of words permits substitution restriction on semantic grounds while retaining the literal meaning (e.g., *eat apples*, where "apples" can be substituted by "oranges, watermelon, spaghetti," and so on) and which collocations are restricted by arbitrary substitution limitations (e.g., *perform a task*, where one can *do* a task, but not *make* a task). More importantly, learners must cognize which collocational sequences of lexical items which habitually co-occur rarely permit substitution of elements and which collocating and colligating lexemic/syntactic sequences fully prohibit elements substitution. In the former, the combination to *do a flip-flop* and *do a U-turn*, for example, evokes a figurative meaning in the sense of "a sudden or unexpected reversal of one's attitude, behavior, belief, direction, mind, or policy" while also preserving a current literal interpretation of "doing a flip-flop," the execution of a backward handspring/somersault or the wearing of any backless, usually open-toed flat shoe or slipper, or "doing a U-turn," the turn made by a vehicle in the shape of a "U," thereby resulting in a complete reversal and change of direction. Such expressions are also termed *figurative idioms* (see Boers, 2001; Boers, Demecheleer, & Eyckmans, 2004a, 2004b; Boers, Eyckmans, & Stengers, 2007). In the latter, elements substitution in sequences such as *blow the gaff, burn the candle at both ends, eat humble pie,* and *hear something straight from the horse's mouth,* for example, is fully prohibited, thereby retaining only the figurative meaning. Such word combinations are referred to as *pure idioms* (Cowie, 1981; Cowie, Mackin, & McCaig, 1983; Mulhall, 2010).

Transparency and *commutability* are thus critical parameters in language learning best practiced in real contexts and across the four language modalities (i.e., speaking, listening, reading, and writing). *Contextualization* and *memorization* based on appropriate meaning, definition, and real-use application must precede instructional attempts to compile long lists of collocations, idioms, and idiomatic expressions *sans* understanding and real-context practice in the target language. Defining the notion of phraseological collocation/colligation in easy-to-understand language; identifying criteria allowing the operationalization of such definitions; describing the characteristic syntactic, semantic, pragmatic, and discoursal properties of collocations/colligations; and delimiting them with respect to other combinatory phenomena are some of the distinct ways teachers may employ to introduce students to these frequent, recurrent, and conventionalized "building blocks" or "essential units" of the lexicon (Lewis, 2000; Nesselhauf, 2003; Zyzik, 2011).

Relating the syntactic, semantic, and pragmatic description of lexemes, teachers should also consider how best to help their students distinguish *collocations* from *free combinations* on the one hand, and from *pure idioms* on the other. Between these two boundaries, they could, for example, ask students to organize exemplars of certain types along the idiomatological/phraseological continuum. Using measurable criteria of definition, description, and lexicographic presentation of collocations, and following the rules of syntax, students apply syntagmatic combination phenomena involving two or more lexemes (of category noun, verb, adjective, or adverb) as they occur (adjacently) in a text. In so doing, they also display their budding understanding of an expression's *compositionality*, *collocability*, and *flexibility*, which, according to Barkema (1996), best capture the various linguistic characteristics of idioms and other lexicalized expressions. Knowledge of lexical combinatorics, especially knowledge displaying suitable combinations of nouns in compounds or noun phrases, is most important for translation, where collocationally correct texts are perceived as "fluent" and "natural" (Barfield & Gyllstad, 2009).

By extension, analysis of vocabulary learning beyond single words must follow within authentic texts, and its meaning must be derived from the given context. For maximum results, to provide for a more systematic account of frequent collocations in English, authentic textual materials are to be employed whenever feasible. In particular, the use of intelligent corpus-querying software that mine and extract collocational data from large text corpora, of the sort employed widely in various computational linguistic studies, is to be encouraged. The availability of collocation lists extracted from texts or machine-readable dictionaries, based on statistical measures of similarity or plausibility of a parameter value (e.g., log-likelihood, mutual information, t-score, z-score) to uncover frequencies and probability distributions of the co-occurrence of word associations based on a key word in context (KWIC) and the ways words are used is a great advantage for the semantic description of all lexical items. Moreover, corpus exploration of the recurring presence of a node and its collocates in a text, combined with a collocational multidimensional description entailing paradigmatic syntactic, semantic, and pragmatic considerations, is certain to exemplify a rich source of meaningful analyses of language form, language meaning, and language in context. Such instructional emphasis will no doubt shed light on important *interlexical* (word length, collocate–node relationship) and *intralexical* factors (L1 influence and/or interference, L1–L2 differences, congruency) which, in turn, may further accelerate the (semi-)automatic acquisition and use of institutionalized idioms and idiomatic expressions in human and computational applications of lexical knowledge sources (Peters, 2016).

The move from a word-centered to a phrase-centered approach to idiomaticity will undoubtedly underscore knowledge of recurrent word combinations as vital for the competent use of a language, for even the most grammatically perfect sentence will stand out as awkward and unnatural if collocational preferences are either deliberately violated or unknowingly avoided. Helping learners to amass (and accurately and appropriately use) commonly used *collocations* and *multiword sequences* of all types and lengths remains a formidable challenge for language professionals at all levels, not least because there are so many in everyday and professional language use across the world's languages (Conklin & Schmitt, 2012). Multiword sequences, according to Jackendoff (1997), are scarcely "a marginal part of our use of language" (p. 156), a view also echoed in the work of many corpus investigation studies (see, for example, Conrad, 2000; De Cock, Granger, Leech, & McEnery, 1998; Walker, 2011) which hold that such sequences account for about 50 percent of all language produced by native speakers in speech and writing. With respect to *formulaic sequences* (FSs), Erman and Warren (2000) and Schmitt and Carter (2004) posit that such sequences make up a large portion of discourse, and that as much as 50 percent of the language may be explainable using idiomatic terms. And according to Foster (2001), more than 30 percent of speech is formulaic. Such accounts, sheer size and idiosyncratic properties aside, naturally pose clear implications for language learning and use, the most important of which are discussed next.

Implications for Teaching Idioms and Idiomatic Language

Given the heterogeneous properties different types of idioms and idiomatic expressions exhibit and the cognitive lexical and grammatical mechanisms at work by which such expressions are processed and produced by native and non-native language speakers alike, albeit with different levels of socio-pragmatic success (see Culicover, Jackendoff, & Audring, 2017; Goldberg, 2006; Wray, 2017), it is only logical to suggest time-tested pedagogical structures that have the potential to support language acquisition and processing beyond single-word vocabulary. To begin with, the ubiquity of idiomaticity, combined with pedagogical measures of comprehension and production known to define and facilitate native language fluency (Pawley & Syder, 1983), is best apprehended in authentic materials and settings that exemplify natural language use. Therein, language learners can discover the multiple functions and pragmatic constraints idioms and idiomatic expressions serve during the achievement of social and communicative goals, as well as their possible variations and recurrent word patterns underlying the pivotal role they play in language and linguistic productivity. Prolonged exposure to usage and practice with idiomatic utterances during sustained discourse helps solidify idiomaticity as a pivotal building block of language acquisition and natural language fluency. *Morphosyntactic form, length, degree of fixedness, level of grammatical acceptability, semantic opaqueness, word association strength, frequency, range, oral and written discourse functions,* and *register* are but some of the most important attributes a sociopragmatic usage-based approach to idiomaticity can reasonably hope to attain. Importantly, a close examination of these attributes, individually or in combination, can lead to improved instructional techniques that are certain to frame the purpose of idiomatic learning and guide philosophical disquisitions of the *breadth and depth of understanding idiomaticity,* the framework of which is discussed next.

Breadth and Depth of Understanding Idiomaticity

Because idiomaticity entails the study of idioms and idiomatic language, all learning associated with it needs to take full account of the graphophonological, morphological, syntactic, semantic, and pragmatic parameters that underlie linguistic productivity and natural language use, including those permitting possible specific elements transformations known to operate through and across levels of language analysis. Such intentional learning, referred to here as the *breadth of idiomatic learning,* anchors knowledge of idiomaticity within pedagogic-technological constructs that promote purposeful practice, assiduous assessment, and authentic evaluation. The systematic integration of such knowledge across the curriculum is referred to here as the *depth of idiomatic learning*. Combined with the breadth of idiomatic learning, these two archetypes of idiomatic learning comprise the framework I call the *breadth and depth of understanding idiomaticity*. As such, the framework covers the full span of knowledge of idiomaticity, including the ubiquity and heterogeneous properties of idioms proper and idiomatic language broadly defined.

To gain *breadth and depth of understanding idiomaticity*, language practitioners and teachers alike are encouraged to cross disciplinary boundaries to take advantage of all knowledge to date that has scrutinized the origin, nature, methods, and limits of idiomaticity. Progress made over the years in each area of investigation, including all epistemological relevance of knowledge pertaining to how idioms and idiomatic language are best practiced purposefully, assessed assiduously, and evaluated authentically, can serve as a guide to fruitful discussions of various classifications and typologies. Following a representative assortment of idiomatic terms and their definition, collaborative effort should address the balance of surface-level knowledge of idiomaticity with deep-level knowledge of idiomaticity.

Specifically, *surface-level knowledge of idiomaticity* (akin to asserted passive knowledge of idiomaticity) involves perfunctory acquaintance with several types of idiomatic expressions without knowing necessarily how to employ them productively in culturally appropriate ways in writing or while speaking, or what rhetorical and communicative effect such expressions hold in various human interactions. Conversely, *deep-level knowledge of idiomaticity* (akin to inferential active knowledge of idiomaticity) embraces knowing and valuing the "creative genius" a great many idiomatic expressions exhibit. Along with knowledge of how idiomatic expressions sound naturally (phonology), deep-level knowledge of idiomaticity also entails knowledge of their written form (orthography) and that of the other constituent parts (morphology), their grammatical use (syntax), their dynamic connotations/denotations and how such lexical senses relate to other words (semantics), and, finally, their non-literal, figurative meanings and the ways by which such meanings are conveyed to others productively across time and space *sans* sociolinguistic and cultural violations (pragmatics) (Bardovi-Harlig & Dörnyei, 1998).

Naturally, attempts at striking the perfect balance of the *breadth and depth of understanding idiomaticity* will depend wholly upon the breadth of the curricular goals espoused at each school grade or language proficiency level and the depth of knowledge empirical investigations targeting idiomaticity seek to uncover. Even so, such attempts may turn out to be as elusive and counterproductive as *putting the cart before the horse.* Put bluntly, as I have stated elsewhere:

> There is no such thing as attaining the perfect balance of the breadth and depth of understanding idiomaticity, only the imperfect attempts of having tried and failed many times over. Perfection is but a state of illusion constantly reminding us of the odyssey that idiomatic learning rightly is. In the end, it is steady progress, not perfection, that determines the breadth and depth of idiomatic learning.
>
> (Liontas, 2018a, p. 7)

Indeed, it is *steady progress in idiomatic learning, not perfection,* that will resolve how healthy (broad and wide) or how robust (deep and strong) any perceived progress toward attaining idiomaticity really is, for, as Strutz (1996) rightly asserts, "No one can be said to be really proficient in another language until he or she possesses an 'idiomatic' control of it" (p. vii). Of course, the perennial question, *depth over breadth* or *breadth over depth*, remains: is it better to learn a lot about a few idiomatic expressions than a little about many? Said another way, is it better to study a broad array of idiomatic expressions and issues associated with their learning than to have a deep understanding of a single area of idiomatic concentration?

Irrespective of answers sought (and I suspect there are many), targeted pursuits of "breadth over depth" are attainable, provided those learning outcomes language practitioners and teachers deem valuable to understanding the vast network of knowledge closely associated with productive manifestations of idiomaticity proper are systematically explored within tenable descriptions (and terminologies) that are authoritative, definitive, and comprehensive. Similarly, "depth over breadth" can be attained if, and only if, idiomatic content is selectively applied and practiced purposefully in settings resembling real-world experiences. Ask yourself, do students need to simply identify and itemize the meaning of idiomatic terms, or do they need to advance, amplify, and apprise both the *idiomatic usage* and *idiomatic use* of particular expressions?

Clearly, both are important, yet both pursue divergent learning goals. Consequently, it is not enough merely to have students know about idioms and idiomatic language, just as it is not enough to have them compile long lists of idioms and idiomatic expressions believed to be frequently and widely used, both noble pursuits by themselves some could argue. More importantly, *idiomatic usage* (the extent to which language users demonstrate their knowledge of idiomaticity) and *idiomatic use* (the extent to which language users demonstrate their ability to use their knowledge of idiomaticity for effective communication in actual social situations) of particular expressions, it bears repeating, need be practiced with a purpose, assessed judiciously, and evaluated authentically in meaningful, pragmatic ways. As I have argued elsewhere (Liontas, 2015, pp. 625–626), the former – *idiomatic usage* – can be studied by focusing attention on the extent to which learners have mastered the formal properties of the linguistic systems of idioms; the latter – *idiomatic use* – can be studied by examining the ways in which learners employ these properties to interpret and produce culturally appropriate meanings during the production of idiomatic phrases. Doing so also epitomizes the cognitive–intellectual needs, wants, and interests of the students who are expected to display their know–how of different facets of literal and non–literal (figurative) language across the elementary, secondary, and tertiary curriculum.

In more ways than one, the curriculum is and remains the epicenter of all learning effort in which the *breadth and depth of understanding idiomaticity* can best be pursued. When engaging in curriculum development, many teachers begin by selecting the standard(s) that will need to be taught at each school grade or language course, the particular knowledge students will need to amass and know during a given lesson or unit plan, and the specific performance skills students will need to demonstrate their understanding of defined content and concepts as higher levels of schooling and language proficiency levels are attained. By their very design, (national and state-mandated) standards contain a wealth of content and skills information. To frame the purpose of idiomatic learning and guide inquiry, oftentimes such curricular undertakings between teachers and curricular teams charged with developing the curriculum result in diverse instructional protocols, lesson and unit plans, activities, tasks, projects, and assessment practices, all of which combine dynamically to evaluate mastery of content and skill development. Finding common ground, or even agreeing on the best practices to attain these curricular goals, is certainly no easy task, and the end result is often much linguistic-idiomatic information, not to mention viable etymological or metaphoric information, that students will need, or are expected, to master as they progress from one grade level to the next. Yet important curricular questions still loom large: How do teachers translate this collaborative-in-nature curricular effort into what they will actually teach in their unit and daily lesson plans? How do they know what to teach and how to teach it? How do they know which resources and materials to apply to scaffold individual and group-based instruction believed to be most suitable for their level of students? And, perhaps even more importantly, how do teachers know that their teaching indeed has a discernible impact on student learning?

It is suggested that teachers begin with "unpacking" the standards to determine the idiomatic content each standard targets. Indeed, a thoughtful review of standards can and does reveal the performance skills students are expected to master to demonstrate their proficiency. To determine the appropriate grade-level skills to be practiced by students, that is, the proper scope and sequence of defined idiomatic knowledge and its application, there is clear and present need to balance breadth of idiomatic knowledge coverage, on the one hand, with depth of idiomatic application, on the other. As a result of articulating such an encompassing balance, a fine-tuned but focused constructive pedagogy of what students "should know" (types of idiomatic expressions, vocabulary words, key concepts and ideas, etc.) and "be able to do" (identify literal/figurative language, recall full idiomatic strings/sentences in form and meaning, critique usage and use of rhetorical devices in different media and genres, apply appropriate (meta)linguistic and pragmatic knowledge within authentic settings of communication, etc.) to showcase their developing breadth and depth of understanding idiomaticity, couched in easy-to-understand user-friendly language, helps teachers to successively author and implement measurable learning targets that decidedly highlight exclusive idiomatic content and skill acquisition. Such intentional-driven targets of what students should know and be able to do, reassuring as they are, also resolve significantly the restricted lessons, activities, and multimodal resources and technology-based tools and platforms teachers will employ to individualize, and scaffold where necessary, student achievement, irrespective of language fluency yet attained. In turn, this will also help in selecting, at times even designing, age-appropriate assessments that, despite their formative, summative, or alternative nature, stand to test attainment of learner outcomes within confirmed research-based practices.

Curricular explorations of the sort envisaged here require foresight, reflection, and untiring dedication to idiomatic learning from day one. When teachers have the opportunity to identify the exact content and skills in a focused and thoughtful way, it allows them to more deeply understand the curricular standards involved in order to plan for and develop suitable teaching-and-learning practices and assessments that truly reflect *breadth and depth of understanding idiomaticity*. Zeroing in on what is essential for idiomatic instruction at each specific grade level helps teachers to design learning activities and real-world settings that will best prepare students for academic and linguistic success, respectively, thereby "unwrapping the riddle" that is idiomaticity proper.

To meet the curricular challenge just discussed, it is imperative that language practitioners use viable research findings to inform their expanding knowledge of idiomaticity and educational practice (Gablasova, Brezina, & McEnery, 2017; Laufer, 2010). In particular, those findings that have been found to positively impact idiomatic learning should be given primary consideration during curricular deliberations and should be implemented strategically across the curriculum. For example, strategies that focus on learning the forms and associative meanings of words (idiomatic expressions) are significant predictors of both vocabulary breadth and depth knowledge (idiomaticity) beyond single-word vocabulary respectively. By extension, research-based arguments held in support of their inclusion in the K–16 curriculum need to establish and uphold the framework comprising the breadth and depth of understanding idiomaticity envisaged herein.

Applying Idiomaticity Across the Second Language Curriculum

The propositions advanced heretofore underscore the *declarative, associative,* and *autonomous stages of idiomatization* I defined as the process of becoming idiomatized to the target culture – that is, the extent to which learners achieve native-like idiom-language norms and practices over time (Liontas, 1999, 2015). The declarative (declarative idiomatic knowledge or receptive control), associative (controlled idiomatic knowledge or partial control), and autonomous (automatic idiomatic knowledge or full control) stages of the idiomatization process are but three distinct stages of idiomatic knowledge control learners attain on their way to gaining full idiomatic control. To reach full control, learners will need to move from *declarative idiomatic knowledge* through *controlled idiomatic knowledge* to *automatic idiomatic knowledge.* Expressed differently, the learners' move from the declarative stage through the associative stage to the autonomous stage is seen as the development of *idiomatic competence* – the ability to understand and use idioms appropriately and accurately in a variety of sociocultural contexts, in a manner similar to that of native speakers, and with the least amount of mental effort (Liontas, 1999, 2002a, 2015). It includes linguistic (phonology, morphology, syntax, semantics) and pragmatic (nonlinguistic, paralinguistic, sociolinguistic/ functional, discourse, personal/world, intra/intercultural) knowledge the speaker-hearer has of what constitutes appropriate and accurate idiomatic language behavior in relation to particular communicative goals. The actual use of these two types of knowledge in understanding and producing appropriate and accurate idiomatic conduct in diverse social contexts is defined as *idiomatic performance.*

Idiomatic competence and *idiomatic performance,* and by extension, *idiomatic usage* and *idiomatic use,* are not linear ends in themselves, but coherent organizing principles of the greater proceduralization process of *idiomatization.* The degree of proceduralization achieved through systematic study, prolonged intentional exposure, and organized practice embedded in authentic, meaningful interaction impacts idiomatization, which, in turn, is attained qualitatively over time, as learners move through higher levels of education and proficiency. The process of idiomatization is an arduous, cumbersome, accumulative process that extends over many years. Development of native-like idiomatic competence thus requires memorization and culturally appropriate active use of a large set of formulaic chunks and patterns in actual social situations. In short, idiomatic competence is not idiomatic performance for the same reason that the *development of idiomatic competence* is not the *competence of idiomatic development.*

Coupled with the curricular goals (exposure, familiarity, mastery) engendered and the learning outcomes targeted, the conditions of learning – nature, type, and range of idioms and idiomatic language learned in (in)formal settings – under which teachers teach and learners learn are of critical import here. Specifically, the type of (implicit/explicit) instruction and (form-oriented/meaning-oriented) experiences learners encounter during dynamic learning and training formats exert strong influence on the learning environment of (structured/random) idiom/idiomatic presentation and (linguistic/communicative) practice. Indeed, the nature and extent of multimodal (naturalistic, interactive, artificial) input learners receive to notice idioms and idiomatic language while engaging in communicative tasks exemplifying natural communication, shaped through reciprocal and spontaneous interaction, directly impacts their level of success. Moreover, the individual learner differences and psychological factors underlying learners' choice of select (meta)cognitive strategies and collaborative work, including the modalities, tools, and digital and (non-)print resources selected for learners to fulfill specific linguicultural intents *sans* sociopragmatic violations, without exception, all have a marked influence, both individually and collectively, on realizing the *breadth and depth of understanding idiomaticity* advocated herein. The dynamic interplay of curricular goals with learning outcomes, conditions of learning with type of instruction/experiences, and learning environments of presentation/practice with nature/extent of multimodal input both exemplify and underscore the individual learner differences and psychological factors commonly pursued in the modalities, tools, and digital and (non-)print resources learners are asked to employ to showcase their budding understanding of idiomatology. There is thus a direct reciprocal relationship between the process of idiomatization applied and the degree of idiomatic competence developed in language comprehension and production. In the end, idiomatic competence is a dynamic, complex, and multifaceted phenomenon of language acquisition best evidenced in the levels of idiomatic performance attained under (un-)planned real operating conditions requiring learners to employ their breadth and depth of understanding idiomaticity to produce appropriate and accurate idiomatic conduct in diverse social contexts.

Where explanatory qualities of breadth and depth do not suffice to drive forward meaningful curricular change, new alternative explanations will need to be assessed and reassessed to uncover and establish the mitigating factors affecting idiomatic learning *per se*, factors that will soon hasten calls for due consideration in the curricula of the future. As a means to attaining the *breadth and depth of understanding idiomaticity*, teachers could have students investigate a wide variety of idiomatic expressions to better understand their use in human interaction. Undeniably, students' (meta) linguistic and sociocultural-pragmatic needs are best served when they have broad and deep knowledge of matters of idiomaticity (Meunier, 2012; Weinert, 2010). The steady accumulation of such knowledge entails a keen understanding of the human condition to use language creatively to create meaning expressed in ways that routinely defy logical deduction. As already suggested, nowhere is this condition better expressed than in the idiomatic expressions omnipresent in the world's languages.

Requiring students to explore and apply the various facets of idiomaticity – from metaphors to idioms to idiomatic expressions, and any other scheme or trope of figurative language in between – broadens their horizons of understanding and, more importantly, solidifies the acquisition of second language skills while offering a viable alternative perspective for the inner workings of their own native language, respectively. For example, through interlingual and intercultural comparisons students are able to exercise greater coherence in knowledge of idiomaticity. Accordingly, they could begin their exploration by first discovering the conceptual constructs underlying the metaphors behind their use. Such metaphoric groundings could then be expanded to include etymological and lexicographical information. Armed with such information, students could pursue in greater detail the syntactic and lexemic variation prevalent in the behavior of a great many idiomatic expressions, including *clefting* (a complex sentence formed by a main clause and a subordinate (dependent) clause that together convey a meaning expressed only by a simple sentence, as in **It was the bucket that John kicked*) and *passivization* (i.e., the transformation of a sentence from an active form to a passive form as in *John kicked the bucket* ("die") vs **the bucket was kicked by John* and *John spilled the beans* ("divulge a secret") vs. *the beans were spilled by John*), and note the various ways in which the literal/figurative meaning is either retained or altered. Both these phrases – *to kick the bucket, to spill the beans* – are VPs and consist of a transitive verb ("kick," "spill") and the direct object theme ("the bucket," "the beans"), and both can undergo certain syntactic transformations. However, in the former example, *to kick the bucket*, the idiomatic interpretation ("die") can neither undergo clefting nor be passivized without losing its idiomatic meaning, while in the latter example, *to spill the beans*, the idiomatic meaning ("divulge a secret") is retained in the passive.

In lower level coursework, in particular, students should be encouraged to build their understanding of specific classes of idiomatic expressions. Locating, recognizing, selecting, defining, and paraphrasing, for example, are all key attributes of meaningful idiomatic learning worthy of intentional instructional attention. And this list is far from complete. As students become more personally invested in their own (grapho)phonological, morphological, syntactic, semantic, and pragmatic discoveries, both big and small, they should be pushed (metaphorically speaking, of course) to begin manipulating the conventionalized manifestations of idiomatic expressions prior to asking them to produce such expressions both "naturally" and "creatively" in speech or in writing. Said another way, students should be encouraged to master and understand the particular properties of each idiomatic expression prior to attempting to productively use said expression for functional or rhetorical purpose. (For additional pedagogic-technological constructs detailing idiomatic learning across the curriculum, see Liontas, 2015, 2017a, 2017b, 2018a, 2018b, 2018c, 2018d, 2018e, 2018f.)

Conclusion

As stated at the outset of this chapter, ID-I-O-MA-TIC-I-TY is much more than a monolexemic word of seven syllables and 12 characters, or a specialized cover term comprised of two elusive sub-terms, *idiom* and *idiomatic*. Notwithstanding the observation that the first four syllables, *idioma*, reference "language" in Spanish, *idiomaticity*, or *idiomatology*, entails the study of idioms and idiomatic language. By all measures, the definition of "idiom" and "idiomatic language" should be as straightforward as looking them up in a dictionary, namely *idiom*, from Ancient Greek ἰδίωμα (*idíōma*, "special feature, special phrasing, a peculiarity"), from ἴδιος (*ídios*, "one's own, private, peculiar"), and *idiomatic*, from Ancient Greek ἰδιωματικός (*idiōmatikós*, "related to an idiom"), from ἰδίωμα (*idíōma*, "idiomatic").

All that is left for us to decipher is what is meant by "special feature," "special phrasing," a "peculiarity" that is derived from "one's own, private, peculiar" language, which, in turn, is "related to an idiom." In attempting to decipher the language behind the intended meanings of "special," "peculiarity," and "private," we may have to *read between the lines* well before we come to cognize that an "idiom" involves a phrase, or a "special phrasing," that is institutionalized by popular usage. As a "special feature/phrasing," it has a unitary, holistic, figurative meaning, which is conventionally understood by native speakers. This "peculiarity" of meaning, often derived from "one's own, private, peculiar" language until it becomes conventionalized and systematized as such in language usage, language use, or both, is unrelated to and undeducible from the individual literal meanings of its constituent elements, or from the general grammatical rules of a language. And it is this "peculiarity" that is characteristic of, or in keeping with, the way a language is ordinarily and naturally used by its native speakers – hence, *idiomatic*.

Yet not all phrases displaying a "special feature, special phrasing, a peculiarity" are "idioms." As shown, the nomenclature to date has become a never-ending labyrinth of terminology and typology that is devoid of clear-cut boundaries with sharp demarcation lines. Anyone attempting to make heads or tails of the various terms, definitions, and categories in use would be hard pressed to offer cogent arguments for or against the exclusive use of a particular name over another. Ask yourself: what is the difference between a *complex lexical unit* and a *multiword unit*, a *phraseological unit* and a *complex lexical unit*, or a *multiword unit* and a *phraseological unit*? Similarly, what is the difference between a *multiword phrase* and a *lexical phrase*?

I can offer many more such examples here, but the point remains. If the resulting definitions are more alike than they are unlike, perhaps the time has come to cull some of those names to make way for a new nomenclature that truly permits investigations of (dis)similar language phenomena. Conversely, if everything is prescriptively defined and classified as "idiom," how do we discriminate and accept or refute research findings among similes (*as old as the hills, as plain as a pikestaff*), proverbs (*out of sight, out of mind*), terse adverbial phrases (*at hand, by far, of late*), phrasal verbs (*keep down, set up*), habitual collocations (*heart and soul, bag and baggage*), somatic idioms (*turn a deaf ear, pay through the nose*), and verb plus particle combinations (*pull through, keep up*), for example? Collectively, these seven categories – *similes, proverbs, terse adverbial phrases, phrasal verbs, habitual collocations, somatic idioms,* and *verb plus particle combinations* – Smith (1925) included in the category "idiom" nearly a century ago. And if these seven categories can indeed be termed "idioms" (and I have not even mentioned the wide range of prepositions he selects as striking peculiarities of the language, for example, *at Oxford, in London*), what argument can then be made in favor of keeping these seven categories as independent stand-alone classifications deserving of their own nomenclature status?

Smith (1925) may well be right when he says, "The forms of phrasing peculiar to English comprise its idiosyncracies" (p. 168), but "idiosyncrasy" alone, however peculiar to a language such forms may be, cannot comprise the sole property by which an entire class of expressions, having a "special feature, special phrasing, a peculiarity," can and should be defined. An all-encompassing definition of the term *idiom* – whether these peculiar forms are literal or not, whether they are, for example, habitual collocations such as *milk and honey* or idiomatic contraventions flouting the laws of language (grammar) such as *try and go* (whereas *★try to go* is the grammatically correct one), or whether they are, as he says, "the life and spirit of language" (p. 277) – is simply too broad and too inclusive to be a useful term to researchers (and language professionals) wishing to investigate narrower senses of language phenomena occurring naturally in the functioning of a language. And while native speakers (and writers) may use many English idioms, as Smith contends, "as expressions of determination, of exasperation and vituperation" (p. 262), not all expressions deemed idiomatic in language use are to be classified as "idioms." As I have argued elsewhere, "All idioms are (idiomatic) expressions, but not all (idiomatic) expressions are idioms proper" (Liontas, 2018a, p. 6).

Similarly, phrasal compounds (*black-mail, eye-opener*), (personal pronoun) substitutes (*he, she,* and *it*), proper names (*Robert and Elizabeth*), abbreviations as parts of quotations (*to be or not to be*), phrasal compounds (*The White House* vs. the white house), figures of speech in homonymy (*he married a lemon*), and slang (*Here's your horn, blow it, vamoose*), for example, Hockett (1958) calls "idiom." For him, *idiom* is an all-pervasive category and includes mono-morphemic lexemes, polylexemic lexemes, phrases, proverbs, private and literal allusions, proper names, abbreviations, even complete conversations. His six-decade-old definition of "idiom" has a catch-all-tendency, where nearly every item in the entire lexicon of a given language is unfortunately an *idiom* or could be characterized as *idiomatic*. Here, too, there is no clear distinction between lexemic and sememic (semanteme) aspects (i.e., the meaning of a morpheme, a minimum, basic unit of intended meaning or content).

If everything in the universe of idiomatic expressions is by default formalized and classified as an "idiom," it is only logical to postulate that every "block," "bundle," "chunk," "cluster," "collocation," "construction," "expression," "pattern," "phrase," "sequence," "stem," "string," "structure," "unit," or "utterance" (and there are many more such constructs available) associated with lexis must also be an *idiom*. And if everything is an "idiom," is there *a priori* reason to research or teach *phrasemes* per se, or are "phrasemes" just another one of those numerous alternative terms standing tall for *phraseologisms, phraseological units, binomials, trinomials, collocations, idioms, idiomatic expressions, idiomatic phrases, metaphors, metonymies, multiword expressions, multiword utterances, multi-morphemic utterances, proverbs, set phrases,* or *sets of thoughts?*

The argument in such *circulus in probando* (circle in proving) fails to persuade however those classroom teachers, language practitioners, or curriculum developers interested in exploring distinct types of idiomatic language if they are to address all those purported weaknesses, difficulties, or problems many English language learners, even those exhibiting advanced levels of language proficiency, allegedly have with non-literal idiomatic or figurative language. One cannot hope to address systematically shortcomings in natural language comprehension or production without proper definition and identification of idiomatic knowledge, knowledge which, by all accounts, is selectionally bound or compelled by linguistic or sociopragmatic convention. Circular reasoning must thus give way to a transparent terminology and palatable concept formation free of logical fallacy and unwarranted convolution if the propositions deliberated heretofore are to ultimately advance the *breadth and depth of understanding idiomaticity* across the second language curriculum for the benefit of all learners. Such aspiring undertakings, promising as they truly are, require descriptions (and terminology) that are authoritative, definitive, and comprehensive. More importantly, they all require rich instructional constructs and contextual conditions that epitomize the sound and natural application of idiomaticity across the second language curriculum in an unapologetic fashion. Devoid of authentic purposes, even the best-laid curricular plans to practice idiomaticity in diverse social contexts will fail to achieve the idiomatic performance envisaged herein.

In closing, language and idiomaticity are indispensable to each other. Nothing primes language more than idiomaticity. Nothing primes idiomaticity more than language. Only when we know what it is we seek shall we give voice to learning that is idiomaticity proper. In the search the answers will reveal themselves, and we shall come to know idiomaticity for the first time. And, thereby, we shall color idiomaticity anew in all its glory – the memory of the people not soon forgotten, the pulse of the times pulsating rhythmically still in the lips of many, the creative genius of language unmistaken. Plain. Simple. Unassuming. This is our heritage. This is idiomaticity. The passage of time moving forward. Our future in the making. *The rest is history* … idiomatically, that is!

References

Abel, B. (2003). English idioms in the first language and second language lexicon: A dual representation approach. *Second Language Research,* 19(4), 329–358.

Alexander, R. J. (1984). Fixed expressions in English: Reference books and the teacher. *ELT Journal,* 38, 127–132.

Alexandropoulos, G. (2012). The function of the set and frozen expressions in the modern Greek language in news, advertising and media: A corpus based approach. *The Buckingham Journal of Language and Linguistics,* 5, 1–8.

Allen, L. Q. (1995). Effects of emblematic gestures on the development and access of mental representations of French expressions. *Modern Language Journal,* 79(4), 521–529.

Altenberg, B. (1998). On the phraseology of spoken English: The evidence of recurrent word-combinations. In A. P. Cowie (Ed.), *Phraseology: Theory, analysis and applications* (pp. 101–122). Oxford: Oxford University Press.

Appel, R., & Trofimovich, P. (2017). Transitional probability predicts native and non-native use of formulaic sequences. *International Journal of Applied Linguistics, 27,* 24–43.

Arnaud, P. J., & Savignon, S. J. (1997). Rare words, complex lexical units and the advanced learner. In J. Coady, & T. Huckin (Eds.), *Second language vocabulary acquisition* (pp. 157–173). Cambridge: Cambridge University Press.

Arnon, I., & Christiansen, M. H. (2017). The role of multiword building blocks in explaining L1–L2 differences. *Topics in Cognitive Science, 9*(3), 621–636.

Arnon, I., & Snider, N. (2010). More than words: Frequency effects for multi-word phrases. *Journal of Memory and Language, 62,* 67–82.

Baker, M., & McCarthy, M. J. (1988). *Multi-word units and things like that. Mimeograph.* Birmingham, AL: University of Birmingham.

Ball, W. J. (1968). *A practical guide to colloquial idiom.* London: Longman.

Bardovi-Harlig, K., & Dörnyei, Z. (1998). Do language learners recognize pragmatic violations? Pragmatic versus grammatical awareness in instructed L2 learning. *TESOL Quarterly, 32,* 233–259.

Barfield, A., & Gyllstad, H. (Eds.). (2009). *Researching collocations in another language: Multiple interpretations.* Basingstoke, UK: Palgrave Macmillan.

Barkema, H. (1996). Idiomaticity and terminology: A multi-dimensional descriptive model. *Studia Linguistica: A Journal of General Linguistics, 50*(2), 125–160.

Bartsch, S. (2004). *Structural and functional properties of collocations in English: A corpus study of lexical and pragmatic constraints on lexical co-occurrence.* Tübingen, Germany: Gunter Narr Verlag.

Bell, R. T. (1991). *Translation and translating: Theory and practice.* London: Longman Group.

Biber, D. (2009). A corpus-driven approach to formulaic language in English: Multi-word patterns in speech and writing. *International Journal of Corpus Linguistics, 14*(3), 275–311.

Biber, D., Johansson, S., Leech, G., Conrad, S., & Finegan, E. (1999). *The Longman grammar of spoken and written English.* London: Longman.

Biber, D., & Barbieri, F. (2007). Lexical bundles in university spoken and written registers. *English for Specific Purposes, 26*(3), 263–286.

Bishop, H. (2004). Noticing formulaic sequences: A problem of measuring the subjective. *LSO Working Papers in Linguistics, 4*, 15–19.

Bobrow, S. A., & Bell, S. M. (1973). On catching on to idiomatic expressions. *Memory and Cognition, 1*, 343–346.

Boers, F. (2001). Remembering figurative idioms by hypothesising about their origin. *Prospect, 16*(3), 35–43.

Boers, F., Demecheleer, M., & Eyckmans, J. (2004a). Cultural variation as a variable in comprehending and remembering figurative idioms. *European Journal of English Studies, 8*, 375–388.

Boers, F., Demecheleer, M., & Eyckmans, J. (2004b). Etymological elaboration as a strategy for learning figurative idioms. In P. Bogaards, & B. Laufer (Eds.), *Vocabulary in a second language: Selection, acquisition and testing* (pp. 53–78). Amsterdam: John Benjamins.

Boers, F., Eyckmans, J., & Stengers, H. (2007). Presenting figurative idioms with a touch of etymology: More than mere mnemonics? *Language Teaching Research, 11*, 43–62.

Boers, F., Eyckmans, J., Kappel, J., Stengers, H., & Demecheleer, M. (2006). Formulaic sequences and perceived oral proficiency: Putting a lexical approach to the test. *Language Teaching Research, 10*(3), 245–261.

Bolinger, D. (1962). Binomials and pitch accent. *Lingua, 11*, 34–44.

Bolinger, D. (1976). Meaning and memory. *Forum Linguisticum I*, 1–14.

Bortfeld, H. (2003). Comprehending idioms cross-linguistically. *Experimental Psychology, 50*(3), 217–230.

Cacciari, C., & Glucksberg, S. (1991). Understanding idiomatic expressions: The contributions of word meanings. In G. B. Simpson (Ed.), *Understanding word and sentence* (pp. 217–240). Amsterdam: Elsevier.

Cacciari, C., & Tabossi, P. (1988). The comprehension of idioms. *Journal of Memory and Language, 27*(6), 668–683.

Caillies, S., & Butcher, K. (2007). Processing of idiomatic expressions: Evidence for a new hybrid view. *Metaphor and Symbol, 22*(1), 79–108.

Carter, R. (1998). *Vocabulary: Applied linguistic perspectives* (2nd ed.). London: Routledge.

Carver, R. P. (1970). Analysis of "chunked" test items as measures of reading and listening comprehension. *Journal of Educational Measurement, 7*, 141–150.

Chafe, W. (1968). Idiomaticity as an anomaly in the Chomskyan paradigm. *Foundations of Language, 4*, 109–126.

Chen, Y. H., & Baker, P. (2010). Lexical bundles in L1 and L2 academic writing. *Language Learning & Technology, 14*(2), 30–49.

Cieślicka, A. B. (2006). Literal salience in on-line processing of idiomatic expressions by second language learners. *Second Language Research,* 22(2), 115–144.

Conklin, K., & Schmitt, N. (2007). Formulaic sequences: Are they processed more quickly than nonformulaic language by native and nonnative speakers? *Applied Linguistics,* 28, 1–18.

Conklin, K., & Schmitt, N. (2012). The processing of formulaic language. *Annual Review of Applied Linguistics,* 32, 45–61.

Conrad, S. (2000). Will corpus linguistics revolutionize grammar teaching in the 21st century? *TESOL Quarterly,* 34(3), 548–560.

Cooper, T. C. (1999). Processing of idioms in L2 learners of English. *TESOL Quarterly,* 33(2), 233–262.

Corder, S. P. (1973). *Introducing applied linguistics.* Harmondsworth, UK: Penguin Books.

Cortes, V. (2002). Lexical bundles in freshman composition. In R. Reppen, S. M. Fitzmaurice, & D. Biber (Eds.), *Using corpora to explore linguistic variation* (pp. 131–145). Amsterdam: John Benjamins.

Cortes, V. (2006). Teaching lexical bundles in the disciplines: An example from a writing intensive history class. *Linguistics and Education,* 17(3), 391–406.

Coulmas, F. (1979). On the sociolinguistic relevance of routine formulae. *Journal of Pragmatics,* 3, 239–266.

Cowie, A. (1981). The treatment of collocations and idioms in learners' dictionaries. *Applied Linguistics,* 2, 223–235.

Cowie, A. (1992). Multiword lexical units and communicative language teaching. In P. Arnaud, & H. Bejoint (Eds.), *Vocabulary and applied linguistics* (pp. 1–12). London: Macmillan.

Cowie, A. P., Mackin, R., & McCaig, I. R. (Eds.). (1983). *Oxford dictionary of current idiomatic English, Vol. 2.* London: Oxford University Press.

Cruse, D. A. (1986). *Lexical semantics.* Cambridge: Cambridge University Press.

Culicover, P. W., Jackendoff, R., & Audring, J. (2017). Multiword constructions in the grammar. *Topics in Cognitive Science,* 9(3), 552–568.

Cutler, A. (1982). Idioms: The older the colder. *Linguistics Inquiry,* 13(2), 317–320.

Cutting, J. C., & Bock, K. (1997). That's the way the cookie bounces: Syntactic and semantic components of experimentally elicited idiom blends. *Memory & Cognition,* 25, 57–71.

De Cock, S. (1998). A recurrent word combination approach to the study of formulae in the speech of native and non-native speakers of English. *International Journal of Corpus Linguistics, 3*(1), 59–80.

De Cock, S., Granger, S., Leech, G., & McEnery, T. (1998). An automated approach to the phrasicon of EFL learners. In S. Granger (Ed.), *Learning English on computer* (pp. 67–79). London: Addison, Wesley, Longman.

Dörnyei, Z., Durow, V., & Zahran, K. (2004). Individual differences and their effects on formulaic sequence acquisition. In N. Schmitt (Ed.), *Formulaic sequences* (pp. 87–106). Amsterdam: John Benjamins.

Ellis, N. C. (2012). Formulaic language and second language acquisition: Zipf and the phrasal teddy bear. *Annual Review of Applied Linguistics, 32*, 17–44.

Ellis, N. C., & Ogden, D. C. (2017). Thinking about multiword constructions: Usage-based approaches to acquisition and processing. *Topics in Cognitive Science, 9*(3), 604–620.

Ellis, N. C., Simpson-Vlach, R., & Maynard, C. (2008). Formulaic language in native and second-language speakers: Psycholinguistics, corpus linguistics, and TESOL. *TESOL Quarterly, 41*, 375–396.

Ellis, R. (1994). *The study of second language acquisition.* Oxford: Oxford University Press.

Erman, B., & Warren, B. (2000). The idiom principle and the open-choice principle. *Text, 20*(1), 29–62.

Eyckmans, J., & Lindstromberg, S. (2016). The power of sound in L2 idiom learning. *Language Teaching Research,* 1–21.

Fernando, C. (1996). *Idioms and idiomaticity.* Oxford: Oxford University Press.

Fernando, C., & Flavell, R. (1981). *On idiom. Critical views and perspectives. Exeter Linguistic Studies, 5.* Exeter, UK: University of Exeter.

Firth, J. R. (1957). *Papers in linguistics 1934–1951.* London: Oxford University Press.

Firth, J. R. (1968). *Selected papers of J. R. Firth 1952–59.* F. R. Palmer (Ed.). London: Longmans.

Foster, P. (2001). Rules and routines: A consideration of their role in the task-based language production of native and non-native speakers. In M. Bygate, P. Skehan, & M. Swain (Eds.), *Researching pedagogic tasks: Second language learning, teaching and testing* (pp. 75–93). Harlow, UK: Longman.

Fraser, B. (1970). Idioms within a transformational grammar. *Foundations of Language, 6*, 22–42.

Gablasova, D., Brezina, V., & McEnery, T. (2017). Collocations in corpus-based language learning research: Identifying, comparing, and interpreting the evidence. *Language Learning, 67*(S1), 155–179.

Geeraert, K., Newman, J., & Baayen, R. H. (2017). Idiom variation: Experimental data and a blueprint of a computational model. *Topics in Cognitive Science, 9*(3), 653–669.

Gibbs, R. W. (1980). Spilling the beans on understanding and memory for idioms in conversation. *Memory and Cognition, 8*, 449–456.

Gibbs, R. W. (1994). *The poetics of mind: Figurative thought, language and understanding*. New York, NY: Cambridge University Press.

Gibbs, R. W. (1995). Idiomaticity and human cognition. In M. Everaert, E.-J. van der Linden, A. Schenk, & R. Schreuder (Eds.), *Idioms: Structural and psychological perspectives* (pp. 97–116). Hillsdale, NJ: Lawrence Erlbaum Associates.

Gibbs, R. W., & Gonzales, G. P. (1985). Syntactic frozenness in processing and remembering idioms. *Cognition, 20*, 243–59.

Gibbs, R. W., & Nayak, N. P. (1989). Psycholinguistic studies on the syntactic behavior of idioms. *Cognitive Psychology, 21*, 100–138.

Gibbs, R. W., Nayak, N. P., & Cutting, C. (1989). How to kick the bucket and not decompose: Analyzability and idiom processing. *Journal of Memory and Language, 28*, 576–593.

Giora, R. (1997). Understanding figurative and literal language: The graded salience hypothesis. *Cognitive Linguistics, 8*(3), 183–206.

Girard, M. (2004). The functions of formulaic speech in the L2 class. *Pragmatics, 14*(1), 31–53.

Gläser, R. (1998). The stylistic potential of phraseological units in the light of genre analysis. In A. P. Cowie (Ed.), *Phraseology*. Oxford: Clarendon Press.

Goldberg, A. (2006). *Constructions at work: The nature of generalization in language*. New York, NY: Oxford University Press.

Granger, S. (1998). Prefabricated patterns in advanced EFL writing: Collocations and formulae. In A. P. Cowie (Ed.), *Phraseology: Theory, analysis and applications* (pp. 145–160). Oxford: Oxford University Press.

Grant, L., & Bauer, L. (2004). Criteria for re-defining idioms: Are we barking up the wrong tree? *Applied Linguistics, 25*(1), 38–61.

Hakuta, K. (1974). Prefabricated patterns and the emergence of structure in second language acquisition. *Language Learning, 24*, 287–298.

Hatami, S. (2015). Teaching formulaic sequences in the ESL classroom. *TESOL Journal, 6*(1), 112–129.

Henriksen, B. (2013). Research on L2 learners' collocational competence and development – A progress report. In C. Bardel, C. Lindqvist, & B. Laufer (Eds.), *L2 vocabulary acquisition, knowledge and use: New perspectives on assessment and corpus analysis* (pp. 29–56). Amsterdam: John Benjamins.

Hinkel, E. (2017). Teaching idiomatic expressions and phrases: Insights and techniques. *Iranian Journal of Language Teaching Research, 5*(3), 45–59.

Hoang, H., & Boers, F. (2016). Re-telling a story in a second language: How well do adult learners mine an input text for multiword expressions? *Studies in Second Language Learning and Teaching, 6*(3), 513–535.

Hockett, C. F. (1958). *A course in modern linguistics*. New York, NY: Macmillan.

Hoey, M. P. (1991). *Patterns of lexis in text*. Oxford: Oxford University Press.

Hoey, M. (2005). *Lexical priming: A new theory of words and language*. London: Routledge.

Hyland, K. (2008a). Academic clusters: Text patterning in published and postgraduate writing. *International Journal of Applied Linguistics, 18*(1), 41–62.

Hyland, K. (2008b). As can be seen: Lexical bundles and disciplinary variation. *English for Specific Purposes, 27*(1), 4–21.

Ibáñez, A., Manes, F., Escobar, J., Trujillo, N., Andreucci, P., & Hurtado, E. (2010). Gesture influences the processing of figurative language in non-native speakers: ERP evidence. *Neuroscience Letters, 471*, 48–52.

Imura, K., & Shimizu, T. (2012). Development of formulaic language in adult second language learners' lexicon through study abroad experience. *Language, Culture, and Communication, 4*, 173–190.

Irujo, S. (1986). Don't put your leg in your mouth: Transfer in the acquisition of idioms in a second language. *TESOL Quarterly, 20*, 287–304.

Irujo, S. (1993). Steering clear: Avoidance in the production of idioms. *IRAL, 31*(3), 205–219.

Jackendoff, R. (1997). *The architecture of the language faculty*. Cambridge, MA: MIT Press.

Jiang, N., & Nekrasova, T. M. (2007). The processing of formulaic sequences by second language speakers. *Modern Language Journal, 91*, 433–445.

Katz, J. J., & Postal, P. M. (1964). *An integrated theory of linguistic descriptions*. Cambridge, MA: MIT Press.

Kecskes, I. (2000). A cognitive-pragmatic approach to situation-bound utterances. *Journal of Pragmatics, 32*(6), 605–625.

Keller, E. (1979). Gambits: Conversational strategy signals. *Journal of Pragmatics, 3*, 219–238.

Keller, E. (1981). Gambits: Conversational strategy signals. In F. Coulmas (Ed.), *Conversational routine: Explorations in standardized communicative situations and prepatterned speech* (pp. 93–113). The Hague: Mouton.

Kenny, D. (2000). Lexical hide-and-seek: Looking for creativity in a parallel corpus. In M. Olohan (Ed.), *Intercultural faultlines. Research models in translation studies I. Textual and cognitive aspects* (pp. 93–104). Manchester, UK: St. Jerome Publishing.

Kövecses, Z., & Szabó, P. (1996). Idioms: A view from cognitive semantics. *Applied Linguistics, 17,* 326–355.

Laufer, B. (2000). Avoidance of idioms in a second language: The effect of L1-L2 degree of similarity. *Studia Linguistica,* 54(2), 186–196.

Laufer, B. (2010). The contribution of dictionary use to the production and retention of collocations in a second language. *International Journal of Lexicography,* 24(1), 29–49.

Lewis, M. (1993). *The lexical approach: The state of ELT and the way forward.* Hove, UK: Language Teaching Publications.

Lewis, M. (Ed.). (2000). *Teaching collocations: Further developments in the lexical approach.* Hove, UK: Language Teaching Publications.

Libben, M. R., & Titone, D. A. (2008). The multidetermined nature of idiom processing. *Memory & Cognition, 36,* 1103–1121.

Lieven, E. (2006). Producing multiword utterances. In B. Kelly, & E. Clark (Eds.), *Constructions in acquisition* (pp. 83–110). Stanford, CA: CSLI Publications.

Lindstromberg, S., Eyckmans, J., & Connabeer, R. (2016). A modified dictogloss for helping learners remember L2 academic English formulaic sequences for use in later writing. *English for Specific Purposes, 41,* 12–21.

Liontas, J. I. (1999). *Developing a pragmatic methodology of idiomaticity: The comprehension and interpretation of SL vivid phrasal idioms during reading* (Unpublished doctoral dissertation). University of Arizona, Tucson, AZ.

Liontas, J. I. (2001). That's all Greek to me! The comprehension and interpretation of modern Greek phrasal idioms. *The Reading Matrix: An International Online Journal,* 1(1), 1–32.

Liontas, J. I. (2002a). Context and idiom understanding in second languages. In S. H. Foster-Cohen, T. Ruthenberg, & M-L. Poschen (Eds.), *EUROSLA Yearbook: Annual conference of the European second language association, Vol. 2* (pp. 155–185). Proceedings of the 2002 Annual Conference of the European Second Language Association. Amsterdam: John Benjamins.

Liontas, J. I. (2002b).Vivid phrasal idioms and the lexical-image continuum. *Issues in Applied Linguistics,* 13(1), 71–109.

Liontas, J. I. (2015). Developing idiomatic competence in the ESOL classroom: A pragmatic account. *TESOL Journal,* 6(4), 621–658.

Liontas, J. I. (2017a). Why teach idioms? A challenge to the profession. *Iranian Journal of Language Teaching Research,* 5(3), 5–25.

Liontas, J. I. (2017b). Through the looking glass: A second look at understanding idiomaticity in CALL. The Messenger of Alfred Nobel University. Series *Pedagogy and Psychology. Pedagogical Sciences,* 2(14), 229–237.

Liontas, J. I. (2018a). Idiomaticity: A riddle wrapped in a mystery inside an enigma. In J. I. Liontas (Ed.), *The TESOL encyclopedia of English language teaching,* First edition. J. I. Liontas (Ed., *Current trends and future directions in English language teaching*). Hoboken, NJ: John Wiley & Sons, Inc. DOI: 10.1002/9781118784235.eelt0947

Liontas, J. I. (2018b). Understanding idiomaticity in CALL. In J. Perren, K. Kelch, J.-S. Byun, S. Cervantes, & S. Safavi (Eds.), *Applications of CALL theory in ESL and EFL environments* (pp. 36–58). Hershey, PA: IGI Global Publishing.

Liontas, J. I. (2018c). Exploring figurative language across the curriculum. In J. I. Liontas (Ed.), *The TESOL encyclopedia of English language teaching,* first edition. K. T. Reynolds (Ed., *Teaching vocabulary,*Vol.V) (pp. 3020–3028). Hoboken, NJ: John Wiley & Sons, Inc.

Liontas, J. I. (2018d). Proverbs and idioms in raising cultural awareness. In J. I. Liontas (Ed.), *The TESOL encyclopedia of English language teaching,* first edition. S. Nero (Ed., *Sociocultural aspects of English language teaching,*Vol.V) (pp. 3641–3650). Hoboken, NJ: John Wiley & Sons, Inc.

Liontas, J. I. (2018e). Teaching idiomatic language in context. In J. I. Liontas (Ed.), *The TESOL encyclopedia of English language teaching,* first edition. K. T. Reynolds (Ed., *Teaching vocabulary,*Vol.V) (pp. 3247–3256). Hoboken, NJ: John Wiley & Sons, Inc.

Liontas, J. I. (2018f, in press). Reflective and effective teaching of idioms. In M. Zeraatpishe, A. Faravani, H. R. Kargozari, & M. Azarnoosh (Eds.), *Issues in applying SLA theories toward creative teaching.* Rotterdam, Netherlands: SENSE Publishers B.V.

Liu, D. (2012).The most frequently-used multi-word constructions in academic written English: A multi-corpus study. *English for Specific Purposes,* 31(1), 25–35.

Makkai, A. (1972). *Idiom structure in English*. The Hague: Mouton.

Makkai, A., Boatner, M. T., & Gates, J. E. (1995). *A dictionary of American idioms* (3rd ed.). Hauppauge, NY: Barron's Educational Series.

Malkiel, Y. (1959). Studies in irreversible binomials. *Lingua, 8*, 113–160.

Malt, B. C., & Eiter, B. (2004). Even with a green card, you can be put out to pasture and still have to work: Non-native intuitions of the transparency of common English idioms. *Journal of Memory and Cognition, 32*(6), 896–904.

Mauranen, A. (2000). Strange strings in translated language: A study on corpora. In M. Olohan (Ed.), *Intercultural faultlines. Research models in translation studies I. Textual and cognitive aspects* (pp. 119–141). Manchester, UK: St. Jerome Publishing.

McCarthy, M. (1998). *Spoken language and applied linguistics*. Cambridge: Cambridge University Press.

McCarthy, M., & O'Dell, F. (2002). *English idioms in use*. Cambridge: Cambridge University Press.

McCauley, S. M., & Christiansen, M. H. (2017). Computational investigations of multiword chunks in language learning. *Topics in Cognitive Science, 9*(3), 637–652.

Meunier, F. (2012). Formulaic language and language teaching. *Annual Review of Applied Linguistics, 32*, 111–129.

Mollin, S. (2012). Revisiting binomial order in English: Ordering constraints and reversibility. *English Language and Linguistics, 16*(1), 81–103.

Moon, R. (1997). Vocabulary connections: Multi-word items in English. In N. Schmitt, & M. McCarthy (Eds.), *Vocabulary: Description, acquisition and pedagogy* (pp. 40–63). Cambridge: Cambridge University Press.

Moon, R. (1998). *Fixed expressions and idioms in English: A corpus-based approach*. Oxford: Clarendon Press.

Mulhall, C. (2010). A semantic and lexical-based approach to the lemmatisation of idioms in bilingual Italian-English dictionaries. In A. Dykstra, & T. Schoonheim (Eds.), *Proceedings of the XIV Euralex International Congress* (pp. 1355–1371). Ljouwert, Netherlands: Fryske Academy.

Myles, F., & Cordier, C. (2017). Formulaic sequence (FS) cannot be an umbrella term in SLA: Focusing on psycholinguistic FSs and their identification. *Studies in Second Language Acquisition, 39*(1), 3–28.

Myles, F., Hooper, J., & Mitchell, R. (1998). Rote or rule? Exploring the role of formulaic language in classroom foreign language learning. *Language Learning, 48*, 323–363.

Nattinger, J. R., & DeCarrico, J. S. (1992). *Lexical phrases and language teaching.* Oxford: Oxford University Press.

Nekrasova, T. (2009). English L1 and L2 speakers' knowledge of lexical bundles. *Language Learning,* 59(3), 647–686.

Nesselhauf, N. (2003). The use of collocations by advanced learners of English and some implications for teaching. *Applied Linguistics,* 24(2), 223–242.

Newmeyer, F. (1972). The insertion of idioms. In P. M. Peranteau, J. N. Levi, & G. C. Phares (Eds.), *Papers from the Eighth Regional Meeting of the Chicago Linguistic Society* (pp. 294–302). Chicago, IL: Chicago Linguistic Society.

Newmeyer, F. (1974). The regularity of idiom behavior. *Lingua,* 34(4), 327–342.

Norrick, N. R. (1988). Binomial meaning in texts. *Journal of English Linguistics,* 21, 71–87.

Nunberg, G. (1978). *The pragmatics of reference.* Bloomington, IN: Indiana University Linguistic Club.

Nunberg, G., Sag, I. A., & Wasow, T. (1994). Idioms. *Language,* 70(3), 491–538.

Omidian, T., Shahriari, H., & Ghonsooly, B. (2017). Evaluating the pedagogic value of multi-word expressions based on EFL teachers' and advanced learners' value judgments. *TESOL Journal,* 8(2), 489–511.

Palmer, H. (1933). *Second interim report on English Collocations … submitted to the Tenth Annual Conference of English Teachers under the auspices of the Institute for Research in English Teaching.* Tokyo: IRET. [3rd (1935) ed. in Selected Writings, Vol. 9.]

Pawley, A., & Syder, F. H. (1983). Two puzzles for linguistic theory: Nativelike selection and nativelike fluency. In J. C. Richards, & R. W. Schmidt (Eds.), *Language and communication* (pp. 191–226). New York, NY: Longman.

Peters, A. M. (1983). *The units of language acquisition.* Cambridge: Cambridge University Press.

Peters, E. (2016). The learning burden of collocations: The role of interlexical and intralexical factors. *Language Teaching Research,* 20(1), 113–138.

Raupach, M. (1984). Formulae in second language speech production. In H. W. Dechert, & D. Mahle (Eds.), *Second language productions* (pp. 114–137). Tübingen, Germany: Gunter Narr Verlag.

Read, J., & Nation, I. S. P. (2004). Measurement of formulaic sequences. In N. Schmitt (Ed.), *Formulaic sequences* (pp. 23–35). Amsterdam: John Benjamins.

Roberts, M. H. (1944). The science of idiom: A method of inquiry into the cognitive design of language. *Publications of the Modern Language Association of America,* 69, 291–306.

Sag, I. A., Baldwin, T., Bond, F., Copestake, A., & Flickinger, D. (2002). Multiword expressions: A pain in the neck for NLP. In A. Gelbukh (Ed.), *Proceedings of the Third International Conference on Intelligent Text Processing and Computational Linguistics* (pp. 1–15). Berlin: Springer.

Schmitt, N. (2000). *Vocabulary in language teaching.* Cambridge: Cambridge University Press.

Schmitt, N. (Ed.) (2004). Formulaic sequences in action: An introduction. In N. Schmitt (Ed.), *Formulaic sequences: Acquisition, processing and use* (pp. 1–22). Amsterdam: John Benjamins.

Schmitt, N. (2010). *Researching vocabulary: A vocabulary research manual.* New York, NY: Palgrave Macmillan.

Schmitt, N., & Carter, R. (2004). Formulaic sequences in action: An introduction. In N. Schmitt (Ed.), *Formulaic sequences: Acquisition, processing and use* (pp. 1–22). Amsterdam: John Benjamins.

Schmitt, N., Dornyei, Z., Adolphs, S., & Durow, V. (2004). Knowledge and acquisition of formulaic sequences. A longitudinal study. In N. Schmitt (Ed.), *Formulaic sequences: Acquisition, processing, and use* (pp. 55–86). Amsterdam: John Benjamins.

Seidl, J., & McMordie, W. (1988). *English idioms* (5th ed.). Oxford: Oxford University Press.

Serrano, R., Stengers, H., & Housen, A. (2014). Acquisition of formulaic sequences in intensive and regular EFL programmes. *Language Teaching Research,* 19(1), 89–106.

Siepmann, D. (2005). Collocation, colligation and encoding dictionaries. Part I: Lexicological aspects. *International Journal of Lexicography,* 18(4), 409–443.

Sinclair, J. (1987). Collocation: A progress report. In R. Steele, & T. Threadgold (Eds.), *Language topics: Essays in honour of Michael Halliday* (pp. 319–331). Amsterdam: John Benjamins.

Sinclair, J. (1991). *Corpus, concordance, collocation.* Oxford: Oxford University Press.

Smith, L. P. (1925). *Words and idioms. Studies in the English language.* Boston, MA: Houghton Mifflin Company.

Sprenger, S. A., Levelt, W. J. M., & Kempen, G. (2006). Lexical access during the production of idiomatic phrases. *Journal of Memory and Language,* 54, 161–184.

Strässler, J. (1982). *Idioms in English: A pragmatic analysis.* Tübingen, Germany: Gunter Narr Verlag.

Strutz, H. (1996). *German idioms.* Hauppauge, NY: Barron's Educational Series, Inc.

Swinney, D. A., & Cutler, A. (1979). The access and processing of idiomatic expressions. *Journal of Verbal Learning and Verbal Behavior, 18,* 523–534.

Swan M. (2006). Chunks in the classroom: Let's not go overboard. *Teacher Trainer, 20,* 5–6.

Theakston, A., & Lieven, E. (2017). Multiunit sequences in first language acquisition. *Topics in Cognitive Science, 9*(3), 588–603.

Titone, D. A., & Connine, C. M. (1999). On the compositional and noncompositional nature of idiomatic expressions. *Journal of Pragmatics, 31*(12), 1655–1674.

Titone, D., Columbus, G., Whitford, V., Mercier, J., & Libben. M. (2015). Contrasting bilingual and monolingual idiom processing. In R. R. Heredia, & A. B. Cieślicka (Eds.), *Bilingual figurative language processing* (pp. 171–207). New York, NY: Cambridge University Press.

Tomasello, M. (2003). *Constructing a language: A usage-based theory of language acquisition.* Cambridge MA: Harvard University Press.

Tremblay, A., Derwing, B., Libben, G., & Westbury, C. (2011). Processing advantages of lexical bundles: Evidence from self-paced reading and sentence recall tasks. *Language Learning, 61*(2), 569–613.

Vale, O. A. (2003). Some regularities of frozen expressions in Brazilian Portuguese. In N. J. Mamede, I. Trancoso, J. Baptista, M. das Graças Volpe Nunes (Eds.), *Computational processing of the Portuguese language* (pp. 98–101). Berlin: Springer.

Vanlancker-Sidtis, D. (2003). Auditory recognition of idioms by native and nonnative speakers of English: It takes one to know one. *Applied Linguistics, 24*(1), 45–57.

Van Lancker Sidtis, D. (2004). When novel sentences spoken or heard for the first time in the history of the universe are not enough (Cf. Pinker, 1995, p. 22): Toward a dual-process model of language. *International Journal of Language Communication Disorders, 39*(1), 1–44.

Van Lancker Sidtis, D. (2012). Two-track mind: Formulaic and novel language support a dual-process model. In M. Faust (Ed.), *The handbook of the neuropsychology of language* (pp. 342–367). Chichester, UK: Wiley-Blackwell.

Van Lancker Sidtis, D., Cameron, K., Bridges, K., & Sidtis, J. J. (2015). The formulaic schema in the minds of two generations of native speakers. *Ampersand, 2,* 39–48.

Vasiljevic, Z. (2015). Teaching and learning idioms in L2: From theory to practice. *MEXTESOL Journal,* 39(4), 1–24.

Walker, C. P. (2011). A corpus-based study of the linguistic features and processes which influence the way collocations are formed: Some implications for the learning of collocations. *TESOL Quarterly,* 45, 291–312.

Weinert, R. (1995). The role of formulaic language in second language acquisition: A review. *Applied Linguistics,* 16(2), 180–205.

Weinert, R. (2010). Formulaicity and usage-based language: Linguistic, psycholinguistic and acquisitional manifestations. In D. Wood (Ed.), *Perspectives on formulaic language* (pp. 1–22). New York, NY: Continuum.

Weinreich, U. (1969). Problems in the amalysis of idioms. In J. Puhvel (Ed.), *Substance and structure of language* (pp. 23–81). Berkeley/Los Angeles, CA: University of California Press.

Wong-Fillmore, L. (1976). *The second time around.* Unpublished doctoral dissertation, Stanford University, CA.

Wood, D., & Appel, R. (2014). Multiword constructions in first year business and engineering university textbooks and EAP textbooks. *Journal of English for Academic Purposes,* 15(1), 1–13.

Wray, A. (1999). Formulaic language in learners and native speakers. *Language Teaching,* 32, 213–231.

Wray, A. (2002). *Formulaic language and the lexicon.* Cambridge: Cambridge University Press.

Wray, A. (2012). What do we (think we) know about formulaic language? An evaluation of the current state of play. *Annual Review of Applied Linguistics,* 32, 231–254.

Wray, A. (2013). Formulaic language. *Language Teaching,* 46(3), 316–334.

Wray, A. (2017). Formulaic sequences as a regulatory mechanism for cognitive perturbations during the achievement of social goals. *Topics in Cognitive Science,* 9(3), 569–587.

Yorio, C. A. (1989). Idiomaticity as an indicator of second language proficiency. In K. Hyltenstam, & L. K. Obler (Eds.), *Bilingualism across the lifespan: Aspects of acquisition, maturity, and loss* (55–72). Cambridge: Cambridge University Press.

Zyzik, E. (2011). Second language idiom learning: The effects of lexical knowledge and pedagogical sequencing. *Language Teaching Research,* 15(4), 413–433.

Part II

TEACHING PRACTICALITIES

Chapter 4

Teaching Strategies and Techniques
Collocations and Multiword Units

Eli Hinkel

Introduction: Collocations Are Everywhere

In language teaching, grammar and vocabulary instruction are typically viewed as two rather separate domains of tools and skills, in addition to listening, speaking, reading, and writing. For learners, becoming fluent and proficient in using vocabulary and grammar takes a great deal of time and work simply because the English grammar system is complex, and the number of words to be learned, retained, and practiced is enormous. An excellent case in point is that English dictionaries intended specifically for language learners are large books, and some have upwards of a couple of hundred thousand words, combinations of words, and examples. It is also a fact that many words are combined in various patterns to create new meanings that cannot be predicted from the meaning of their component parts, e.g. *look after, look up to, look into, drop by, come by, come around, come into view, come to a stop, come to an agreement.*

In language analyses, combinations of words that frequently occur and re-occur together are called collocations and multiword units. These can be laborious to learn and use correctly because they consist of two or more component parts (Howarth, 1998; Hinkel, 2002, 2004; Nation, Shin, & Grant, 2016).

Although in English teaching, phrasal verbs, for example, such as those in the examples above, routinely receive a good deal of attention, other types of multiword constructions are often slighted and go unnoticed (this is a collocation), e.g.:

big deal/news/noise/excitement/improvement/disappointment/mistake/problem
large amount/number/population/scale/size
heavy rain/snow/fog/coat/traffic/load/meal/losses (plural)

However, due to the fact that many recurrent word combinations can have unpredictable meanings and grammatically irregular structures – these units of language cannot be derived and formed according to grammar rules – noticing their occurrences and components is very important if learners are to increase their linguistic repertoire, fluency, and proficiency. Most proficient first language and second language (L2) users attain their facility with collocations over time and through encountering them in all manner of interactions, reading, and writing (Cowie, 1992; Durrant, 2014; Hinkel, 2015, 2016; Nation, 2011).

One of the key issues with collocations and multiword units is that they are extremely frequent. Some researchers have claimed that "up to 70% of everything we say, hear, read, or write is to be found in some form of fixed expression" (Hill, 2000, p. 53). Others have counted their occurrences in the hundreds of thousands, but the point is that these units of language are so numerous that their exact numbers are unknown (Martinez & Schmitt, 2012; Nation, 2011, 2013; Webb & Nation, 2017). In language teaching and research, at present, a clear consensus has been achieved that understanding and producing language is in fact impossible without the use of collocations (see the Preamble earlier in this volume). Another and equally important finding is that, without explicit instruction, most language learners cannot always identify the occurrence or prevalence of multiword units in either spoken or written English, and in part for this reason have restricted opportunities of learning how and when to deploy them in language comprehension or production.

To add to the complexity, in English many words, particularly frequent ones, are polysemous, that is, they have multiple meanings, and the more meanings words have, the more frequently they occur, e.g. dozens of combinations with the verbs *make* and *take* can be encountered in speech and writing: *make an appointment, make time, make coffee, make a phone call, make a promise, make a mistake, take your time, take turns, take a break, take a bus/train, take a minute, take a picture, take a seat, take a walk, take care, take notes.*

> Word combinations can have deducible meanings that can be transparent and thus figured out even if approximately, as in *take* (have) *a shower/taxi/test/class*, but then the meanings of other collocations are opaque, e.g. *find ~~ out/a way/success/value/interesting/hard/time/a minute/words/a solution.*

Although various definitions of collocations and multiword units have been investigated, examined, explored, proposed, debated, reviewed, refuted, deliberated, and discussed, what represents a collocation is likely to be immaterial in the classroom. On the other hand, for teaching and learning, a few pedagogical considerations are of crucial importance. Collocations and multiword units have a few specific attributes that make them difficult for learners to remember and use correctly. Two of their features that are directly relevant to teaching are noted here.

(1) A key characteristic of collocations is that most (but certainly not all) have a rigid word order that cannot be altered or re-arranged, e.g.:
- *one or the other*, but not **the other or one*
- *here and there/up and down*, but not **there and here/*down and up*
- *near and far*, but not **far and near*
- *a verb/noun phrase*, but not **a phrase of verb/noun*
- *a drop in the bucket*, but not **a bucket drop*
- *birds of prey*, but not **prey birds*
- *a couple of pencils*, but not **a pencil couple*

(2) Another indelible attribute of collocations is that their lexical components cannot be replaced even when the meanings of phrases are transparent; "the problem is that native speakers do not say it in that way" (Shin & Nation, 2008, p. 340), e.g.:
- **heavy wind*, instead of *strong wind*
- **past night,* instead of *last night*

- *fall into parts, instead of *fall apart*
- *take a looking/a talk/for walking, instead of *take a look/walk, have a talk,* or *take [someone/something] for walk*
- *get loss/tire/hunger/a dress, instead of *get lost/tired/hungry/dressed*

> Because the structure of collocations does not follow grammar rules and because their meanings are unpredictable, multiword constructions cannot be assembled in the process of comprehension or communication. By and large, their forms, meanings, and functions have to be learned and memorized.

Due to the fact that the number of collocations is very large, in L2 teaching and learning, there is not a moment to lose. When it comes to collocations and multiword units by any other name the teacher's job is essential:

- To bring learners' attention to word combinations as they occur in context.
- To focus on more valuable, frequent, and useful collocations and to avoid spending time on those that are low frequency.
- To provide learning strategies and techniques to help learners remember and practice collocations.

This chapter presents several teaching strategies, techniques, and activities that can be implemented at any level of learners' proficiencies from beginning to advanced. Instruction in collocations can take place in the teaching of listening, speaking, reading, and writing, and their uses can be highlighted in practically any context, as the sample teaching activities demonstrate. As has been mentioned, collocations, recurrent phrases, and multiword units are so frequent and ubiquitous that they can be found anywhere. A few teaching activities and ideas exemplified here can be further modified and adapted in any language classroom and beyond it. Because practically all collocations and phrases are idiomatic and highly conventionalized, their instructional applications can contribute to learners' strategic language development in learners' receptive and productive skills in various instructional settings.

Noticing Collocations and Raising Learners' Awareness

The first order of priority is to select multiword units that are frequent and recurrent. Beginning and intermediate learners can be asked to notice words that tend to co-occur in short and simple texts (Arnon & Snider, 2010; Shin & Nation, 2008). Many samples can be easily found in student textbooks and materials, and even on textbook covers. A few common and transparent word combinations found on student textbooks covers are provided in Example 1.

Example 1

⇒ *Learn the words* you *need to* *improve your English*
⇒ *Learn* conversational *expressions* *by looking at* the *pictures*
⇒ *Improve* your *vocabulary* and *learn* new *grammar* *structures*
⇒ *Look at* the examples and *learn* useful *words* and *phrases*
⇒ *Improve* your speaking *skills* *in five minutes a day*

In such short and clear examples, collocations are easy to identify, notice, and highlight: *learn* + noun, *improve* + noun, and *need to* + verb. Additional opportunities for noticing multiword units can also arise if the teacher chooses to focus learners' attention on, say, *look at* and *in five/ten* [number] *minutes/one hour/two hours* [*in* + time], or *a day/a week/a month* [per day/ week/month].

Example 2

For high-intermediate and advanced learners who are required to take tests and exams, a similar noticing practice can take place in the course of L2 learning and preparation. In most cases of students who are working toward formal assessments and exams, a great deal of attention, time, and effort is devoted to teaching and learning academic vocabulary and grammar. However, as Lewis (2000) comments astutely, one of the reasons that learners do not notice or learn collocations is that teachers do not point them out in the text. That is, the vocabulary that students encounter may not be new, but word combinations in which it occurs are likely to be, e.g. *you know/see*, *the fact is*, or *in this/that way*.

In most texts where collocations can be found and identified, some are more frequent and valuable to learn, but others might be less so. Example 2 includes two sets: those that are common with transparent meanings and that are suitable for learners at any level, and those that are less frequent.

Sea eagles are the <u>one of the</u> largest <u>birds of prey</u> <u>in the world</u>. You might think that life is good <u>at the top</u> of <u>the food chain</u>, and that all the smaller, less powerful birds would <u>stay away from</u> these predators. <u>Not so</u>. Crows, <u>for example</u>, often harass eagles <u>in flight</u>, and you can frequently see <u>a group of</u> three or four crows circling and <u>driving off</u> an eagle. Crows usually noisily follow an eagle <u>to add insult to injury</u>. <u>Once in a while</u>, a crow who's <u>not on the ball</u> will feel the larger bird's talons, but mostly the crows <u>get the better of</u> the eagles in these battles <u>in the air</u>. Eagles are big and powerful, but crows <u>are able to</u> maneuver quickly. Crows <u>are</u> also more intelligent and <u>able to</u> work together <u>in social groups</u>.

The teacher's job is to identify and highlight multiword units, focus learners' attention on their form, structure, and meaning, point out lexical and grammatical patterns, and explain their uses in contest. Pointing out, identifying, and discussing collocations in context is an essential step in teaching multiword units: these word combinations are difficult and work-consuming to learn, and noticing them in text can ease the task.

As is the case with most vocabulary learning, collocations can be frequent and valuable for teaching and learning, or less frequent and productive. The teacher's guidance is almost always required to identify high frequency multiword units, as well as those that might be already partly familiar, and separating valuable word combinations from those that are not. The two sets of collocations presented here provide an example of those found in the text on sea eagles.

Frequent and transparent: *one of the* [+ noun], *in the world, at the top, stay away (from), not so, for example, a group of* [+ noun], *drive off/away, once in a while, in the air, are [be] able to* [+ verb], *in social* [adjective or noun, e.g. *big, large, small, study, family, reading] groups*
Infrequent and opaque: *the food chain, in flight, to add insult to injury, on the ball, to get the better of* [+ noun]

In addition to helping students notice co-occurring word combinations, it is relatively easy to design exercises and practice activities with frequent and essential multiword units that can be employed productively in the long run (a few exemplars are discussed later in this chapter). Since most L2 teaching takes place with the aid of spoken or written texts, noticing and collecting frequent or less prevalent word combinations lends itself to instruction when working in any language skill. For instance, when collocations are encountered in textbooks on listening and speaking, a supplemental writing practice can further promote remembering and retention, or those that are found in reading texts excerpts can come in handy in practicing L2 listening and speaking (Hinkel, 2015, 2016, 2018).

In classroom instruction and with the teacher's guidance, many L2 learners can become experienced and proficient in noticing word co-occurrences and phrase patterns, and this is considered to be one of the foundational language learning skills (Foster, 2001; Yorio, 1989).

- In language teaching, it is important to note collocations and bring learners' attention to their uses, forms, and functions: essential multiword units can be productively added to learning grammar and vocabulary in context.
- The teacher's guidance and contextualized discussion is paramount to determine which co-occurrences are common and thus should be learned, or those that are rare and that may not be worth the time and work that learning them requires.

Carefully selecting collocations for learning can become an ongoing task for both teachers and learners, and a few criteria for deciding what collocations to choose are discussed in the next section.

Research has demonstrated that flash cards or electronic applications and tools (e.g. mini self-quizzes, review lists, or phrase collections) represent the single most efficient way of learning and practicing vocabulary and collocations for retention (Hinkel, 2004, 2013; Webb & Nation, 2017). Numerous electronic applications send automatic and timed review notifications and reminders – a great convenience for teachers and learners. When it comes to learning vocabulary of any type, be it single words or multiword units, students should be asked to make lists of valuable, frequent, and productive collocations and put them on flash cards. Examples with these words, phrases, and synonyms can be added to the lists and flash cards of any variety. Vocabulary and multiword unit notebooks are also a very useful, efficient, and practical learning aid because reviewing the items that have been covered and learned previously can be made easier when they are collected in one place.

Highly Frequent and Absolutely Essential Multiword Units

Typically, collocations consist of two elements: a pivot word and accompanying word(s) (one or more). A pivot word is the main/focal word in the collocation, and its meanings are crucial to the meaning of the entire collocation. Accompanying word(s) can come before or after the pivot word. For example, *reach* is the pivot word in the following multiword units:

> *reach for/over/out, beyond/within* [someone's] *reach, long reach, reach the point, reach the end/limit, reach a goal/an aim, reach your* [one's] *destination, reach a conclusion, reach* [someone] *on the phone, reach* [place/location/height], *reach an agreement*

According to a large corpus study by Shin & Nation (2008), the number of collocations of the most frequent 100 pivot words accounts for 53 percent of collocations in spoken English, and the top 200 most frequent pivots for approximately 70 percent. Shin and Nation explain that the shorter collocations are, the more frequent they are, and 77 percent of all spoken collocations consist of two words. In fact, most common collocations are encountered so frequently that they do not need to be specially taught or learned, e.g.:

> *you know, I think, a bit, as well, a lot of, thank you, very much, talk about, at the moment, a little bit, this morning, come on, come in, come back, have a look, last year, this year, last night, go back, very good, that way, at the end, for example, all the time, too much, over there, make sure, very well, in the morning*

One of thorniest problems with L2 uses of multiword units, however, is that they can be difficult and laborious to learn, and many are error-prone. An immediately obvious consideration in learning them is that they contain more (and more complex) component parts than single-word vocabulary. Many L2 students know from experience that learning collocations is tedious and work-consuming. Their L2 uses often lead to a high rate of errors because of the irregularity of their grammatical and lexical forms, mis-applications of translated L1 collocations with similar meanings, or simple old-fashioned confusion of which collocational component goes with which (Boers & Lindstromberg, 2012; Boers, 2000). However, most frequent collocations are so ubiquitous that they are encountered in any context, and without these no L2 learner can survive.

As mentioned earlier, short collocations are encountered highly frequently, and most have transparent meanings and functions. For this reason, they can be a suitable starting point for teaching beginners or learners at any proficiency level. However, many short collocations have complex structures and can be challenging for L2 learners to use correctly (Hinkel, 2002, 2004, 2013; Nation, 2011, 2013).

Two samples of complex multiword units with prepositions are presented in Examples 3 and 4, and these require a great deal of attention and practice. English prepositions are famously (notoriously, extremely, incredibly, tremendously) difficult to teach, learn, and use correctly. Even for highly advanced and proficient L2 English users prepositions represent on ongoing problem. There are many reasons that make prepositions onerous to use correctly, but at least a couple may be worth mentioning:

(1) Prepositions can have different functions in different contexts, and for instance, *in the house, in June, in class, in time, in the book, in the evening, in the picture.*

(2) Almost all uses of prepositions are idiomatic and lexicalized, and they do not follow grammar or vocabulary rules.

(3) Many (most?) uses and functions of prepositions are un-derivable, illogical, and opaque, that is, their meanings cannot be guessed from context.

> The uses, functions, and meanings of most prepositions and prepositional phrases are collocational (and idiomatic), and they cannot be assembled in the process of speaking or writing.

Example 3

Frequent Multiword Units That Need to Be Taught and Practiced (and Practiced)	
Quantity Collocations	Time Collocations
a couple of [+ noun plural], e.g. *a couple of apples/hours* ~~ *a couple of times*	*in* + month/year, e.g. *in June, in 2000* *in the* + season, e.g. *in the fall/winter*
a few [+ noun plural] *(vs. few)*, e.g. *books, pens, people*	*on* + day of the week/date, e.g. *on Monday, on June 1*
a little [+ noncount noun, e.g. *milk, water, information, attention, work*]	*at* + hour, e.g. *at 12 o'clock, at noon, at 1:30*

Frequent Multiword Units That Need to Be Taught and Practiced (and Practiced)	
a great deal of [+ noncount noun]	at night/midnight ~~ late at night
a number of [+ noun plural] ~~ lots of	in the afternoon/evening
a great/large/high number of [+ noun plural]	Ø next time/week/month (e.g. June)/year
much [+ noncount noun] vs. many [+ noun plural]	Ø last time/week/month (e.g. May)/year ~~ last night
plenty of [+ noun plural or noncount]	in + amount of time, e.g. in a minute/hour/day/week in a couple of days/weeks/months
each/every [+ noun singular], e.g. each person/every student	on/for the weekend
one/two of the [+ noun plural] some of the [+ noncount noun]	once a day/week/month/year once in a while twice a day/week/month/year

In addition to the frequent expressions of quantity and time, two- and three-word collocations with transparent meanings are also appropriate for beginners, as in Example 4. These can be productive in teaching with follow-up review activities to facilitate their retention (see Suggested Teaching Activities below).

Example 4

Two- and Three-word Multiword Units with Transparent Meanings		
in and out	this and that	far away/nearby/close to
up and down	(thank you) very much ~~ OR thanks a lot [but not *thank you a lot]	peace and quiet
come and go	off and on	here and there
more or less [but not *more and less]	a/the difference between [noun and noun]	back and forth
true or false	in a distance/at the distance of [+ noun/number & noun], e.g. a mile, five kilometers	day and night/all day/ all night/all morning
once or twice	one way or another	sooner or later

In much L2 vocabulary and grammar teaching, phrasal verbs, e.g. *take on, take out, take along, come by, come out, look forward to, look for, look in*, typically occupy a prominent place. In addition to these and multiword units of quantity and time, large collocational patterns with unpredictable and un-derivable meanings can also be found in the following contexts, with, for example:

- Prepositions of location (e.g. *in/on the corner, on xxx street, on the left/right, in/from* [city], *across, on the wall/desk, at the terminal/station/airport/stop/Sony building*)
- Prepositions of movement and direction (e.g. *walk for* [distance]/*toward/along, through, out/out of, to, into, up, down, around, on/off, away/away from, back/back to*)
- Prepositions of instruments and transportation (e.g. *with (a spoon/knife), by bus/car/taxi*, vs. *on the bus/in a car, by email/phone/text*) ∼ BUT ∼ *a novel/poem by John Smith* ∼ *xxx invented by Thomas Edison*

Checking the Frequency (and Accuracy) of Collocations

A very useful and practical technique for checking the accuracy and frequency of collocations, multiword units, and expressions of any kind is to perform an online search (illustrative examples are provided in the Appendix to this chapter). Some popular search engines permit searches for a specific phrase exactly in the form that it takes when the search term is surrounded by quotation marks.

For instance, it is easy to check which form of an expression is more frequent, e.g. "each and every" or "each or every." The number of search hits serves as a good guide to demonstrate whether the first or the second string is prevalent. For instance, "each and every" gets 117 million hits, but "each or every" – only around 56 thousand. So, clearly, "each and every" is the more frequent (and probably more linguistically accurate) form of this expression. It is not a pristine corpus query, of course, but it is indicative, cheap, and easy.

This search technique takes only a couple of seconds, and the results are instant and usually pretty clear-cut. It can be useful for both teachers and learners for any type of an expression and in any context (see the Appendix).

Suggested Teaching Activities for Highly Frequent Collocations

An Important Note on Learning and Retention of Vocabulary, Collocations, and Grammar

Spaced repetition is the single most important factor in all remembering/ vocabulary retention. Review, review, review the collocations and words learned. For example, effective vocabulary reviews can take place at regular intervals, such as one, two, three, and seven days apart. Vocabulary practice and review is the essential foundation of vocabulary learning and remembering.

Providing opportunities for regular spaced repetition is the single most important technique in all vocabulary teaching and learning.

The need for spaced repetition for language learning and retention has been widely recognized by the vast expanse of the language learning enterprise. Dozens of online and offline applications are available for vocabulary and collocation reviews, and many are free to use while others require a nominal charge. As always, however, old-fashioned flash cards may be convenient in the settings where electronic tools are not immediately accessible or available.

(1)   Ask students to write a letter to someone to describe what they did the previous day or week (past tense practice), what they usually do every day or week (present tense practice), or what they do during their class/ at school.

An alternative: Students can provide a detailed explanation of the school activities that take place during a day/week in order to clarify the schedule for a new student who is not familiar with the structure of the school day.

(2)   To make a careful shopping (or grocery) list for someone else who can do their shopping, students receive a list of items where they need to supply the quantity of what the helpful shopper is requested to buy. Ask students specifically to use quantity collocations in Example 3. For instance:

_____ *tomatoes*	_____ *orange juice*
_____ *cucumbers*	_____ *snacks*
_____ *blue pens*	_____ *pencils*
_____ *bottles of water/milk/soft drinks*	
_____ *notebooks*	_____ *sandwiches*

(3) For speaking and dictation practice, working in pairs or small groups, students can dictate their schedules or shopping lists to someone on an imaginary phone. While one or two students are dictating, their partners can write down the schedules or the lists.

(4) With and–or expressions (Example 4), students receive a list with one half of the pair, with the conjunction for beginners, but without it for intermediate learners (Ur, 2012). Then students are asked to complete the collocations, e.g.

in (and) _____   *once (or)* _____   *here* _____

An alternative: Students receive a list with ten (and not more than this) collocations of quantity and/or time. In pairs or small groups, they are asked to write out food preparation instructions that include timing and recipes, make weekend or vacation plans, or create timetables for buses, trains, guided tours of interesting or well-known locations, or exercise routines.

(5) The number of highly frequent quantity and time collocations that students need to learn is actually pretty small, that is, around 12–15 of each type. A mini-quiz for six to ten minutes during each class can become an excellent opportunity for Spaced Repetition.

(6) Students can make up questions with each collocation (interrogative/ question construction practice) and take turns asking one another in pairs, e.g. *What do you usually have for breakfast/lunch/dinner? What time does your favorite TV show start? When do leave your house in the morning? How often do you go out with your friends?* (Collocations are underlined.)

Collocations with a Purpose, Part I: Speaking and Conversations

A large body of research has demonstrated that conversational exchanges and routines are highly pre-patterned, structured, and stereotyped (Coulmas, 1981; Hinkel, 2013, 2014). Analyses of conversational discourse and their findings are almost universally reflected in student textbooks for teaching L2 listening and speaking. In everyday spoken interactions, pre-patterned exchanges can be readily identified in casual conversations, small talk, meetings, discussions, or service encounters, and most include highly frequent collocations. These can be deployed with a practically unlimited range of functions, such as greetings, openings, introductions, answering the phone, requesting information, pre-closings, closings, asking for directions or clarifications, or making requests.

Recurrent word combinations can be utilized to develop learners' strategic language skills, spoken fluency, and easily accessible collocation substitutions, e.g. *We had a great/wonderful/fantastic time.*

> In L2 speaking skills, fluency refers to the amount of attention and effort required to produce stretches of speech without communicative breakdowns and important misunderstandings.

The uses of pre-patterned expressions clearly provide a great resource when L2 speaking takes place in real time and under pressure (Hinkel, 2014; Nation & Webb, 2011). Collocational expressions typically mark discourse and conversation organizational structure. In this example of a conversation starter, a few multiword substitutions can be available in context:

- *Hi/Hello! How are you?/How is everything? How is your morning/day/week/class going?*
- *Hi! Good/great/excellent/fantastic. Can't complain/Doing well/Everything is going well. How about you?/What's going on with you?/How's everything with you?*
- *Doing (very) well/Great so far/My morning/day/class is pretty good.*

Collocations play a prominent role in short two-turn exchanges (also called adjacency pairs in spoken discourse analysis), and these are almost always pre-patterned and routinized.

Collocational two- (or three-) turn conversations can be found in a great range of conversations, and they are typically constructed with multiword units to structure discourse:

greeting – greeting, compliments – thanks, requests – grant/apologize and deny, information question – response, apologize – accept

For example:

(1) *Good morning! How's everything going?*
   ● *Great, can't complain. How's everything with you?*
(2) *Thank you.*
   ● *You are welcome.*
(3) *Sorry, wrong number. / Sorry, I am late. / Sorry, I am lost. / Sorry, I missed my bus.*
   ● *No problem.*

To help learners develop conversational fluency, multiword units are also highly frequent in nominating, maintaining, and expanding conversational topics.

For example (collocations with topic nominations are underlined):

● *Nice day/weather today …/Looks like more rain today ….*
● *I've been watching/following the soccer/football game/TV show ….*
● *I am taking a cooking/French class ….*
● *Have you seen the xxx movie/read the xxx book/noticed the xxx announcement?*
● *Do you live close to xxx?//Where do you live?*
● *The bus/train is late again/is on time today ….*

In general terms, routines and collocations are employed in most conversational or speaking contexts, and these multiword units have an enormous array of interactional and social purposes and functions (Ur, 2014). In spoken contexts, routinized expressions have transparent meanings, and for this reason, they readily lend themselves to teaching and learning. However, an important consideration in instruction is that interaction participants have to be able to understand their linguistic forms and highly predictable social functions.

Communicative breakdowns can occur if and when the interactional purpose of a collocational exchange is misinterpreted or misunderstood (Cowie, 1992; Fernando, 1996). For example, the expressions, such as *Okay, I'll see you there* or *Sorry, I have a bus to catch*, are not in fact announcements of plans or schedules, but they have the function of pre-closing a conversation, and these expressions are usually followed by good-byes.

A further benefit of noticing and learning collocations applies directly to the improved grasp of their interactional functions. As has been mentioned, a critical characteristic of collocations is that they do not follow grammar and lexical rules, and their communicative goals, as well as routinized responses, also require explicit teaching and learning (Hinkel, 2014). Conversational and spoken fluency can be addressed, for example, in a variety of in-class and out-of-class activities:

- Analyzing collocations in textbook dialogs, test preparation materials, and authentic interactions
- Identifying pre-patterned expressions and adding substitutions
- Re-working or re-stating frequent collocations in teaching materials, role plays, paired practice, and rehearsing

In more formal presentations and lectures, multiword expressions are also very common, and their typical functions are to highlight discourse organization or transitions from one section to the next. Among the most frequent are such collocations as *on the one hand, on the other hand, in the case of, as a result of, it is important to, take a look at, going to talk, at the same time, for this reason, a little bit, in the end, the best way,* or *the role of the* (Carter & McCarthy, 2006; Nattinger & DeCarrico, 1992). Since these collocations are longer and more complex than conversational expressions, typically, learning their forms and discourse features is more laborious and challenging. Although many of these multiword units are suitable for high intermediate and advanced learners, a few highly frequent expressions can be useful even to beginning learners, nonetheless.

Specifically, the ubiquitous collocations that are worth the work and effort include just a handful, but for learners, these are very useful simply because they are very frequent and relatively inflexible in their forms. Examples of high frequency multiword units include the following.

on the one hand/on the other hand	*I think (that)//I don't think so*
the most important thing	*I would like to//would you like to?*
my point is that …	*my first point/second point/final point the next/second point*
for example/for instance	*another thing//the other thing*

Suggested Teaching Activities for Collocations in Speaking and Conversations

(1) Matching conversational collocations and possible responses. For example:

Hi! How's everything going?	*Thank you! I study very hard.*
I missed class yesterday. Could I borrow your class notes?	*I think, but I am not sure, that it's on zzz (day) at xxx (time).* (Note: The preposition *on* is used with days and dates, and *at* with time points.)
When is the xxx? (day and time)?	*Sure! I am afraid, though, that they are a little bit messy.*
Where is the yyy?/How far is xxx? (location)	*I am sorry, but I don't know. Maybe, yyy could tell you?*
Your English/Spanish/French is great!	*Great/good/fine. How about you?*

(2) Short talks/presentations, between one and four minutes. Students can be divided into pairs or small groups when they prepare short and timed presentations. The teacher prepares in advance a list of ten (and no more than ten) collocations that learners are required to use in each talk. When their preparations are completed, students make presentations to one another in groups of three to five while the listeners make notes of effective or less effective talk elements.

It is paramount to vary topics, rotate groups, and provide partially overlapping collocation lists. Initially, such presentations can be scheduled for one or two minutes a piece. Then the time limit can be gradually extended to four or five minutes each and practiced on several occasions. After several presentations, each student can have opportunities to learn and practice around 40 or more frequent spoken collocations.

Experience has shown that with regular rotations of student groups and different presentation topics, students usually enjoy these short talks and can become quite skilled at giving mini-talks.

> Planned and prepared short talks are excellent activities for reviewing high-frequency collocations and vocabulary, as well as developing spoken fluency.

(3) Dictogloss is a language teaching activity when the teacher reads a short text, usually more than once, while learners are required to reconstruct it after listening. The first step is for students to listen and write down key words, expressions, or grammar constructions. Then these noted language components are used as a base for reconstructing as much of the text as possible.

The text can be a story or an excerpt as short as one paragraph and as long as several depending on students' proficiency levels. Students are asked to write down all the collocations that they can identify. A good practice can take two to four repeated readings. Then, based on their collocation notes, in pairs or small groups, students can be asked to re-tell or reconstruct the story to the best of their ability. When they have finished, the entire story or the list of collocations is handed to students for checking.

A classroom dictogloss can be take as little as five to ten minutes, and it can be used as often as necessary during a school term. An excerpted example is presented below (collocations are underlined).

My brother called <u>last night</u>, but I was <u>too busy</u> to <u>answer the phone</u>. So, he <u>left a message</u>. He said that he was <u>nearby</u> and <u>on his way</u> to my house. He <u>showed up</u> <u>a little while</u> later <u>together with</u> his five friends. They <u>decided to</u> visit me because they were <u>looking for something to eat</u>. But all I had <u>in my refrigerator</u> was <u>a couple of</u> cucumbers, <u>a little</u> orange juice, and <u>a bottle of</u> soda. <u>Needless to say</u>, my brother and his friends were <u>very disappointed</u>. <u>I hope</u> that they <u>learned their lesson</u> about <u>coming by</u> uninvited.

Collocations with a Purpose, Part II: Academic Writing

At present, a great deal is known about frequent collocations and multiword units typically required L2 academic writing, such as common phrases (e.g. *in general…, on the whole …, for this reason …*), non-referential *it*-constructions (e.g. *it is interesting/clear/has been established*), or complex inflexible prepositions (e.g. *except for, in spite of/despite, by means of, in regard to, on top of, together with, prior to, such as*).

The teaching of academic writing – other than to absolute beginners – may be difficult to carry out without teaching recurrent academic collocations and multiword units, as well as longer stretches of text, such as *for a long time xxx, it has been the case that*, or *recent evidence/findings suggest(s) that* …. In most (if not all) student academic writing, such multiword expressions and their variations can be simply unavoidable (Hinkel, 2015, 2016, 2018).

As with conversational routines, in formal academic prose, what is appropriate and inappropriate in written discourse is also highly conventionalized (Swales, 1990). To a great extent, academic writing is also highly patterned, stereotyped, and rigidly structured, and particularly so in the case of student essays and written assignments (Hinkel, 2015; Nattinger & DeCarrico, 1992). The stereotypical structure of most academic writing usually begins with an opening or an introductory statement, followed by the topic nomination, then moving on to the main points, and some sort of closing statement at the end. Generally speaking, the progression of writing from one rhetorical section to the next is clearly identified by means of flexible collocations, such as *To begin/start with/First, The main idea/point/question,* and *To conclude/sum up, In sum/conclusion, Finally.*

In academic writing, many conventional and highly predictable phrases that mark discourse junctures are called "institutionalized" because they occur more frequently in certain types of texts than in others (Howarth, 1996, 1998; Pawley & Syder, 1983; Swales, 1990). In writing instruction, learning frequent multiword units can take place in the context of L2 writing, say, when constructing predictable essay openings with variants and substitutions, e.g. *Many authors/books/articles state/say/that ....*

For example, the number of reporting verbs that can be employed to mark paraphrases is around a dozen, and they can be learned with relative ease while working on a writing assignment, e.g.

> *the author says/states/indicates/comments/notes/observes/believes/points out/ emphasizes/advocates/reports/concludes/underscores/mentions/finds*

Additionally, frequent academic collocations with similar meanings and textual functions can also be learned and practiced:

> *according to the author/article/book, as the author states/indicates, in the author's view/opinion/understanding, as noted/stated/mentioned (in the book/ article), based on the article/author's opinion*

A large number of academic collocations can have transparent meanings, and these can be useful for learners at any proficiency level. Although some are longer than two or three words, typically, such multiword units consist of only

one or two content words accompanied by function words, such as articles
(*a, an, the*) and highly recurrent prepositions (e.g. *of, in, to, for, with, on, at, from*).

Highly Frequent Academic Multiword Units with Transparent Meanings		
the end of the ~ *at the end of* ~ *at the end of the*	*the beginning of the* ~ *at the beginning of* ~ *at the beginning of the*	*a number of the* ~ *a large/small number of the* ~ *in a number of* *(in) a total number (of)*
one of the ~ *one of the most* *most of the* *some of the* *(a) part of the*	*at the same time* *for the first time* *at this/that time* *at the time of*	*the size of the* *the amount of the* *the type of the* *the rate/frequency of the* *the value of the* *the form of the*
(is/are) the same as *the same way (as)*	*is similar to*	*as well (as)* *as well as the*
a wide range of	*based on (the)* ~ *is/are based on the* *on the basis of the*	*in addition* ~ *in addition to the* ~ *in addition to this/that*
as a result (of)	*for this reason*	*because of (the)~ due to (the)*

(Adapted from Biber, et al. (1999) and Simpson-Vlach & Ellis (2010))

Essential and frequent collocations can become an efficient means of
expanding L2 learners' language range, particularly when they are also
taught how to substitute their elements appropriately and in practical ways.

> When working with frequent academic collocations, it is important to
> bring learners' attention to fundamental distinctions between conver-
> sational and informal language units that are distinct from those found
> in formal writing.

Although both conversational and academic collocations are usually
encountered in instruction, pointing out the differences in these two types
of multiword units is of the essence: without explicit teaching, learners may
simply miss conversational vs. academic language components.

Suggested Teaching Activities for Collocations in Academic Writing

(1) Present students with a short set of numerical or survey data of, say, a population description, languages/dialects spoken, educational backgrounds,

or shopping preferences in a city, region, or country. Provide the list of academic collocations that are required in a written description of the data. Students can work individually or in pairs.

(2) Give the students a list of necessary collocations before they begin working. Assign students to measure (however approximately) the size of the classroom, the school (or public) library, cafeteria, study area, their houses, rooms, or hallways; or count books in a bookcase, or attendees in a lecture hall or a large classroom, or types of drinks, vegetables, or snacks in a grocery store, various kinds of souvenirs sold to tourists, vehicles in a parking lot, or shoes sold in a shoe store. That is, the students' task is to come up with a set of numerical data that can be described and written up in a short survey report.

As a starting point, students can begin by answering specific questions to guide their data collecting: who/what? for what purpose? where? at what time/when? Some suitable versions of these questions are usually sufficient for students to begin working as a data or writing prompt.

(3) Have students read a short editorial or an opinion on a popular topic. The task is to present the writer's views, e.g.

> the author states that ~~~ the author also says that
> the writer explains that ~~~ in addition, the writer reports that
> the article shows that ~~~ at the beginning, the data demonstrates that

An alternative: The teacher reads aloud a short text slowly, sentence by sentence. The students write down each sentence with their own restatements/versions of the text (see Dictogloss earlier in this chapter). This activity can be very productive because it addresses a number of language skills at one time, e.g. spelling, collocations, vocabulary, grammar, and sentence constructions.

A Final Comment

As with all language learning, repeated exposures and practice lead to long-term memory retention and subsequent production in speaking and writing. Many L2 learners have great difficulty using collocations and becoming fluent simply because most collocations and multiword units cannot be pieced together in the process of communication, and due to their length, they are laborious to remember and use correctly. It is also well-known that collocations require instruction accompanied by contextualized uses, practice, and more practice.

Although most collocations do not have immediately comprehensible and transparent meanings and grammar structure, a good number that are very common can be deducible and appropriate for learners at any level. When it comes to multiword units, a reliable rule of thumb is that the shorter the phrase is, the more likely it is to have a transparent meaning and grammatical structure (Nation, 2013; Nation, Shin, & Grant, 2016).

- Two- or three-word collocations and multiword units are the easiest to understand and learn
- This principle applies to collocations of practically any kind, including those that consist of a function word and a content word or two content words
- For teaching and learning, the short collocations and multiword units are encountered far more frequently than longer ones, and thus, can be easier to learn and practice

---

Examples of frequent collocations and multiword units are easy to locate – they are everywhere:

in fact, you know, I suppose, at the moment, work on, no way, used to, about right, on sale, feel free, save/spend/waste time, (have) no time, just now, right now, fast food, good start, for sure, any more, over there, I see/bet, it seems, and so on, let me see, (not) really, would like to

Because two-word collocations are highly common and can be found in both speech and writing, they are also relatively straightforward to come up with online, in dictionaries, and various teaching materials, such as picture books, textbooks, and electronic texts (Hinkel, 2014, 2015, 2018). On the whole, teaching and learning short collocations and multiword units is not a very demanding task due to their frequency: for example, they are almost always included in student textbooks on listening, speaking, reading, and writing. For beginners, for example, a small number of fixed (e.g. *hold on, call me*) or minimally variable (e.g. *See you later/tomorrow/next week*) expressions could be a good place to start. For more advanced learners, the collocational expressions that mark conversational sequences or written discourse structure are essential to learn.

In general terms, ubiquitous multiword units can be well-suited for practice in conversations or formal academic writing when they are added, omitted, and modified to match different types of contexts, formality levels, teaching and learning goals, and learners' proficiencies, from beginning to advanced. All in all, a great range of concepts, ideas, and functions are expressed by means of collocations and multiword units, and language usage is impossible without them.

References

Arnon, I., & Snider, N. (2010). More than words: Frequency effects for multi-word phrases. *Journal of Memory and Language, 62*, 67–82.

Biber, D., Johansson, S., Leech, G., Conrad, S., & Finegan, E. (1999). *Longman grammar of spoken and written English*. Harlow, UK: Pearson.

Boers, F. (2000). Metaphor awareness and vocabulary retention. *Applied Linguistics, 21*, 553–571.

Boers, F., & Lindstromberg, S. (2012). Experimental and intervention studies on formulaic sequences in a second language. *Annual Review of Applied Linguistics, 32*, 83–110.

Carter, R., & McCarthy, M. (2006). *Cambridge grammar of English*. Cambridge: Cambridge University Press.

Coulmas, F. (1981). *Conversational routines*. The Hague: Mouton.

Cowie, A. (1992). Multiword lexical units and communicative language teaching. In P. Arnaud, & H. Bejoint (Eds.), *Vocabulary and applied linguistics* (pp. 1–12). London: Macmillan.

Durrant, P. (2014). Corpus frequency and second language learners' knowledge of collocations: A meta-analysis. *International Journal of Corpus Linguistics, 19*, 443–477.

Fernando, C. (1996). *Idioms and idiomaticity*. Oxford: Oxford University Press.

Foster, P. (2001). Rules and routines: A consideration of their role in the task-based language production of native and non-native speakers. In M. Bygate, P. Skehan, & M. Swain (Eds.), *Researching pedagogic tasks: Second language learning, teaching and testing* (pp. 75–93). Harlow, UK: Longman.

Hill, J. (2000). Revising priorities: From grammatical failure to collocational success. In M. Lewis (Ed.), *Teaching collocation: Further developments in the lexical approach* (pp. 47–69). Hove, UK: Language Teaching Publications.

Hinkel, E. (2002). *Second language writers' text*. New York, NY: Routledge.

Hinkel, E. (2004). *Teaching academic ESL writing: Practical techniques in vocabulary and grammar*. New York, NY: Routledge.

Hinkel, E. (2013). Cultures of learning and writing in the US academy. In L. Jin, & M. Cortazzi (Eds.), *Researching intercultural learning: Investigations in language and education* (pp. 21–35). New York, NY: Palgrave Macmillan

Hinkel, E. (2014). Culture and pragmatics in second language teaching and learning. In M. Celce-Murcia, D. Brinton, & M. Snow (Eds.), *Teaching*

English as a second or foreign language (4th ed., pp. 394–408). Boston, MA: National Geographic Learning.

Hinkel, E. (2015). *Effective curriculum for teaching L2 writing: Principles and techniques.* New York, NY: Routledge.

Hinkel, E. (2016). Practical grammar teaching: Grammar constructions and their relatives. In E. Hinkel (Ed.), *Teaching English grammar to speakers of other languages* (pp. 171–191). New York, NY: Routledge.

Hinkel, E. (2018). Teaching and learning formulaic sequences and prefabs. In J. Liontas (Ed.), *The TESOL encyclopedia of English language teaching* (pp. 500–508). Malden, MA: Wiley/Blackwell.

Howarth, P. (1996). *Phraseology in English academic writing: Some implications for language learning and dictionary making.* Tübingen: Max Niemeyer.

Howarth, P. (1998). Phraseology and second language proficiency. *Applied Linguistics,* 19 (1), 24–44.

Lewis, M. (2000). There is nothing as practical as a good theory. In M. Lewis (Ed.), *Teaching collocation: Further developments in the lexical approach* (pp. 10–27). Hove, UK: Language Teaching Publications.

Martinez, R., & Schmitt, N. (2012). A phrasal expressions list. *Applied Linguistics,* 33(3), 299–320.

Nation, P., & Webb, S. (2011). Content-based instruction and vocabulary learning. In E. Hinkel (Ed.), *Handbook of research in second language teaching and learning, Vol. 2* (pp. 631–644). New York, NY: Routledge.

Nation, P. (2011). Research into practice: Vocabulary. *Language Teaching,* 44, 529–539.

Nation, P. (2013). *Learning vocabulary in another language* (2nd ed.). Cambridge: Cambridge University Press.

Nation, P., Shin, D., & Grant, L. (2016). Multiword units. In Nation, P. (Ed.), *Making and using word lists for language learning and testing* (pp. 71–79). Amsterdam: John Benjamins.

Nattinger, J., & DeCarrico, J. (1992). *Lexical phrases and language teaching.* Oxford: Oxford University Press.

Pawley, A., & Syder, F. (1983). Two puzzles for linguistic theory: Nativelike selection and nativelike fluency. In J. Richards, & R. Schmidt (Eds.), *Language and communication* (pp. 191–225). London: Longman.

Shin, D., & Nation, P. (2008). Beyond single words: The most frequent collocations in spoken English. *English Language Teaching Journal,* 62(4), 339–348.

Simpson-Vlach, R., & Ellis, N. (2010). An academic formulas list: New methods in phraseology research. *Applied Linguistics,* 31(4), 487–512.

Swales, J. (1990). *Genre analysis.* Cambridge: Cambridge University Press.

Ur, P. (2012). *Vocabulary activities.* Cambridge: Cambridge University Press.

Ur, P. (2014). Practice and research-based theory in English teacher development. *The European Journal of Applied Linguistics and TEFL,* 3(2), 143–155.

Webb, S., & Nation, P. (2017). *How vocabulary is learned.* Oxford: Oxford University Press.

Yorio, C. (1989). Idiomaticity as an indicator of second language proficiency. In K. Hyltenstam, & L. Obler (Eds.), *Bilingualism across the lifespan* (pp. 55–72). Cambridge: Cambridge University Press.

Appendix

By ~~ Large

"by and large"

About 43,300,000 results (0.46 seconds)

"by or large"

About 3 results (0.34 seconds)

Thank you

"thank you very much"

About 83,300,000 results (0.31 seconds)

"thank you a lot"

About 3,710,000 results (0.40 seconds)

More ~~ Less

"more or less"

About 128,000,000 results (0.56 seconds)

"more and less"

About 35,800,000 results (0.44 seconds)

Chapter 5

Teaching and Assessing Multiword Expressions Using an Open Educational Resources Academic English Corpus

Brent A. Green

Introduction

Fundamental work in applied and corpus linguistics (Biber, 2009; Biber et al., 1999; Biber and Barbieri, 2007; Boers et al., 2006; Nattinger & Decarrico, 1992; Schmitt, 2004; Sinclair, 1996: Wray, 1999, 2002, 2008, 2012) has highlighted the importance of multiword expressions in second language learners' spoken and written language. Erman and Warren's (2000) corpus analysis of the London Lund Corpus of Spoken English (LLC) and the Lancaster-Oslo–Bergen corpus (LOB), where nearly 60 percent of spoken and over 50 percent of written language were multiword expressions, illustrates the prevalence of multiword units in spoken and written English. In fact, Sinclair (2004) claims, based on years of corpus research, that "for every distinct unit of meaning there is a full phrasal expression …" If this is true, one would expect that becoming competent in a second language would require the acquisition of such forms. Cowie (1992) asserts that it "is impossible to perform at a level acceptable to native users, in writing or in speech, without controlling an appropriate range of multiword units" (p. 10). The challenge for the modern language teacher in a world where very few textbooks include knowledge of or practice with multiword expressions (Romer, 2011) is understanding how her learners acquire such expressions in another language and how she might effectively teach them.

While there are abundant resources for second language vocabulary and grammar acquisition teaching and learning practices found in the literature (see Christison, Christian, Duff, and Spada, 2015; and Nation, 2008, 2013), one approach is to engage learners in corpus-based learning tasks which align along a teacher/learner-centered continuum (Sripicharn, 2003). In this chapter I will discuss how teachers can access or build their own corpora using open educational resources and create multiword expressions acquisition tasks for their students, engage them in collaborative tasks, and teach them the tools for answering their own multiword expressions inquiries. Additionally, I will provide some guidelines and examples of how teachers can use OER corpus data to create assessment tasks which are designed to help them make valid decisions about learners' knowledge of multiword forms, meanings, and uses.

Why a Corpus-Based Approach to Teaching Multiword Expressions?

Classroom concordancing is a teaching approach in which corpus data are used in the language classroom to help learners notice and practice language patterns in target language domains. This teaching approach is sometimes referred to as Data-driven Learning (DDL) or a Corpus-based Approach (CBA) to language learning.[1] In a CBA, learners use authentic language data, presented in the form of concordance lines, to act as "linguistic detectives" as they find answers to their language questions (Johns 1988; 1991a, 1991b). Using a CBA is about helping students to recognize particular language forms, understand language meanings, and see patterns in language use with the ultimate goal of successfully using them in communicative situations. In fact, the advantage of using corpora in the language classroom is that students learn how to use tools that give them access to a vast resource of language data that they can use to discover how language is used by real people in real situations.

In addition to the language learning benefits mentioned above, O'Sullivan (2007) lists several cognitive and metacognitive skills that corpus-based approaches promote, including "predicting, observing, noticing, thinking, reasoning, analysing, interpreting, reflecting, exploring, making inferences (inductively or deductively), focusing, guessing, comparing, differentiating, theorizing, hypothesizing, and verifying" (p. 277). While the extent to which these skills are employed in corpus-based approaches by language learners needs to be examined more fully, this is, nonetheless, an impressive list of skills. Additionally, Aston et al. (2001) list three benefits for learners when corpora are used as resources for language learning activities: improved competence, engaged capacity, and increased autonomy.

Despite a trend towards the use of corpora and corpus tools in second language acquisition research and while applied linguists have come to embrace the value of corpus linguistics in terms of what it can offer language teachers, corpora and corpus tools are still not being widely implemented in the language classroom (Romer, 2011). Boulton (2009, 2010) believes that language practitioners' failure to employ a CBA in their classrooms can be attributed to three misperceptions. The first is the belief that the investment in time, effort, money, and resources is not worth the results. The second is the misperception that most CBAs focus on advanced learners working on complex language points. The final misperception is that lots of computers in a dedicated computer lab are needed in order to effectively implement a CBA. Given these misperceptions, it is perhaps not surprising that other teachers may not see the relevance of a CBA to their own local circumstances, but as Mauranen (2004) states "to make a serious contribution to language teaching, corpora must be adopted by ordinary teachers and learners in ordinary classrooms" (p. 208)

In addressing the complexity misperception above, Johns (1991a) clearly illustrates the value of DDL used with students from a variety of contexts and language levels:

> Talking about the DDL approach with other language teachers I am
> sometimes reproached that while this way of language-teaching by

stimulating student questions and by doing linguistic research in the classroom on a cooperative basis may be all very well for students as intelligent, sophisticated, and well-motivated as ours at Birmingham University, it would not work with students as unintelligent, unsophisticated, and poorly-motivated as theirs. I would be the last to deny that our students at Birmingham are very remarkable indeed: what I suspect, however, is that most students given the opportunity to show what they are capable of might be (almost) as remarkable.

(Johns, 1991a, p. 12)

A final benefit of classroom concordancing is helping teachers and students uncover the mysteries of language use which are often absent from reference grammars and textbooks (O'Keefe & Farr, 2003; Romer, 2011).

Which Corpus Should Be Used in the Classroom?

We now turn to a discussion of which corpus or corpora should be used in the language classroom to teach multiword expressions. Many ESL teachers and researchers are familiar with and use readily accessible web-based corpora like the British National Corpus (BNC) and the Corpus of Contemporary American English (COCA). These web-based corpora have specific built-in tools which allow teachers and learners to search for individual and multiword expressions within large language databases. The Corpus of Contemporary American English (Davies, 2008–), for example, boasts a database of over 560 million words. Most experts would agree that such large corpora provide opportunities for teachers and learners to engage in meaningful learning tasks. However, there are some limitations to using web-based corpora which can impact the teaching and learning of multiword expressions.

First, large corpora may be considered too big if a user wants to examine a specific language domain and perform simple analyses, and web-based corpora are sometimes too big for this purpose (Anthony, 2013). Also, while accessing web-based corpora is relatively easy, it may require registering for the service and possibly paying a monthly subscription charge, especially for institutional access.[2] A third issue relates to the fact that some web-based corpora, due to copyright laws,[3] do not allow access to the broader contexts where particular forms are found. This makes the task of finding discourse-related patterns which extend beyond the normal 100 or more words given in web-based corpora context windows difficult. This limitation also impacts discourse-level assessment tasks. An additional issue with some web-based corpora is that learners cannot view a "true" key word in context (KWIC) frame with search terms situated in the center of the screen, nor can they sort the search results in the variety of ways needed to construct a full picture of language use. As we will see later, KWIC and sorting the data are important processes for learners to engage in when searching for specific multiword language patterns.

Each one of these limitations can be overcome with the development of open educational resources (OER) corpora which, when paired with a freeware concordancing program like AntConc (Anthony, 2018), can be accessed by anyone using a Windows, Macintosh, or Linux computer operating system.

The OER Academic English Corpus

The corpus which is referenced in this chapter and which was compiled by the author is named the Open Educational Resources – Academic English Corpus or OER-AEC. It is a collection of introductory-level college texts written in English. There are nearly 10.5 million words in the OER-AEC, and it's a very rich resource for teachers who are teaching in academic English programs. An additional benefit is that the data represents textbook language from introductory-level credit-bearing college courses from a variety of disciplines. The corpus is comprised of language from four broad disciplines: math, science, social science, and humanities. The source texts are licensed under a Creative Commons Attribution 4.0 International license, which means users are free to share (copy and redistribute the material in any medium or format) and adapt (remix, transform, and build upon the material) for any purpose, even commercially. Individuals who share or adapt are required to give appropriate credit, provide a link to the license, and indicate any changes that are made (see *When we share, everyone wins*, n.d.). The actual texts are free to download in pdf and html formats from the OpenStax.org[4] website (see OpenStax, n.d.).

Table 5.1 lists the texts found in the corpus. Teachers and students may choose to use the complete corpus or select specific texts for their language teaching/learning purposes. The number to the right represents the number of words/tokens found in each text.

Table 5.1 OER-AEC Corpus Texts and Word Counts

Math		Social Science		Science		Humanities	
Algebra and Trigonometry	395,081	American Government	345,782	Anatomy and Physiology	527,449	U.S. History	404,956
Calculus Volume 1	184,197	Economics 2e	454,436	Astronomy	509,335		
Calculus Volume 2	172,170	Introduction to Sociology 2e	265,863	Biology	528,877		
Calculus Volume 3	237,566	Macroeconomics 2e	244,003	Chemistry Atoms First	371,412		
College Algebra	294,034	Microeconomics 2e	226,588	Chemistry	369,251		
Elementary Algebra	215,122	Principles of Economics	450,629	College Physics	673,920		
Intermediate Algebra	231,146	Principles of Macroeconomics	285,932	Concepts of Biology	231,860		
Introductory Business Statistics	176,748	Principles of Microeconomics	264,536	Microbiology	418,073		
Prealgebra	171,837	Psychology	297,282	University Physics Volume 1	392,024		
Precalculus	376,563			University Physics Volume 2	305,246		
Statistics	217,823			University Physics Volume 3	216,497		
Total	2,672,287		2,835,051		4,543,944		404,956

Individual corpus files can be downloaded from the Internet (see Green, 2018). Building the corpus was quite simple and was facilitated with the use of a variety of tools freely available from corpus linguist Laurence Anthony's website.[5] Figure 5.1 lists the tools that were used and describes their basic functions.

Software Tool	Basic Functions
AntFileConverter (Anthony, 2017a)	AntFileConverter is a very easy to use freeware tool for converting PDF and Microsoft Word (.docx) files to plain text (in the UTF-8 encoding).
AntFileSplitter (Anthony, 2017b)	AntFileSplitter is a freeware file-splitting tool. It takes an input list of text files (e.g. .txt) and divides them up into equally sized smaller text chunks according to a predefined size setting. AntConc seems to function faster when files are split into smaller chunks of data.
AntConc (Anthony, 2018)	AntConc is a freeware, multiplatform tool for carrying out corpus linguistics research and data-driven learning. It runs on any computer running Microsoft Windows (tested on Win 98/ME/2000/NT, XP, Vista, Win 7), Macintosh OS X (tested on 10.4.x, 10.5.x, 10.6.x), and Linux (tested on Ubuntu 10, Linux Mint).

Figure 5.1 Laurence Anthony's Corpus Tools

Creating and using an OER corpus involves three basic steps. These steps can be followed to create teacher and learner custom corpora from Word and PDF files. Each step along with a detail explanation is listed below:

1. **Create folders on your desktop.**
   Create a folder and name it "Corpus" with three subfolders, "Concordancers," "Corpora," and "Other Programs."
2. **Download files and save them in your folders.**
   Download OER-AEC files from the Internet (see Green, 2018) to the "Corpora" subfolder on your hard drive. In the "Concordancers" subfolder place the freeware concordancing program AntConc, which can be downloaded from www.laurenceanthony.net. Finally, download AntFileConverter and AntFileSplitter from the same website and put them in the "Other Programs" subfolder.
3. **Prepare files for analysis.**
   Downloaded corpus files from the OER-AEC site have already been converted to the UTF-8 text format and split into 100,000-word files needed to work with the AntConc concordancing program. More files can be added to your "Corpora" subfolder by downloading Word or

PDF files and using the AntFileConverter program to create UTF-8[6] formatted text. Large files should be split to facilitate faster processing. Splitting files into separate 10,000- or 100,000-word files has been found to be most effective when conducting corpus-based searches.

Teachers and students who want to use corpora in the classroom need to know how concordancing software works on a basic level,[7] including opening concordancing software, loading corpus files, completing basic and wild card searches and sorting data using left and right search parameters. It is recommended that teachers view Laurence Anthony's YouTube videos (see Anthony, n.d.) on how to use AntConc or download and possibly adapt the *AntConc Basics* worksheet found on the Internet (see Green, 2018) for specific learner needs.

Which Multiword Expressions Should Be Taught/Learned?

The determination of which multiword expression to focus on with a particular group of learners depends on several factors. It requires not only knowledge of the learners' goals, but also an understanding of the target language domain. Teachers need to know what language knowledge the learner can already use appropriately and understand how to establish pedagogical priorities appropriate for their learners. Nation, Shin, and Grant (2016) point out that while "deliberately learning multiword units can be an effective way of increasing knowledge, most learning of multiword units is likely to come from extensive reading and listening" (p. 79). It is in fact the texts from the target language domain that should drive corpus-based learning. Additionally, Flowerdew's (1996) survey of EAP concordance-derived materials found that they were developed because of what teachers viewed as salient, what they perceived as areas of weakness for students, and/ or areas that students themselves perceived to be their own weaknesses.

In terms of pedagogical priorities, Flowerdew (2001) recommends three areas of focus which intersect with the study of multiword units: 1) collocation patterning, 2) pragmatic appropriacy, and 3) discourse features. She goes on to share techniques for helping students identify salient patterns and raise their awareness of their importance through corpus-based activities. While specific texts will present varying patterns of multiword expressions use, a list of salient features found in the literature on multiword expressions is a good starting point for teachers. Table 5.2 lists various multiword

Table 5.2 Multiword Expressions

Multiword Expressions	Examples
Collocation patterning	look into the matter
Semantic irregularity	pull someone's leg
Grammatical irregularity	by and large
Phrase structure	NP – the best example VP – represented an opportunity PP – from the point of view AdjP – chronic tension-type AdvP – silently along
Closed and open slot phrase patterns	make _____ go _____ the answer to this _____ is/depends on
Referential expressions	based on in the form of
Identification and focus	a variety of (an/the) example of (a)
Contrast and comparison	and the same different from the
Deictics and locatives	a and b the real world
Vagueness markers	and so on and so forth
Hedges	(more) likely to (be) it may be
Epistemic stance	according to the we can see
Obligation and directive	do you want (me) (to) I want you to tell me
Expressions of ability and possibility	can be used to allows us to
Metadiscourse and textual reference	as shown in in this article
Topic introduction and focus	let's look at first of all
Topic elaboration	are as follows in more detail
Discourse markers	at the same time (in) other words

expressions. After the first four, Simpson-Vlach and Ellis' (2010) functional classification system is used. They argue that such a system can be quite useful for pedagogical purposes.

Ultimately, the decision of which patterns to teach comes down to what learners already know, what they need to know to be effective language users, and how effectively what they need to know can be taught using a corpus-based approach. In terms of setting forth course objectives using a CBA, Aston (2001) describes three which he feels are important:

> First, ... microscopic features can be noticed without sophisticated analyses of enormous amounts of data. Second, as there is rarely only one descriptive insight to be gained ... users can decide for themselves what to focus on, according to their own criteria of relevance and learnability. Third, such descriptions need not be fully accurate: since learning a language involves gradual approximation to the target system, then provided users are aware that their descriptions are partial and approximate, these may still be of value to them.
>
> (Aston, 2001, pp. 12–13)

Teaching Multiword Expressions Aligned to a Teacher/Learner-Centered Continuum

According to Mukherjee (2006), corpus-based activities should be "plotted on a cline of learner autonomy, ranging from teacher-led and relatively closed concordance-based activities to entirely learner-centered corpus-browsing projects" (p. 12). The description of the continuum (see Figure 5.2 below), adapted from Sripicharn (2003), provides details of the various methods teachers may want to use in their CBA classrooms. It should be noted that several example tasks below, while situated along the continuum, can be adapted depending on the desire for more or less teacher/student control.

Figure 5.2 Teacher/Learner Centered Continuum

Teacher-Centered Corpus Tasks for Multiword Expressions

In a *teacher-centered* task, the teacher selects the words or phrases to be investigated from the target language context. The teacher searches for and selects concordance lines that provide clear examples of the target form and designs concordance-based tasks with different degrees of control. While learners are engaged in the tasks, the teacher gives clues and hints to help learners complete the tasks successfully, or guides learners to an appropriate generalization or conclusion.

It is important to remember when creating teacher-centered tasks that first-time students are not used to seeing a KWIC view (see Figure 5.3 below) and can become confused by the lack of clear sentence structure. Tribble (2001) recommends at the early stages of introducing a corpus-based approach that students be shown sentence-view data. This can be accomplished using teacher-made worksheets created with corpus data. This approach lends itself well to teacher-centered activities.

The following task illustrates ways in which teachers can provide computer-free corpus-based multiword expressions learning activities in a teacher-centered approach. First, teachers can search the OER-AEC for specific examples of a lexical or grammatical multiword phenomenon and then create a worksheet like the following.

Look and Its Multiple Forms in Academic Text

Instructions: *Look* has both noun and verb forms and occurs quite frequently with other words in academic texts. In this task, you are going to examine example sentences with *look* taken from the OER-AEC and answer questions about them. What patterns do you see in the use of *look*? Some guiding questions have been provided to help you guess the patterns. You may work with a partner or in a small group if you wish.

1. Take a <u>look</u> at the following figure.
2. Let's take a <u>look</u> at the history of mental health treatment from the past.
3. Now let's take a <u>look</u> at the three errors of distortion: misattribution, suggestibility, and bias.

4. Let's take a <u>look</u> at two examples of common learning disabilities: dysgraphia and dyslexia.
5. When Lucia responded with a puzzled and then angry <u>look</u>, Alejandro realized he'd committed a mistake.
6. Read the following sentences, then <u>look</u> away and count backwards from 30 by threes to zero.
7. Archival research relies on looking at past records or data sets to <u>look</u> for interesting patterns or relationships.
8. In psychoanalysis, therapists help their patients <u>look</u> into their past to uncover repressed feelings.
9. In the following section, we will <u>look</u> more closely at the neuroscience of emotional response.
10. There has also been much work suggesting that optimism – the general tendency to <u>look</u> on the bright side of things – is also a significant predictor of positive health outcomes.

1. Can you find some examples of *look* as a verb? Write the number of the sentences where *look* is a verb.

_____

2. Can you find some examples of *look* as a noun? Write the number of the sentences where *look* is a noun.

_____

3. What are the most frequent words that occur before or after *look* as a verb?

_____

_____

4. What are the most frequent words that occur before or after *look* as a noun?

_____

_____

5. What else do you notice about the use of *look* in academic texts?

_____

_____

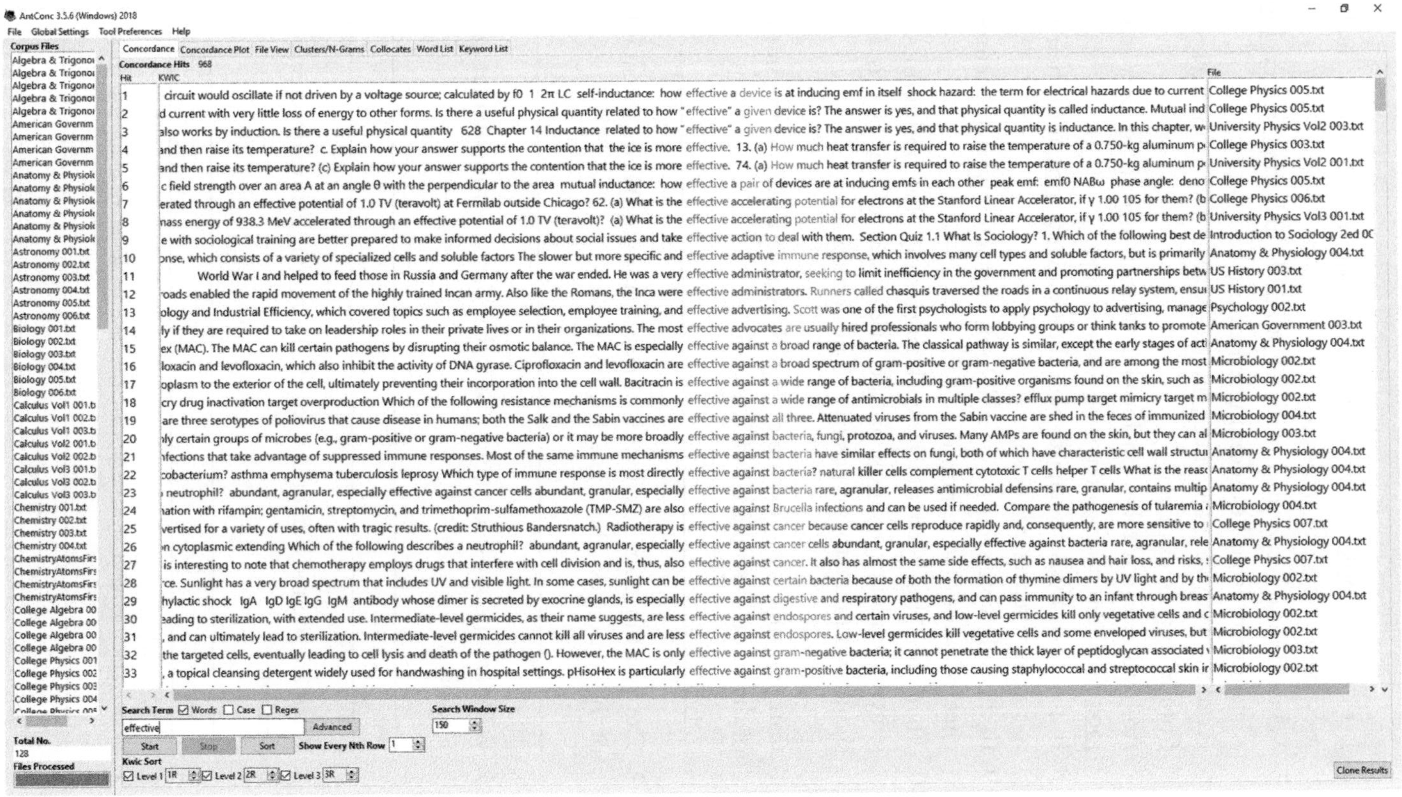

Figure 5.3 KWIC

As the students engage in the tasks, the teacher should be helping them answer the questions on the worksheet.

Collaborative Corpus Tasks for Multiword Expressions

In a *collaborative* task, the teacher and the learners agree on the language to be studied, which may come from course texts or be based on language-related situations learners encounter outside the classroom. The teacher and the learners browse the corpus to find specific instances of the word or phrases encountered and examine the language data together. Throughout the process, the teacher comments on and helps refine the learners' generalizations.

In order for collaborative corpus tasks to work, however, students will need a general introduction to concordancing software. Alternatively, the teacher can project sample concordance lines in the classroom so all students can participate in the collaborative task. Romer (2011) recommends engaging students in a collaborative task where learners and the teacher work out the collocation and phraseological behavior of pairs of near-synonyms like *speak* and *talk*. The OER-AEC has several examples of these two terms. The task is to show the data sorted in a variety of ways. The teacher can either do the sorting herself in the classroom or require the students to do the sorting on their own computers in a lab setting. Figures 5.4 and 5.5 illustrate the concordance samples of *talk* and *speak* from the OER-AEC.

After viewing the data, the teacher and students look for collocational patterns. In the case of *talk* and *speak,* the teacher can help the learners generate generalizations like the following:

Generalizations about *talk* and *speak*:
- *about* appears to collocate with *talk* (Lines 1–19) more frequently than with *speak* (Line 7)
- Verbs which occur before *to + talk* are *allow, tend, expect, want, refuse* (Lines 3, 12, 14, 15, 17)
- *talk* occurs idiomatically in *talk the talk* and co-occurs with *walk the walk* (Line 23)
- *speak* occurs idiomatically in Line 27 with the expression *so to speak*
- We can *speak a language* (Lines 1–5) or *speak another language* (Lines 10–11) but we do not *talk a language*

AntConc 3.5.6 (Windows) 2018

File Global Settings Tool Preferences Help

Corpus Files:
American Government
American Government
Anatomy & Physiology
Biology 001.txt
College Physics 001.txt
Economics 2ed 001.txt
Intro to Business Statist
Psychology 001.txt
Psychology 002.txt
Psychology 003.txt
Psychology 004.txt
Statistics 001.txt
University Physics Vol1

Concordance Concordance Plot File View Clusters/N-Grams Collocates Word List Keyword List

Concordance Hits 48

Hit	KWIC	File
1	lemanded! In economic terminology, demand is not the same as quantity demanded. When economists talk about demand, they mean the relationship between a range of prices and the quantities demanded a	Economics 2ed 001.txt
2	uantity demanded always move in opposite directions (on the demand curve). By convention, we always talk about elasticities as positive numbers. Mathematically, we take the absolute value of the result. We w	Economics 2ed 001.txt
3	d to Breuer for help. He spent 2 years (1880–1882) treating Anna O. and discovered that allowing her to talk about her experiences seemed to bring some relief of her symptoms. Anna O. called his treatment th	Psychology 002.txt
4	uble them up." For example, if you have measurements in petameters (1 Pm 1015 m), it is not proper to talk about megagigameters, although 106 109 1015. In practice, the This OpenStax book is available for	University Physics Vol1 001.txt
5	ry storage system: recall, recognition, and relearning. Recall is what we most often think about when we talk about memory retrieval: it means you can access information without cues. For example, you would	Psychology 001.txt
6	e ways, which allow us to communicate information about both concrete and abstract concepts. We can talk about our immediate and observable surroundings as well as the surface of unseen planets: We can	Psychology 001.txt
7	rvice to the community. Group activities can be as simple as hosting a book club or discussion group to talk about politics. Coffee Party USA provides an online forum for people from a variety of political persp	American Government 001.txt
8	s to celebrities. These examples represent an interesting facet of demand and supply. When economists talk about prices, they are less interested in making judgments than in gaining a practical understanding	Economics 2ed 001.txt
9	ural product, like wheat, we would include the farmer used for crops here. • Labor – When we talk about production, labor means human effort, both physical and mental. The pizzaiolo was the primary	Economics 2ed 001.txt
10	es demanded at those prices, as illustrated by a demand curve or a demand schedule. When economists talk about quantity demanded, they mean only a certain point on the demand curve, or one quantity on t	Economics 2ed 001.txt
11	y demanded refers to the (specific) point on the curve. Supply of Goods and Services When economists talk about supply, they mean the amount of some good or service a producer is willing to supply at each	Economics 2ed 001.txt
12	typical to support your team by wearing the team colors and sitting behind their bench. People tend to talk about the things that are important to them or the things they think about the most. What we talk ab	Psychology 003.txt
13	to talk about the things that are important to them or the things they think about the most. What we talk about the most. What we talk about, therefore, is a reflection of our values. Grammatical errors that involve overgeneralization of	Psychology 003.txt
14	the way that English and Mandarin Chinese speakers talk and think about time. English speakers tend to talk about time using terms that describe changes along a horizontal dimension, for example, saying son	Psychology 001.txt
15	think (Deutsch & Gerard, 1955; Berkowitz, 2004). How are we expected to act? What are we expected to wear? In our discussion of social roles we noted that colleges have t	Psychology 002.txt
16	and for dermatologists to specialize exclusively in these procedures. Consider visiting a dermatologist to talk about why, he or she entered the field and what the field of dermatology is like. Visit this for addition	Anatomy & Physiology 001.txt
17	do, Dan. Rather: No—no, sir, I don't. Bush: This is not a great night, because I want to talk about why I want to be president, why those 41 percent of the people are supporting me. And I don't	American Government 002.txt
18	nt) feedback to the president." (p. 6.3). Self-regulation is also known as will power. When we talk about will power, we tend to think of it as the ability to delay gratification. For example, Bettina's teer	Psychology 002.txt
19	you want, your children to read, then read to them. Let them see you reading. Keep books in your home. Talk about your favorite books. If you want your children to be healthy, then let them see you eat right ar	Psychology 001.txt
20	must select sites and voters carefully to ensure a representative and random poll. Some people refuse to talk to a representative of the people who do so until well after their first birthday; Each child's	Psychology 003.txt
21	ration of this phenomenon involved differences in the way that English and Mandarin Chinese speakers talk and think about time. English speakers tend to talk about time using terms that describe changes alo	Psychology 001.txt
22	s skill, as in Achè culture. ... Children develop at different rates. For example, some children may walk and talk as early as 8 months old, while others may not do so until well after their first birthday; Each child's	Psychology 003.txt
23	do in a situation where we actually do in that situation. In other words, we might "talk the talk," but not "walk the walk." How does this theory apply to males and females? Kohlberg (1969) felt tha	Psychology 002.txt
24	anks. He delivered his first radio speech eight days after assuming the presidency: "My friends! I want to talk for a few minutes with the people of the United States about banking—to talk with the comparative!	American Government 002.txt
25	ow famous last lecture called "Really Achieving Your Childhood Dreams." In his moving, yet humorous talk, he shares his insights on seeing the good in others, overcoming obstacles, and experiencing zero gr	Psychology 002.txt
26	y what a person says: The person might ramble, exhibit loose associations (jump from topic to topic), or talk in a way that is so disorganized and incomprehensible that it seems as though the person is random	Psychology 003.txt
27	strangers; others become excessively irritable and complain or make hostile comments. The person may talk loudly and rapidly, exhibiting flight of ideas, abruptly switching from one topic to another. These indi	Psychology 003.txt
28	because of shared experiences, concerns, and ideas. Citizens who are comfortable with one another will talk more and share opinions, leading to more opportunities to influence or reinforce one another. This	American Government 002.txt
29	m cues that help voters pay closer attention to a political debate and make decisions about it. Through a talk program or opinion column, the elite commentator tells people when and how to react to a current	American Government 002.txt
30	esidents, to reach out to citizens. While the increased use of television decreased the popularity of radio, talk radio still provides political information. Modern presidents also use television to rally people in time	American Government 002.txt
31	s, leaving presidents with no sure way to communicate with the public.49 Other voices, such as those of talk show hosts and political pundits, now fill the gap. Electoral candidates have also lost some media gr	American Government 002.txt
32	) Eric Cantor, a representative from Virginia, was at the top of his game. He was handsome, popular with talk show hosts and powerful insiders, an impressive campaign fundraiser and speaker, and apparently c	American Government 002.txt
33	ference for streaming video may overtake physical DVD disks. Netflix, the source of numerous late night talk show laughs and jabs in 2011, may yet have the last laugh. This OpenStax book is available for free	Economics 2ed 001.txt

Search Term ☑ Words ☐ Case ☐ Regex

Search Term: talk

Search Window Size: 150

Start Stop Sort Advanced Show Every Nth Row: 1

Kwic Sort
☑ Level 1 1R ☐ Level 2 2R ☐ Level 3 3R

Total No.
13

Files Processed

Close Results

Figure 5.4 OER-AEC Concordance Samples of Talk

File Global Settings Tool Preferences Help

Corpus Files | Concordance Concordance Plot File View Clusters/N-Grams Collocates Word List Keyword List

Corpus Files
American Government
Biology 001.txt
College Physics 001.txt
Economics 2nd 001.txt
Elementary Algebra 0...
Intro to Business Stati...
Principles of Economic...
Principles of Macroec...
Psychology 001.txt
Statistics 001.txt
University Physics Vol1

Concordance Hits 31

Hit	KWIC	File
1	of the batteries last at least how long? The percent of persons (ages five and older) in each state who speak a language at home other than English is approximately exponentially distributed with a mean of...	Intro to Business Statistics 001.t...
2	ty that the percent is between eight and 14. The percent of all individuals living in the United States who speak a language at home other than English is 13.8. Why is this number different from 9.848%? What...	Intro to Business Statistics 001.t...
3	of the batteries last at least how long? The percent of persons (ages five and older) in each state who speak a language at home other than English is approximately exponentially distributed with a mean of...	Statistics 001.txt
4	ty that the percent is between eight and 14. The percent of all individuals living in the United States who speak a language at home other than English is 13.8. Why is this number different from 9.848%? What...	Statistics 001.txt
5	Approximately 281,000,000 people over age five live in the United States. Of these people, 55,000,000 speak a language other than English at home. Of those who speak another language at home. 62.3% spe...	Intro to Business Statistics 001.t...
6	e. Approximately 281,000,000 people over age five live in the United States. Of these people, 55,000,000 speak a language other than English at home. Of those who speak another language at home. 62.3% spe...	Intro to Business Statistics 001.t...
7	nfluences thought compared how English speakers and the Dani people of Papua New Guinea think and speak about color. The Dani have two words for color: one word for light and one word for dark. In contr...	Psychology 001.txt
8	like school children—adult participants can distinguish between the government's allowing someone to speak and endorsing that person's allowing someone to speak and endorsing that person's speech. Yet, while some displays of religious codes (e.g.. Ten Commar...	American Government 001.txt
9	she was in a car accident and suffered brain damage to her Broca's area. She completely lost the ability to speak and form any kind of meaningful language. There is nothing wrong with her mouth or her vocal c...	Psychology 001.txt
10	e United States. Of these people, 55,000,000 speak a language other than English at home. Of those who speak another language at home, 62.3% speak English at home; E... speaks another...	Intro to Business Statistics 001.t...
11	e United States. Of these people, 55,000,000 speak a language other than English at home. Of those who speak another language at home, 62.3% speak Spanish. Let E speaks English at home; E... speaks another...	Statistics 001.txt
12	es such as abortion, euthanasia, the death penalty, and military involvement abroad. Political candidates speak at religious centers and institutions in an effort to meet like-minded voters. For example, Senator...	American Government 001.txt
13	own blood with brain matter emerging from his head, Gage was conscious and able to get up, walk, and speak. But in the months following his accident, people noticed that his personality had changed. Many...	Psychology 001.txt
14	m their parents and sent to boarding schools, many of them run by churches, where they were forced to speak English and abandon their traditional cultures.97 In 1887, the Dawes Severalty Act, another effort t...	American Government 001.txt
15	most people lack the inclination, time, or expertise necessary to decide political issues, these groups will speak for them. As groups compete with one another and find themselves in conflict regarding importan...	American Government 001.txt
16	DRUGS There are several different types of neurotransmitters released by different neurons, and we can speak in broad terms about the kinds of functions associated with different neurotransmitters (). Much o...	Psychology 001.txt
17	U THINK? The Meaning of Language Think about what you know of other languages; perhaps you even speak multiple languages. Imagine for a moment that your closest friend fluently speaks more than one...	Psychology 001.txt
18	usually the case that an 's' is added to the end of a word to indicate plurality. For example, we speak of one dog versus two dogs. Young children will overgeneralize this rule to cases that are exceptio...	Psychology 001.txt
19	er problem (hints are given), but it does fit the major features of projectile range as described. When we speak of the range of a projectile on level ground, we assume that R is very small compared with the circ...	College Physics 001.txt
20	xample 4.9 were launched at the same speed, 4.4 which shot would have the greatest range? When we speak of the range of a projectile on level ground, we assume R is very small compared with the circumf...	University Physics Vol1 001.txt
21	n of weight used by NASA and the popular media in relation to space travel and exploration. When they speak of "weightlessness" and "microgravity," they are really referring to the phenomenon we call "free-...	College Physics 001.txt
22	e of politics by watching a parent or guardian vote, for instance, or by hearing presidents and candidates speak on television or the internet, or seeing adults honor the American flag at an event (Figure 6.2). As s...	American Government 001.txt
23	exceptions to the rules are still being learned (Moskowitz, 1978). LANGUAGE AND THOUGHT When we speak one language, we agree that words are representations of ideas, people, places, and events. The gir...	Psychology 001.txt
24	e the late 1700s. When President John Adams signed the Sedition Act in 1798, which made it a crime to speak openly against the government, the Kentucky and Virginia legislatures passed resolutions declari...	American Government 001.txt
25	the courts. The right to freedom of expression is not absolute; several key restrictions limit our ability to speak or publish opinions under certain circumstances. We have seen that the Constitution protects mos...	American Government 001.txt
26	the substrate binds is called the enzyme's active site. The active site is where the "action" happens, so to speak. Since enzymes are proteins, there is a unique combination of amino acid residues (also called side...	Biology 001.txt
27	better education for students of Mexican ancestry. Los Angeles schools did not allow Latino students to speak Spanish in class and gave no place to study Mexican history in the curriculum. Guidance counselor...	American Government 001.txt
28	00 speak a language other than English at home. Of those who speak another language at home, 62.3% speak Spanish. Let E speaks English at home; E... speaks another language at home; E speaks another...	Intro to Business Statistics 001.t...
29	00 speak a language other than English at home. Of those who speak another language at home, 62.3% speak Spanish. Let E speaks English at home; E... speaks another language at home; E speaks another...	Statistics 001.txt
30	learned. Whitney took Spanish in high school, but after high school she did not have the opportunity to speak Spanish. Whitney is now 31, and her company has offered her an opportunity to work in their Me...	Psychology 001.txt
31	lected. All of the methods described thus far are correlational in nature. This means that researchers can speak to important relationships that might exist between two or more variables of interest. However, co...	Psychology 001.txt

Search Term ☑ Words ☐ Case ☐ Regex

Advanced

Search Window Size 150

Kwic Sort
☑ Level 1 1R ☑ Level 2 2R ☑ Level 3 3R

Total No. 31
Files Processed

Close Results

Figure 5.5 OER-AEC Concordance Samples of Speak

While there are many more generalizations that can be co-constructed in a collaborative corpus task like the one presented above, it is important to emphasize Aston's (2001) observation that these types of descriptions do not need to be completely accurate, because "learning a language involves gradual approximation to the target system" (p. 12). These activities can also segue into more language analyses with teachers and students collaborating or learners exploring their own strands of inquiry. An example from the *talk* and *speak* contexts above might include examining contexts where the idiomatic expression *talk the talk* might occur.

Learner-Centered Corpus Tasks for Multiword Expressions

In a *learner-centered* task, students are left on their own to answer the form-, meaning-, and use-related questions they may have about multiword expressions. Learners who are well versed in using concordancers and corpora can often do this work at home using their own computer. In a lab setting, the teacher can make herself available to the students to help guide them towards independent learning if help is needed. Since learners need a firm understanding of how to use corpora and concordancing tools in order for this task to work as intended, learner-centered tasks should occur later in a course schedule after students have acquired the corpus research skills needed for this task to be effective. An example of how to help structure learner-centered corpus tasks can be in the form of a handout in which students are asked to write down what they discovered in their independent searches. This is also a way for students to demonstrate that they are doing independent corpus work.

Multiword Expressions Form, Meaning, and Use Handout

Instructions: As you engage in your linguistic "detective" work, take notes on the patterns you see. Try to make distinctions between the structure's form, meaning, and use.

Structure under investigation: _____

Form (How is this structure formed?):

_____

_____

_____

_____

Meaning (What does this structure mean?):

_____

_____

_____

Use (How is this structure used?):

_____

_____

_____

Reflect on what you learned in your language discovery session today.

_____

_____

_____

Using Corpora to Develop Assessment Tasks

The most fundamental consideration in planning and developing any language assessment task is the purpose for which the results might be used (Bachman, 1990; Bachman & Palmer, 1996, 2010). If, for example, a classroom teacher wants to determine whether or not a group of learners have acquired a particular multiword form, a form-based assessment task should be generated. Student performance on multiword meaning tasks should help teachers make valid decisions about learners' progress in linking forms to meaning. Finally, learner performance on tasks which require learners to use multiword expression in target language use situations should inform decisions about students' abilities to use language appropriately in those domains. A simple approach to assessing multiword expressions in the classroom can be conceptualized using a form, meaning, and use framework (Larsen-Freeman, 2014). Examples of multiword assessment tasks developed from the OER-AEC are discussed below. In addition, it is important for teachers to recognize and practice using concordancers like AntConc to generate form, meaning, and use tasks, thus saving teachers time in creating such tasks. Examples which illustrate the various test item types and how they were derived from corpus data will be explained below.

Form-Focused Assessment Tasks for Multiword Expressions

In a *form-focused* assessment task, teachers are most concerned with whether or not students can recognize and produce the correct forms. This can be accomplished by using the corpus to find specific target forms, selecting appropriate passages of text, and then copying them to a word processing program. What is left to do is to create the instructions outlining what is expected from the test-taker. A simple example of this is asking students to find and underline modals plus verb forms in an academic passage retrieved from the OER-AEC. This is shown in the example below.

Modal Forms

Instructions: Find and underline all modal forms and their accompanying verbs in the paragraphs below. Paragraphs were extracted from the Psychology textbook in the OER-AEC Corpus. (One point for each underlined modal and one point for each underlined verb.) (Hint: Paragraph #1 contains four modals with verbs; Paragraph #2 contains five modals with verbs.)

1. Imagine that you are on the admissions committee of a major university. You are faced with a huge number of applications but you are able to accommodate only a small percentage of the applicant pool. How might you decide who should be admitted? You might try to correlate your current students' college GPA with their scores on standardized tests like the SAT or ACT. By observing which correlations were strongest for your current students, you could use this information to predict relative success of those students who have applied for admission into the university.

2. Sexism is prejudice and discrimination toward individuals based on their sex. Typically sexism takes the form of men holding biases

against women, but either sex can show sexism toward their own or their opposite sex. Like racism sexism may be subtle and difficult to detect. Common forms of sexism in modern society include gender role expectations such as expecting women to be the caretakers of the household. Sexism also includes people's expectations for how members of a gender group should behave. For example women are expected to be friendly, passive and nurturing and when women behave in an unfriendly, assertive or neglectful manner, they often are disliked for violating their gender role. Research by Laurie Rudman finds that when female job applicants self-promote, they are likely to be viewed as competent, but they may be disliked and are less likely to be hired because they violated gender expectations for modesty. Sexism can exist on a societal level such as in hiring employment opportunities and education. Women are less likely to be hired or promoted in male dominated professions such as engineering, aviation and construction.

Meaning-Focused Assessment Tasks for Multiword Expressions

Meaning-focused assessment tasks can take many different forms. Teachers should remember that the primary purpose of a meaning-focused task is to determine whether or not learners know what a particular phrase means. An example of a meaning-focused assessment task with common phrases found in academic writing could take the form of a gap-fill task with sentences extracted from the corpus (see example below). It should be noted that providing as much context as possible greatly facilitates learner success with this type of test item.

Academic Phrases

Instructions: Choose a common academic phrase from the word bank to complete the sentences below. Phrases and sentences have been taken from the OER–AEC. (One point each.)

as well as	because of	compared to	consist of
impact on	lack of	on the other hand	point of view

1. Fishing provides income, _____ food, for many Americans. However, without government restrictions on the kinds and number of fish that can be caught, the fish population would decline and certain species could become instinct.

2. Look at your watch. Wait fifteen seconds. Then wait another fifteen seconds. In that time, two children have died from _____ access to clean drinking water. Access to safe water is one of the most basic human needs, and it is woefully out of reach for millions of people on the planet.

3. How well do our pets recall the fond memories we share with them? There is an urban legend that a goldfish has a memory of three seconds, but this is just a myth. Goldfish can remember up to three months, while the beta fish has a memory of up to five months. And while a puppy's memory span is no longer than 30 seconds, the adult dog can remember for five minutes. This is meager _____ _____ a cat, whose memory span lasts for 16 hours.

4. Janet Saltzman Chafetz (1941–2006) presented a model of feminist theory that attempts to explain the forces that maintain gender inequality as well as a theory of how such a system can be changed (Turner 2003). Similarly, critical race theory grew out of a critical analysis of race and racism from a legal _____. Critical race theory looks at structural inequality based on white privilege and associated wealth, power, and prestige.

5. Two important countries in terms of their potential impact that did not ratify the Kyoto Protocol were the United States and China. The United States rejected it as a result of a powerful fossil fuel industry and China _____ a concern it would stifle the nation's growth.

6. The mucous membranes lining the nose, mouth, lungs, and urinary and digestive tracts provide another nonspecific barrier against potential pathogens. Mucous membranes _____ a layer of epithelial cells bound by tight junctions. The epithelial cells secrete a moist, sticky substance called mucus, which covers and protects the more fragile cell layers beneath it and traps debris and particulate matter, including microbes. Mucus secretions also contain antimicrobial peptides.

7. Netflix officials had anticipated the price increase would have little _____ attracting new customers. Netflix

anticipated adding up to 1.29 million new subscribers in the third quarter of 2011. It is true this was slower growth than the firm had experienced – about 2 million per quarter.

8.   Given that voters will want to find quick, useful information about each, candidates will try to get the media's attention and pick up momentum. Media attention is especially important for newer candidates. Most voters assume a candidate's website and other campaign material will be skewed, showing only the most positive information. The media, _____, are generally considered more reliable and unbiased than a candidate's campaign materials, so voters turn to news networks and journalists to pick up information about the candidates' histories and issue positions. Candidates are aware of voters' preference for quick information and news and try to get interviews or news coverage for themselves. Candidates also benefit from news coverage that is longer and cheaper than campaign ads.

Answers: 1) as well as; 2) lack of; 3) compared to; 4) point of view; 5) because of; 6) consist of; 7) impact on; 8) on the other hand

Use-Focused Assessment Tasks for Multiword Expressions

Use-focused assessment tasks for multiword expressions should be designed to elicit learner knowledge of how to use such expressions in real world language tasks. For this reason, a use-based assessment task will allow students to construct their responses rather than select them. Teachers wishing to know how students can use multiword expressions can create text-based writing tasks where the teacher selects a short, cohesive extract from the corpus and then asks the students to respond in writing to questions related to general interpretations of the reading. Here is an example of this type of task:

Verb + Infinitive

Instructions: Read the short passage on happiness taken from the Psychology Text in the OER-AEC Corpus. Then answer **ONE** of the following questions related to the reading. Write a paragraph of at least five sentences. Use at least five verbs listed below in your response.

(believe, assume, find, know, perceive, prove, show, think, understand, advise, allow, cause, enable, force, get, help, permit, persuade, tell, urge, attempt, tend, fail, proceed, manage, refuse, promise, offer, decide, try, want, intend, expect, prefer, hate, like, love, hope, desire, admit, appreciate, avoid, begin, continue, defend, deny, enjoy, feel, finish, forget, hear, like, prefer, quit, recall, regret, remember, resume, risk, see, smell, stop, have, make, let)

HAPPINESS

America's founders declared that its citizens have an unalienable right to pursue happiness. But what is happiness? When asked to define the term, people emphasize different aspects of this elusive state. Indeed, happiness is somewhat ambiguous and can be defined from different perspectives (Martin, 2012). Some people, especially those who are highly committed to their religious faith, view happiness in ways that emphasize virtuosity, reverence, and enlightened spirituality. Others see happiness as primarily contentment – the inner peace and joy that come from deep satisfaction with one's surroundings, relationships with others, accomplishments, and oneself. Still others view happiness mainly as pleasurable engagement with their personal environment – having a career and hobbies that are engaging, meaningful, rewarding, and exciting. These differences, of course, are merely differences in emphasis. Most people would probably agree that each of these views, in some respects, captures the essence of happiness.

1. Which aspects of happiness described above do you feel are important? Explain your answer with specific details.
2. Your friend says that she is unhappy in her life. What would you do to help her out?

_____

_____

_____

_____

_____

_____

_____

_____

_____

_____

_____

_____

_____

_____

_____

_____

_____

Another example would be to provide a writing topic and give learners a list of target phrases previously covered in the coursework. Here is an example of this task with phrasal verbs. Grading this task would probably be based on a number of considerations, including how well the test-takers used the target phrases in their writing.

Phrasal Verbs

Instructions: Use at least five two-word verbs listed below to describe a recent conversation you have had on the phone with someone. (Ten points.)

> cash in, hang up, put down, get to, go after, find out, make up, miss out, pay off, turn down, fall for, find out, leave out, make up, pick up, light up, look after, pass over, put away, tear down, tear up, try on, try out, turn down, come back, keep away, lie down, light up

_____

_____

_____

_____

_____

_____

Concordancers as Assessment Task Creation Tools

In a final note, it is important for teachers to become familiar with all of the features concordancing programs like AntConc have to offer. These features can be useful tools in helping to create form, meaning, and use test tasks. A corpus, for example, can be used to find contexts where the target structures occur more frequently. The Concordance Plot feature in AntConc greatly facilitates this. Finding these frequently occurring structures allows the teacher to identify specific real-world contexts where they are used.

Additionally, if teachers want to use a particular language text which they have selected independently, like a newspaper article or a passage from a textbook, they can load it in AntConc and search for target structures they are interested in assessing. Once found, they can easily select them to create specific test items. This approach is much more efficient than looking for target structures by hand.

Finally, for fill-in-the blank items, AntConc allows teachers to hide the structures. This makes creating this type of test item very easy and much less time consuming. Figures 5.6 and 5.7, for example, show two screens respectively before and after hiding the KWIC for the multiword hedge *more likely* as found in the OER-AEC.

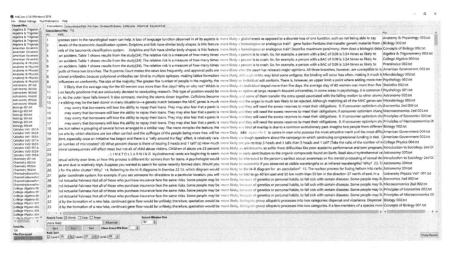

Figure 5.6 More Likely KWIC

Figure 5.7 More Likely with KWIC Hidden

Conclusion

This chapter has focused on the specific ways in which teachers can access or create open educational resources corpora to help their learners engage in corpus-based multiword expressions activities. Example tasks were presented along a teacher/learner-centered continuum. A general discussion of creating meaningful assessment tasks was also included. It is hoped that this discussion will encourage more teachers to recognize the value of OER corpora and concordancing tools and to begin using a CBA in their language classrooms.

Notes

1 For the purposes of this chapter, both DDL and CBA will be used interchangeably to refer to the application of corpora in L2 classrooms.
2 See www.sketchengine.eu/prices-for-academic-individual-users/ and https://corpus.byu.edu/premium.asp and https://corpus.byu.edu/academic_license.asp for information about licensing requirements from Sketchengine and COCA.
3 See https://corpus.byu.edu/faq.asp#x3 for discussion of COCA Copyright Policy.
4 OpenStax is a nonprofit organization based at Rice University whose mission is to improve student access to education. They do this by facilitating

the writing of college textbooks and making them available online under a Creative Commons Attribution 4.0 International license. This means that anyone is able to copy and redistribute the material in any medium or format and/or remix, transform, and build upon the material for any purpose, even commercially. OpenStax textbook development is funded through partnerships with Rice University and philanthropic foundations such the William & Flora Hewlett Foundation, Bill & Melinda Gates Foundation, Michelson 20MM Foundation, Maxfield Foundation, and Open Society Foundation.

5 Laurence Anthony is a professor in the Faculty of Science and Engineering at Waseda University, Japan who has an extensive series of free software programs which are invaluable to the language teacher and learner using a corpus-based approach. The url www.laurenceanthony.net/ will allow you to access his site.

6 AntConc works best with UTF-8 formatted text files.

7 Most concordancing programs have many word and phrase analysis tools which are not typically needed for teachers or learners to conduct searches and sorts in the process of becoming familiar with language patterns.

References

Anthony, L. (n.d.). AntConc Tutorial (Ver. 3.4.0) [YouTube Playlist]. Retrieved from www.youtube.com/playlist?list=PLiRIDpYmiC0Ta0-Hdvc1D7hG6dmiS_TZj

Anthony, L. (2013). A critical look at software tools in corpus linguistics. *Linguistic Research,* 30(2), 141–161.

Anthony, L. (2017a). AntFileConverter (Version 1.2.1) [Computer Software]. Tokyo, Japan: Waseda University. Available from www.laurenceanthony. net/software

Anthony, L. (2017b). AntFileSplitter (Version 1.2.1) [Computer Software]. Tokyo, Japan: Waseda University. Available from www.laurenceanthony. net/software

Anthony, L. (2018). AntConc (Version 3.5.7) [Computer Software]. Tokyo, Japan: Waseda University. Available from www.laurenceanthony.net/software

Aston, G. (2001). (Ed.). *Learning with corpora.* Houston, TX: Athelstan.

Bachman, L. F. (1990). *Fundamental considerations in language testing.* Oxford: Oxford University Press.

Bachman, L., & Palmer, A. (1996). *Language testing in practice*. Oxford: Oxford University Press.

Bachman, L., & Palmer, A. (2010). Language assessment in practice. Oxford: Oxford University Press.

Biber, D. (2009). A corpus-driven approach to formulaic language in English. *International Journal of Corpus Linguistics, 14*, 275–311.

Biber, D., & Barbieri, F. (2007). Lexical bundles in university spoken and written registers. *English for Specific Purposes, 26*, 263–286.

Biber, D., Johansson, S., Leech, G., Conrad, S., & Finegan, E. (1999). *Longman grammar of spoken and written English*. Harlow, UK: Pearson Education.

Boers, F., Eyckmans, J., Kappel, J., Stengers, H., & Demecheleer, M. (2006). Formulaic sequences and perceived oral proficiency: Putting a lexical approach to the test. *Language Teaching Research, 10*, 245–261.

Boulton, A. (2009). Testing the limits of data-driven learning: Language proficiency and training. *ReCALL, 21*(1), 37–51.

Boulton, A. (2010). Data-driven learning: Taking the computer out of the equation. *Language Learning, 60*(3), 534–572.

Christison, M. A., Christian, D., Spada, N., & Duff, P. (2015). *Research on teaching and learning English grammar*. New York, NY: Routledge/Taylor & Francis.

Cowie, A. P. (1992). Multiword lexical units and communicative language teaching. In P. J. Arnaud, & H. Bejoint (Eds.), *Vocabulary and applied linguistics* (pp. 1–12). London: Macmillan.

Davies, M. (2008–). *The corpus of contemporary American English (COCA): 560 million words, 1990-present*. https://corpus.byu.edu/coca/.

Erman, B., & Warren, B. (2000). The idiom principle and the open choice principle. *Text, 20*, 29–62.

Flowerdew, J. (1996). Concordancing in language learning. In M. Pennington (Ed.), *The power of CALL* (pp. 97–113). Houston TX: Athelstan.

Flowerdew, L. (2001). The exploitation of small learner corpora in EAP materials design. In M. Ghadessy, A. Henry, & R. L. Roseberry (Eds.), *Small corpus studies and ELT: Theory and practice* (pp. 363–379). Amsterdam: John Benjamins.

Green, B. A. (2018, May 13). *OER Corpus for EAP*. https://sites.google.com/site/oercorpusforeap

Johns, T. (1988). Whence and whither classroom concordancing? In T. Bongaerts, P. de Hann, S. Lobbe, & H. Wekker (Eds.), *Computer applications in language learning* (pp. 9–27). Dordrecht: Forbis Publications.

Johns, T. (1991a). Should you be persuaded – two samples of data-driven learning materials. In T. Johns, & P. King (Eds.), *Classroom concordancing* (pp. 1–16). Birmingham: University of Birmingham.

Johns, T. (1991b). From printout to handout: Grammar and vocabulary teaching in the context of data-driven learning. In T. Johns, & P. King (Eds.), *Classroom concordancing* (pp. 27–45). Birmingham: University of Birmingham.

Larsen-Freeman, D. (2014). Teaching grammar. In M. Celce-Murcia, D. M. Brinton, & M. A. Snow (Eds.), *Teaching English as a second or foreign language* (4th ed. pp. 256–270). Boston, MA: Heinle/Cengage Learning.

Mauranen, A. (2004). *Spoken corpus for an ordinary learner.* In J. Sinclair (Ed.), *How to use corpora in language teaching* (pp. 89–105). Amsterdam and Philadelphia: John Benjamins.

Mukherjee, J. (2006). Corpus linguistics and language pedagogy: The state of the art – and beyond. *English Corpus Linguistics, 3,* 5–24.

Nation, I. S. P. (2008). *Teaching vocabulary: Strategies and techniques.* Boston, MA: Heinle Cengage Learning.

Nation, I. S. P. (2013). *Learning vocabulary in another language.* Cambridge: Cambridge University Press.

Nation, I. S. P., Shin, D., & Grant, L. (2016). Multiword units. In I. S. P. Nation (Ed.), *Making and using word lists for language learning and testing* (pp. 71–79). Amsterdam: John Benjamins.

Nattinger, J. R. and DeCarrico, J. S. (1992). *Lexical phrases and language teaching.* Oxford: Oxford University Press.

O'Keefe, A., & Farr, F. (2003). Using language corpora in initial teacher education: Pedagogic issues and practical applications. *TESOL Quarterly, 37*(3), 389–413.

O'Sullivan, I. (2007). Enhancing a process-oriented approach to literacy and language learning: The role of corpus consultation literacy. *ReCALL, 19,* 269–286.

OpenStax. (n.d.). Retrieved from https://openstax.org/

Romer, U. (2011). Corpus research applications in second language teaching. *Annual Review of Applied Linguistics, 31,* 205–225.

Simpson-Vlach, R., & Ellis, N. C. (2010). An academic formulas list: New methods in phraseology research. *Applied Linguistics, 31,* 487–512.

Sinclair, J. M. (1996). The search for units of meaning. *Textus, 9*(1), 75–106.

Sinclair, J. (2004) *Trust the text: Language, corpus and discourse.* London: Routledge.

Sripicharn, P. (2003). *Implementing collaborative concordancing between teacher and learners in the writing class.* Paper presented at the 5th CULI International Conference, Bangkok, Thailand.

Tribble, C. (2001). Small corpora and teaching writing. In M. Ghadessy, A. Henry, & R. L. Roseberry (Eds.), *Small corpus studies and ELT* (pp. 381–408). Amsterdam: John Benjamins.

Wray, A. (1999). Formulaic language in learners and native speakers. *Language Teaching, 32,* 213–231.

Wray, A. (2002). *Formulaic language and the lexicon.* Cambridge: Cambridge University Press.

Wray, A. (2008). *Formulaic language: Pushing the boundaries.* Oxford: Oxford University Press.

Wray, A. (2012). What do we (think we) know about formulaic language? An evaluation of the current state of play. *Annual Review of Applied Linguistics, 32,* 231–254.

Schmitt, N. (2004). *Formulaic sequences: Acquisition, processing, and use.* Amsterdam: John Benjamins.

When we share, everyone wins – Creative Commons. (n.d.). Retrieved from https://creativecommons.org/

Chapter 6

Functions of Formulaic Expressions at School

From the Coffee Shop to the Classroom

Cheryl Boyd Zimmerman

1. What is the meaning of each of the following *formulaic sequences* (in italics)?
   - *By and large.*
   - *In spite of this.*
   - *For the most part.*
2. Compare the following passages. What differences do the formulaic sequences make?
   - *By and large* university life is challenging. *In spite of this,* we persevere. *For the most part,* it opens doors.
   - University life is challenging. We persevere. It opens doors.

Formulaic sequences such as those above are difficult to define, but their presence changes a passage. *By and large* refers to the statement that follows, showing this is a general statement. *In spite of this* signals an exception, and *for the most part* indicates that the statement that follows doesn't apply to everyone. Known as *discourse organizers,* these formulaic sequences don't add new subject matter to the passage, but they make considerable differences in meaning: they show how one thought relates to another. Three- and four-word formulaic expressions are very frequent in English, making up 28 percent of words in conversation, and 20 percent in academic prose (Biber & Conrad, par 22). For that reason and others, they present a considerable challenge to English language learners.

Why do formulaic sequences occur? It has been suggested that whenever there is a frequently occurring language need (the need to apologize, compare ideas, introduce a new topic, show gratitude, complain), it is likely there will be a conventionalized expression to express it (Nattinger & DeCarrico, 1992, p. 62). We use formulaic sequences to maintain conversation (*How are you?*) organize our thoughts (*First and foremost*) and introduce requests (*I wonder if you'd mind*). Each formulaic sequence is used for a reason and associated with an identifiable function such as expressing a lack of certainty (*I don't know if*), or describing time (*a month ago*).

Formulaic sequences range from discourse markers (*by and large, in spite of this, for the most part*) to a wide variety of commonly occurring expressions with social (e.g., apologies) and academic functions (e.g., enumerating). They are so common in speaking and writing that proficient speakers expect them; when sequences do not conform to the norm of the speech community, they sound unnatural or inappropriate (e.g., *a lot of people* sounds natural; *★a sum of people* does not). There is growing agreement amongst language educators that an understanding of formulaic language is central to L2 learning and that students need to acquire them in large numbers (Nattinger & DeCarrico, 1992; Boers and Lindstromberg, 2008).

In this chapter we will explore formulaic sequences' *pragmatic functions,* or the practical purposes for which they are used. The focus will be on those sequences most likely to be encountered in a school setting in both speaking and writing, including conversation, classroom teaching/academic lectures, and academic prose and will be directed to intermediate and advanced English learners. There are many terms used to refer to these structures (e.g., *chunks, clusters, lexical phrases, lexical bundles); we will use the term *formulaic sequences* as used by Wray, 1992. When discussing specific researchers, their terminology will be explained and used.

I. Background

What Role Do Formulaic Sequences Play in Language Use?

Why is it that a non-formulaic utterance can sound unnatural to us when we are expecting a formulaic one? For example, why do we find the statement *I am really glad you could come* more natural than *I'm in a very glad state as a result of your coming* (Pawley & Syder, 1983, as cited in Wray & Perkins, 2000, p. 10). One explanation is that certain strings of words are stored in our mental lexicons and treated as single units. Thus, we store the sequence and treat it as one item, no longer analyzing its structure. This was first described by John Sinclair in the "Idiom Principle"; he proposed that language users draw not only upon individual words to express themselves, but also upon many " ... semi-preconstructed phrases that constitute single choices" (1991, p. 110). Strings of words are stored and accessed as units in long-term memory in the same way as individual words, instead of being "subject to generation or analysis by the language grammar" (Wray, 2000, p. 465). This results in an economy of effort and a short-cut in processing.

What Is Difficult About Learning Formulaic Sequences?

The challenges that these sequences pose for English learners begin with looking beyond the traditional single-word boundary and knowing when several words in a specific sequence represent one meaning. For example, in the sequence *by the way,* one might stop at the individual familiar words, and miss that this specific phrase has a specialized function, that of singling out an attribute or focusing attention (*By the way, did you notice the time?*). The challenge continues in identifying the meaning of the sequence or its discourse function. For example, *take a look at* can be used to introduce a topic, and *I think it was ...* expresses uncertainty. Many frequent formulaic sequences are misleading because learners easily know the individual words, making the structure deceptively transparent (*to come up with, by and large, be that as it may*). Other frequent sequences may be transparent in meaning, but used less frequently by English learners because of the challenge of memorizing them accurately (**up to down* rather than *top to bottom* or **according to me* rather than *in my opinion* and **all to all* rather than *all in all*).

English learners may be familiar with the concept of formulaic sequences operating as single units because such structures are frequent in most other languages (Nattinger & DeCarrico, 1992). Nonetheless, there can be confusion in L1 translation. For example, in English, the sequence *on the other hand* introduces a contrastive relationship, while in Chinese, the sequences *on the one hand* and *on the other hand (yi fang mian … ling yi fang mian* 一方面,另一方面) signal an addition rather than a contrast. That is, the second statement is an additional or parallel point to the first: "*On the one hand* the population keeps rising. *On the other hand* the factories use more water." The translated forms are the same but the usage is different (Lu, 2016, p. 99).

What Does It Mean to Know a Formulaic Sequence?

The learning of both words and formulaic sequences is incremental; to *know* a word or a sequence means to know a great deal about it: this includes how it operates grammatically, its meaning or functions, its pronunciation, formality or domain of use, collocations, and more. For example, for *On the other hand*:

How it operates grammatically :	It's a complete prepositional phrase, usually used before a sentence or clause.
Meaning or function:	*Used for explicit comparison and contrast.*
Pronunciation:	*Stress is often placed on other.*
Formality or domain:	*Used in academic prose, textbooks, and classroom teaching.*
Frequency:	On the other hand is more frequent in textbooks than in classroom teaching (Biber, Cortes, & Conrad, 2004).

Learning a word or formulaic expression does not happen all at once; it builds incrementally. To begin, one learns to recognize an item in reading or listening. This receptive knowledge includes spelling, pronunciation, recognizable word parts, grammatical patterns, and its meaning or function. When learners need to use an item in speaking or writing (productive knowledge), they will need further knowledge of these aspects and also will need to know its collocations (What other items often occur with this one?), frequency (How often is it used and where?) and more about its meanings or functions (What is included in the concept? Does the sequence have more than one meaning or function?). For a detailed chart explaining what is involved with knowing a formulaic sequence, see Nation and Webb, 2011, p. 190. To encourage learners to notice the incremental nature of lexical learning, introduce a self-assessment tool such as the one in Table 6.1.

Table 6.1 Self-Assessment Practice for Learners

1. Teacher explains that knowledge of a formulaic sequence includes knowing a lot about it. How does its grammar operate? How is it pronounced (including stress)? What other words often occur with it? Is it formal or informal? Where, when, and how frequently will we see it? Provide examples as needed.
2. Teacher selects five to seven formulaic sequences (FS), such as those listed here. Pronounce them but don't provide examples yet.
3. Students complete this chart for self-assessment at the beginning of the unit in which the FSs are introduced. Re-assess at the end of the unit and as needed to assess retention.

	I've never seen the FS	I've heard or seen the FS but am not sure what it means	I've heard or seen the FS and understand what it means	I've used the word confidently in either speaking or writing.
By and large				
Time after time				
In the meantime				

Adapted from Zimmerman, 2016

II. The Functions of Formulaic Sequences

As seen above, it's hard to define a formulaic sequence such as *in a nutshell*, but it is important to a sentence because of the discourse function of "summarizing" it signals. In 1992, Nattinger and DeCarrico brought attention to the importance of these sequences for English language teaching. Their work provided an unprecedented, thorough, and teaching-oriented analysis of the functions performed by these structures, which they referred to as *lexical phrases* (defined as "'chunks' of language of varying lengths ... Each is associated with a discourse function" 1992, p. 1). They demonstrated that lexical phrases are critical to language use and useful to language learners when organized by pragmatic categories rather than by key words, as had been done in the past. They identified lexical phrases intuitively, selecting those they considered most frequent and useful. The major divisions for their function–based typology are found in Table 6.2.

The lexical phrase approach raised educators' awareness just as it intended. The importance of lexical phrases to natural language use and the explanations

Table 6.2 Categories for Functional Categorization, Nattinger & DeCarrico, 1992

I. Social interactions:
    A. Conversational maintenance, including:
        a. Summoning (e.g. *how are you; I didn't catch your name*)
        b. Clarifying (e.g. *what did you mean by X?*)
        c. Shifting turns (e.g. *could I say something here?*)
    B. Conversational purpose, including:
        a. Questioning (e.g. *do you X?*)
        b. Refusing (e.g. *I'm sorry but*)
        c. Expressing sympathy (e.g. *I'm very sorry to hear about X*)

I. Necessary topics – frequently heard conversation needs, including:
    A. Autobiography (e.g. *my name is*)
    B. Language (e.g. *Do you speak ___?*)
    C. Time (e.g. *for a long time*)
    D. Shopping (e.g. *I want to buy X*)

II. Discourse devices, including
    A. Logical connectors (e.g. *as a result of*)
    B. Fluency devices (e.g. *you know*)
    C. Exemplifiers (e.g. *in other words*)
    D. Evaluators (e.g. *as far as I know; at least*)

Adapted from Nattinger & DeCarrico, 1992, pp. 61–65

of their discourse functions helped teachers explain English usage to L2 learners. Nevertheless, important questions were raised about the frequency and purposes of the phrases in natural discourse. That is, the lexical phrase approach did not quantify or describe the occurrences of the phrases, leaving many questions: Which lexical phrases were most frequent in conversation, academic lectures, and academic writing? Which functions were most useful to each of these registers? These questions are amongst those that have been subsequently addressed by corpus research methods, which study language through large samples of natural discourse as it is used in selected registers.

One example of this work was done by Biber, Conrad, and Cortes (2004). Referring to formulaic sequences as *lexical bundles* (defined as "the most frequent sequences of words in a register"), they examined four registers (conversation, classroom teaching, textbooks, and academic prose), using large corpora from each register (760,000–5,300,000 words). They wanted to know which lexical bundles were most frequent in each register and to identify their functions. This approach prioritizes frequency, fixedness, and sequences longer than two words in its identification of formulaic sequences, and provides a principled means to make comparisons between the targeted types of discourse. Based on corpus findings, Biber et al. identified four functional categories as noted in Table 6.3.

Table 6.3 Categories of Functional Classification

> • stance expressions: indicate certainty or probability (*I don't know*) and attitude
> (*it is important to*)
> • discourse organizers: introduce topic or focus (*in this chapter we*) and elaborate or
> clarify topic or focus (*as well as the*)
> • referential expressions: identify an entity or single out a particular attribute of
> an entity as especially important. Sub-catego ries here include identification/
> focus (e.g. *that's one of the*), specification of attributes (e.g., *in the case of*), quantity
> specification (e.g., _ *percent of the*) and time/place reference (e.g., *at the same time*)
> • special conversational functions: includes politeness (*thank you very much*), simple
> inquiry (*what are you doing?*) and reporting (*I said to him/her*)

Adapted from Biber, Conrad, and Cortes, 2004; Biber and Conrad, 2004 (pp. 384–388)

The corpus research by Biber et al. represents considerable progress in the understanding of formulaic sequences and how they operate. It defines "lexical bundles" explicitly:

> Lexical bundles are identified using a frequency-driven approach: They are simply the most frequently occurring sequences of words, such as *do you want to* and *I don't know what*. These examples illustrate two typical characteristics of lexical bundles: they are usually not idiomatic in meaning, and they are usually not complete grammatical structures.
>
> (Biber, 2006, p. 134)

It also adheres to this definition in its searching and counting of the bundles and uses large corpora that represent the fields that they claim to represent (Nation & Webb, 2011, p. 184). As a result, their findings inform teachers and materials developers of the natural occurrence of these target items in specific registers.

III. Formulaic Sequences in Writing

Formulaic sequences are frequent in both spoken and written language; just as the purposes of speaking and writing differ, so do the functions of the formulaic sequences. For example, the most frequent instance among the three- to four- word formulaic sequences in conversation expresses a personal opinion (*I don't know*) and the most frequent in academic prose are expressions which help organize the information (*in order to, one of the, part of the*; Biber and Conrad, 2004).

Formulaic Sequences and the Purposes of Writing

A main goal of academic writing is to pass along information with clarity and precision; these priorities are reflected in the nature of their most frequent formulaic sequences. In a study comparing their use in conversation and academic prose, again using the term *lexical bundles,* Biber and Conrad found that most of the common four-word bundles are referential; that is, they identify something or single out a particular attribute as especially important (see Table 6.3). The most common of these bundles specify quantities (*80 percent of the*) and attributes (*on the basis of, the extent to which*). In addition, the bundles in academic prose are less personal and more precise than those in conversation. In fact, there are few similarities between the common four-word bundles in conversation and academic prose. The only four-word bundles the two registers share are *the end of the* and *at the end of* (Biber & Conrad 2004, para. 30).

Academic prose has only three common four-word bundles that express stance (which indicates certainty, probability, and attitude), and none of them are personal. The most frequent one is *the fact that* and its focus is on certainty, reflecting an important feature of academic prose. This is in stark contrast to conversation, where the majority of bundles express stance, used for purposes related to personal communication. Both academic prose and conversation have a large number of discourse-organizing lexical bundles; the most frequent of these in academic prose is *on the other hand* (Biber & Conrad, paras. 33–35).

Formulaic sequences in speech and academic writing are very different structurally. For example, 15 percent of the lexical bundles in conversation are complete phrases or clauses, while less than 5 percent of the bundles in academic prose are complete structural units (Biber, et al. 1999). 60 percent of the bundles in academic prose are parts of noun phrases and/or prepositional phrases: the most frequent are *in order to, one of the, part of the* (Biber & Conrad, 2004, para. 22).

These differences in structure are important for learners of English who need exposure to both written and spoken registers in order to contact the range of formulaic sequences in natural English use. For example, an independent learner who is trying to learn formulaic sequences from reading academic prose will encounter mostly referential sequences which prioritize clarity and precision. They will have very little exposure to the formulaic sequences of stance which facilitate interaction and the communication of personal thoughts and attitudes. Input from both spoken and written registers is needed for complete natural exposure to formulaic sequences in English.

Formulaic Sequence Challenges Experienced by L2 Writers

Schenck & Choi (2014) found that American university students used formulaic sequences not only for straightforward functions such as sequencing and comparison, but also for pragmatic purposes that led to interesting and well-developed writing. This included putting examples into a larger perspective (*as part of, as a whole*), adding connotation (*in no way, just as importantly*), incorporating themes (*as a whole, draws together*) and indicating new viewpoints (*open our eyes to, one wonders how*). On the other hand, Korean EFL students tended not to consider pragmatic functions of the sequences; instead, they used formulaic sequences primarily for more mechanical functions such as explicitly stating sequences and maintaining unity (p. 149). The authors concluded that in EFL contexts, students need to pay particular attention to the meaningful and useful roles played by formulaic sequences in writing.

Hyland (2008) compared the use of formulaic sequences in research articles with Hong Kong students' master's theses and dissertations. He found that master's students used the most formulaic sequences in their writing while professional writers used the fewest. He also saw a considerable difference in the structures and functions used. He suggested that the differences don't necessarily signal lesser proficiency or confidence in the master's student writers, but signal that the writing tasks are different in nature. Though all three genres are persuasive, the nature of the master's thesis is different. As a result of its purpose, it emphasizes the writer's ability to describe their "research skills and practical disciplinary competence" (p. 61). Hyland concludes that teachers should focus on the types of texts that students need to write rather than assuming that all research is the same.

IV. Formulaic Sequences in Spoken Discourse

All spoken English at the university is not the same. In presentations or lectures the purpose is to convey factual or propositional information, falling under the category of *transactional discourse*. In conversations the purpose, known as *interactional discourse,* is primarily to establish and maintain social relationships. There are circumstances where the purposes of speakers overlap both categories, such as lectures aimed at both conveying information and establishing some kind of relationship with the audience. The various purposes of any given speaker dictate how they choose the formulaic sequences they need.

Formulaic Sequences in Classroom Teaching or Academic Lectures

Traditional lectures are examples of *transactional discourse* and they vary greatly in language formality and style. Nattinger and DeCarrico's description of how lectures are organized identified such functions as topic markers (formal: *Let us begin with X;* informal: *We'll be looking at*), summarizers (formal: *In summary/conclusion;* informal: *OK so* − level intonation) and evaluators (formal: *I would (like to) suggest that;* informal: *X is fine/OK by me*). They suggest that lecturers who read their notes or have memorized parts of the lecture tend to use formal, literal forms (e.g., *The main point is, that is, in fact*). More conversational lecturers seek a more relaxed atmosphere and more interaction (*OK, now; OK, so there you've got X; so what do you think? same way here;* 1992, pp. 136–140).

Biber, Conrad, and Cortes (2004) as already mentioned, based their analysis on actual counts of the occurrences of lexical bundles in different registers and found that classroom teaching relies on bundles from both academic prose and conversation. This suggests that classroom teaching prioritizes both the organizational functions of informational written discourse and the communicative functions of other spoken discourse. As a result of using bundles from both registers, classroom teaching relies on about "twice as many different lexical bundles as conversation and about four times as many as textbooks" (p. 382). They also note that both the grammatical structure and lexical bundles of classroom teaching had more in common with spoken registers than with informational ones. That is, classroom teaching is influenced more by its spoken constraints (real-time production, focus on personal and interpersonal purposes, etc.) than informational constraints (p. 399).

Formulaic sequences are critical to lecture comprehension. In spite of apparent fluency, even advanced learners have trouble navigating the content of classroom teaching because they don't follow how the material is organized; that is they don't recognize the signals distinguishing a main topic from an example, or summary from elaboration. Khuwaileh (1999) examined lecture comprehension by Arabic-speaking university students in Jordan. Two groups of students were compared, each of which heard a comparable lecture by a different lecturer. The students' comprehension of the two different lectures was compared. Better results were found among the students of the first lecturer, who used formulaic sequences (*Let me turn to …, now I would like to talk about …, that is to say*) with more frequency and more variety. The same lecturer used more interactive and comprehension questions during the lecture ("Why do we see cements of different colors ..." p. 255). The researcher concluded that the use of formulaic sequences and classroom interaction led to greater lecture comprehension by EFL students.

Formulaic Sequences in Conversation

Conversation is interactional discourse, used to establish and maintain social relationships. Examples of common functions used here are maintaining conversations (*How are you?, See you later*); expressing sympathy (*I'm (very) sorry to hear about* ___) and daily conversational topics such as time (*When is X?*) and location (*How far is X?* Nattinger & DeCarrico, 1992).

Other researchers had different ways of describing the functions of conversation. Wray and Perkins identify three central functions of formulaic sequences in social interaction: 1) manipulation of others (includes commands, requests, politeness markers, bargains, etc.; 2) asserting separate identity (includes story-telling, turn claimers, turn holders, etc.); and 3) asserting group identity (includes 'In' phrases, group chants – *We are the champions*, threats, forms of address) (2000, pp. 13–14).

A study of formulaic sequences in British English conversation found "a focus on interaction and conveying personal thoughts and attitudes, and the concern for politeness and not imposing on others" (Biber & Conrad, 2004, para. 31). A surprisingly high percentage of the sequences were stance expressions, that is, they framed the interpretation of the following proposition by describing the knowledge status of the information (*I don't know what, I don't think so*) or the attitude toward the information (*I don't want to, you don't have to*, para. 28). The sequences expressing stance are useful in interaction because, for example, they can decrease the amount of imposition of a statement (*I don't think so, anyway*), draw others into a conversation ("There was a program on this morning. *I don't know if you saw it.*"), and encourage interaction ("*So what do you think I should do* when I see Mary tomorrow?"). As we have seen in the registers of academic prose and classroom lectures, formulaic sequences accomplish the communicative functions that are important for each situation.

A communicative purpose of unique importance in spoken discourse is politeness, a system of *rules* that arise from social norms in a given community (Culpepper, 2010, p. 3239). Polite questions can be made with a formulaic use of modals (*could you pass the salt?, would you be willing to*). Other formulaic expressions of politeness are found in many categories: apologies (*I'm so sorry*), requests (*I wonder if you'd mind*), denials/refusals (*I'm not sure*), etc. One feature found with (im)politeness is that *breaking a rule* can be as meaningful as keeping one. For example, a British corpus study of conventional phrases marking politeness (*with all due respect, sir, with great/all' due respect, I don't mean to be rude/impolite*) demonstrated that these markers did not necessarily signal the expected polite form or *face-saving remark*. In fact, they were more often followed by an insult or other *face-threatening remark*. To illustrate this tendency, the authors cited two characters in a British sit-com:

Humphries: Minister, with the greatest possible respect –
Hacker: Oh, are you going to insult me again?
Humphries: Yes, Minister.

The functions of such phrases become conventionalized so much so that, in spite of their literal or historical meanings, one expects a negative comment to follow. The researchers conclude that one form can complete different functions, in spite of their literal meanings, and that this usage is often deliberate. They referred to this as "when 'politeness' is not being polite" (Partington, Duguid, & Taylor, 2013, p. 241).

Formulaic sequences in conversation are distinct in structure from those found in other registers. They contain more personal pronouns and more questions. In conversation 90 percent of sequences are declarative clauses or questions. The bundles used in conversation are less varied but more frequent than those either in classroom teaching or academic prose (Biber, Conrad, & Cortes, 2004, p. 382).

In conversation 28 percent of the words used are parts of three- and four-word formulaic sequences, leading some to suggest conversation as the best medium for teaching formulaic sequences. However, Biber and Conrad found that lexical bundles perform very different functions and have different structures in different registers (2004). As for the differences between academic prose and conversation, the only shared functions are elaboration/clarification and one example of time reference (*at the end of* and *the end of the;* Biber & Conrad, 2004). In order to have authentic exposure to the natural use of formulaic sequences in English, learners clearly need exposure to how they are used in both written and spoken input.

V. Considerations for Teaching Formulaic Sequences

To begin, teachers can encourage the use of formulaic sequences by simply "sanctioning their holistic use" (Wray, 2002, p. 191). That is, rather than encouraging listening or composing word by word, encourage a focus on sequences of words; remind learners to look beyond individual word boundaries and notice that, just like words, sequences function as important building blocks of texts.

Raising Awareness

Learners often don't recognize their comprehension problems with the formulaic sequences in academic materials. For example, while listening to a lecture, they might understand the content words and think they are following the important points. What they might be missing, without knowing it, is "a sense of the flow and direction of the lecture, and a sense of what counted as important information and what did not" (Nattinger & DeCarrico, 1992, p. 132). Teachers need to help students *notice* formulaic sequences and be aware of the functions they perform. Keep this in mind when selecting target items: the factors found to influence noticing are salience of the word in the input, previous contact with the word, and realization that the word "fills a gap in the learner's knowledge" (Nation, 2013, p. 103).

In addition, teachers can help learners notice formulaic sequences through strategy training. For example, Nguyen first encouraged noticing by explaining the meanings of the sequences in the input and describing common mistakes made by learners. Learners also benefited from overt strategy instruction designed to help them notice the sequences, such as highlighting and categorizing target structures (2014, p. 129). Examples of other learning strategies designed to optimize noticing of formulaic sequences include various enhancement methods such as using boldface and glossing (Nation, 2013).

Teaching Methods

Alali and Schmitt (2012) investigated whether the same teaching methods were effective for learning single words as well as formulaic sequences. They found that direct instruction, translation, and review were effective for both, but that they led to greater gains and more recall with single words. First, they concluded that, as with all vocabulary learning, repetition was important regardless of the specific method used. Many of the successful interventions include repetition as a secondary effect (e.g. direct instruction, strategy instruction, review, word cards, etc.). In addition, they found that review (especially written review) was beneficial. As suggested by Nguyen (2014) the learning of all vocabulary is incremental: learners need numerous encounters for acquisition; it's a teacher's job to "create opportunities for repeated exposure" (p. 130).

Different methodologies provide different advantages to formulaic sequence learning. For example, Nguyen (2014) found that direct instruction of new formulaic sequence meanings led to the retention of meaning, while strategy training led to gains in noticing formulaic sequences in input. Jones and Haywood (2004) stressed the importance of learners studying not only the meaning of a formulaic sequence but also its form and suggested that activities required time spent focusing on the form of the sequence in order to encourage deep processing. Their suggested activities included classifying sequences into meaning-based groups or structural groups (p. 277).

Negotiation between learners or learners and teachers has repeatedly been shown effective with formulaic sequences (Ellis, Tanaka, & Yamazaki, 1994; Newton, 2014, as cited in Nation, 2013). The negotiations covered target vocabulary items after they had been presented in input; care was taken not to negotiate other items but to focus on a few target words at a time. These studies and others found that negotiation benefited not only the participants in the task, but the observers as well; this suggests that "it is not the negotiation itself which is important but the learning conditions of noticing and gaining information that negotiation sets up" (Nation, 2013, p. 104).

Boers and Lindstromberg (2009) suggest drawing learners' attention to various types of patterns, and encouraging learners' conscious attention to them. Examples of patterns that might be included are: word repetition (*so and so, such and such*); alliteration (*through thick and thin*); assonance (*high and dry*); and consonance (*further afield, wide awake,* pp. 106–107). The same authors have found that dual coding also helps learning (i.e., associating verbal and non-verbal stimuli, such as the meaning of a word with a visual image; Boers & Lindstromberg, 2009, p. 79).

Because of their structure as "unanalyzed wholes," rote learning or memorizing is often relied upon for learning formulaic sequences (FS), just as it is for single words. Nation recommends the use of word cards, following these guidelines:

- Write each FS on a small card with its L1 translation on the opposite side.
- Repeat each FS aloud while memorizing it.
- Don't learn FSs with similar words or meanings together. They will interfere with each other.
- Change the order of the cards to avoid serial learning.

(Nation, 2013, pp. 500–501)

The Role of Meaning in Learning Formulaic Sequences

Most of the studies that refer to meaning and the learning of formulaic sequences are studies of idioms (*out of the blue*). Techniques that have led to gains related to strengthening the form-meaning connection include guessing the historical roots of an idiom (Where does *know the ropes come from?*), making learners aware of literal meanings and letting them make the connection to the figurative meaning (*going for the jugular*, Boers & Lindstromberg, 2009, pp. 87–89). Likewise, in a study of 40 Mandarin-speaking graduate students, where the target words were idioms (*mull over* and *on the books*), it was found that when learners were engaged in understanding the meaning of new idioms in context, productive knowledge increased and retention improved (Nguyen, 2014).

VI. Conclusion

A major consideration for the effective language teacher is to represent the target language accurately in terms of natural use in a variety of registers. Language teachers should strive to observe and better understand the realities of the language we teach; this is done by paying attention both to intuitive language use and to language research. Given the high frequency of formulaic sequences and the variation in how they are used in different domains, they deserve our careful attention.

VII. Teaching Activities

I. **Background**

1. With a partner, list ten formulaic sequences that you think are most frequently used in 1) both speaking and writing, 2) conversation, and 3) academic writing. Compare your lists with the Academic Formulas List (AFL): www.eapfoundation.com/vocab/academic/afl/). Discuss any findings that surprised you.

2. Collocations and formulaic sequences occur in all languages but the translations can cause confusion and lead to errors. Work with a group of speakers of several languages. How would you translate the following?

put on your coat	turn off the light	back up the car
take off your coat	in other words	from the point of view of
back and forth	in a nutshell	once and for all

II. The Functions of Formulaic Sequences

3. Compare Nattinger and DeCarrico's definition of *lexical phrases* with Biber's definition of *lexical bundles* (See Section II above). Realizing that they are referring to the same formulaic sequences, how do you explain the differences? What are the ramifications of the differences for research? For classroom use?

4. Use corpora to find lexical patterning:
   a. Imagine that a student has asked you to explain the difference in use between *think of* and *think about*. Use your experience and intuition to come up with an answer. When do we say *think of*? When do we say *think about*?
   b. Locate an online concordance (www.lextutor.ca – see *Concordance* or *www.corpus2.byu.edu* or see Appendices 6.2A & 6.2B)
   c. Look up the two forms (*think of* and *think about*) and compare the differences.

III. Formulaic Sequences in Writing

5. Practice with classroom writing:
   a. Find a sample paragraph from classroom materials, a news article, high interest website, etc. Review some of the functions found in the register of your sample (See Section III).
   b. Working as a class, highlight the formulaic sequences.
   c. Pairs work together to identify the functions. Discuss such issues as clarity, the number of formulaic sequences, and the readability of the paragraph.

6. Hyland (2008) compared the use of formulaic sequences in the writing of master's students, PhD dissertation writers, and professional writers in the same field. He found that master's students used the most formulaic sequences in their writing and that professional writers used the fewest (see Section III). How would you explain this finding?

IV. Formulaic Sequences in Spoken Discourse

7. Practice with writing and conversation:

> Following are frequency lists of the ten most frequent four-word formulaic sequences from four registers of the British National Corpus Baby edition (Hyland, 2008, Table 1).

   a. With a partner, identify the functions of the sequences. That is, what does each one signal? See Tables 6.2 and 6.3 as needed.

   b. How do you explain the items for each register, referring to the purposes of each register and the functions needed in each. How do you explain the differences and similarities?

Academic	Fiction	News	Conversation
1. on the one hand	1. the end of the	1. the end of the	1. I don't know what
2. in terms of the	2. at the end of	2. at the end of	2. no no no no
3. in the case of	3. the rest of the	3. for the first time	3. do you want to
4. the end of the	4. for the first time	4. percent of the	4. I thought it was
5. on the basis of	5. at the same time	5. the rest of the	5. what do you want
6. as a result of	6. in the middle of	6. as a result of	6. da da da da
7. the way in which	7. the edge of the	7. one of the most	7. thank you very much
8. it is possible to	8. the top of the	8. is one of the	8. I don't know whether
9. at the end of	9. I don't want to	9. at the same time	9. have a look at
10. percent of the	10. he was going to	10. in the second half	10. are you going to

Adapted from Hyland, 2008, Table 1

V. Considerations for Teaching

8. Research suggests that the formulaic sequences used in college teaching are more like spoken language than academic writing. Is this true in your experience? What are some formulaic sequences that you have heard that support your view? Based on your experience as a student in classroom lectures, what are some sequences you would select to teach your students?

9. Following is a list of practice types recommended for the learning of formulaic sequences. According to your experience as a learner,

select the three you consider most valuable. Which do you consider least valuable? Which seem most effective for beginning students? Advanced? Discuss your answers with a partner.

- Direct instruction
- Translation
- Written review
- Repetition (repeated exposure)
- Strategy instruction
- Review
- Word cards
- Emphasizing the study of form
- Classifying formulaic sequences into meaning-based groups or structural groups
- Negotiation of meaning and form between learners or learners and teachers
- Observation of other students negotiating meaning and form

Appendix 6.1 Academic Formulas List (AFL)

www.eapfoundation.com/vocab/academic/afl/

Top-ten Academic Formulaic sequences – written and spoken	Top-ten Academic Formulaic sequences – Spoken	Top-ten Academic Formulaic sequences – Written
1. in terms of	1. be able to	1. on the other hand
2. at the same time	2. blah blah blah	2. due to the fact that
3. from the point of view	3. this is the	3. on the other hand the
4. in order to	4. you know what I mean	4. it should be noted
5. as well as	5. you can see	5. it is not possible to
6. part of the	6. trying to figure it out	6. a wide range of
7. the fact that	7. a little bit about	7. there are a number of
8. in other words	8. does that make sense	8. in such a way that
9. the point of view of	9. you know what	9. take into account the
10. there is a	10. the University of Michigan	10. as can be seen

Adapted from Simpson-Vlach & Ellis, 2010

Appendix 6.2A

think of
stank. Then, as he was trying to **think of** something to say to her (all yes, wedding presents. We must **think of** something. You probably don't racking my brains for three hours to **think of** something, I simply cannot last a second catastrophe. I tried to **think of** something to say myself, but my offered frills. Nicandra tried to **think of** something pleasing to say: only you were here, then we could **think of** something to do. "Christopher groaning quietly, perhaps trying to **think of** something that summed up what let said nothing. He had tried to **think of** something to say, but the only lunch? "Ah me, the young! You **think of** nothing but your stomachs. Sympathy and collusion. But I can **think of** nothing to say. Perdie says, she tried to speak, but she could **think of** nothing, and her mother, shifting anything so familiar, and he could **think of** nothing on earth to say. It man in the world.'"As he could **think of** nothing else, Martin repeated But try as she might, she could **think of** nothing to say like that, fierce listening. Can we ourselves **think of** nothing that needs to be done

Illustration courtesy of Norbert Schmitt (personal communication)

Appendix 6.2B

think about
You wouldn't just **think about** it it's just gone isn't it Well that's a good way, if you **think about** it he's got, he's got four more, I mean they can wear, if you **think about** it they were suits in the When you **think about** it, yeah he was So what ' it seems easier that way when you **think about** it dunnit? Mm it's a lot be oes that come from? Oh when you **think about** it Pledge, why do they call wasn't the money really when you **think about** it because at end of day, week! And why, they don't need to **think about** it, they can talk you out of penetrating as lasers. 'We might **think about** that,' I say at last. I'll have to start and **think about** that train, Dwight. see it. That's the way I like to **think about** that sort of place. It's another way, but I don't want to **think about** that for a while. 'Timothy get eight to twenty – five. Now **think about** that. The district attorney

Illustration courtesy of Norbert Schmitt (personal communication)

References

Alali, F. A., & Schmitt, N. (2012). Teaching formulaic sequences: The same as or different from teaching single words? *TESOL Journal, 3*, 153–180. doi:10.1002/tesj.13

Biber, D. (2006). *University language: A corpus-based study of spoken and written registers.* Amsterdam: John Benjamins. Retrieved from http://ebookcentral.proquest.com/lib/fullerton/detail.action?docID=623257.

Biber, D. (2009). A corpus-driven approach to formulaic language in English: Multi-word patterns in speech and writing. *International Journal of Corpus Linguistics, 14* (3), 275–311.

Biber, D., & Conrad, S. (1999). Lexical bundles in conversation and academic prose. In H. Hasselard, & S. Oksefjell (Eds.), *Out of corpora: Studies in honor of Stig Johansson* (pp. 181–189). Amsterdam: Rodopi.

Biber, D., & Conrad, S. (2004). The frequency and use of lexical bundles in conversation and academic prose. *Lexicographica, 20.*

Biber, D., Conrad, S., & Cortes, V. (2004). If you look at …: Lexical bundles in university teaching and textbooks. *Applied Linguistics, 25*, 371–405.

Boers, F., & Lindstromberg, S. (2008). How cognitive linguistics can further vocabulary teaching. In F. Boers, & S. Lindstromberg (Eds.), *Cognitive linguistic approaches to teaching vocabulary and phraseology* (pp. 1–61). Berlin: Mouton.

Boers, F., & Lindstromberg, S. (2009). *Optimizing a lexical approach to instructed second language acquisition.* London: Palgrave Macmillan.

Culpeper, J. (2010). Impoliteness: Using language to cause offence. *Journal of Pragmatics, 42*, 3232–3245. Retrieved from https://ebookcentral.proquest.com

Hatami, S. (2014). Teaching formulaic sequences in the ESL classroom. *TESOL Journal, 6*(1), 112–129.

Hyland, K. (2008). As can be seen: Lexical bundles and disciplinary variation. *English for Specific Purposes, 27*, 4–21.

Jones, M., & Haywood, S. (2004). Facilitating the acquisition of formulaic sequences: An exploratory study in an EAP context. In N. Schmitt (Ed.), *Formulaic sequences: Acquisition, processing and use* (pp. 269–292). Amsterdam: John Benjamins. Retrieved from https://ebookcentral.proquest.com/lib/fullerton/detail.action?docID=622575

Khuwaileh, A. A. (1999). The role of chunks, phrases and body language in understanding coordinated academic lectures. *System, 27*, 249–260.

Lu, Y. (2016). *A corpus study of collocation in Chinese learner English.* New York, NY: Routledge.

Nation, I. S. P. (2013). *Learning vocabulary in another language.* Cambridge: Cambridge University Press.

Nation, I. S. P., & Webb S. (2011). *Researching and analyzing vocabulary.* Boston, MA: Heinle Cengage Learning.

Nattinger, J., & DeCarrico, J. (1992). *Lexical phrases and language teaching.* Oxford: Oxford University Press.

Nguyen, H. (2014). *The acquisition of formulaic sequences in high-intermediate ESL learners* (Doctoral dissertation). Publicly Accessible Penn Dissertations, 1385. Retrieved from http://repository.upenn.edu/edissertations/1385

Partington, A., Duguid, A., & Taylor, C. (2013). Interactive spoken discourse 2: CADS and (im)politeness. In A. Partington (Ed.), *Patterns and meanings in discourse: Theory and practice in corpus-assisted discourse studies (CADS)* (pp. 239–262). Retrieved from http://ebookcentral.proquest.com

Schenck, A. D., & Choi, W. (2014). Improving EFL writing through study of semantic concepts in formulaic language. *English Language Teaching,* 8(1), 142–154.

Simpson-Vlach, R., & Ellis, N. C. (2010). An academic formulas list: New methods in phraseology research. *Applied Linguistics,* 31, 487–512. Doi:10.1093/applin/amp058.

Sinclair, J. (1991). *Corpus, concordance, collocation.* Oxford: Oxford University Press.

Wray, A. (1992). *The focusing hypothesis: The theory of left hemisphere lateralised language re-examined.* Amsterdam: John Benjamins.

Wray, A. (2000) Formulaic sequences in second language teaching: principle and practice. *Applied Linguistics,* 21(4), 463–489. Retrieved from https://doi-org.lib-proxy.fullerton.edu/10.1093/applin/21.4.463

Wray, A. (2002). *Formulaic language and the lexicon.* Cambridge: Cambridge University Press.

Wray, A., & Perkins, M. R. (2000). The functions of formulaic language: An integrated model. *Language & Communication,* 20(1), 1–28. Retrieved from https://search-proquest-com.lib-proxy.fullerton.edu/docview/219609271?accountid=9840

Zimmerman, C. B. (Series director) (2016). *Inside listening and speaking: Levels Introduction–4.* New York, NY: Oxford University Press.

Chapter 7

Teaching Lexical Bundles

Which Ones and How?

Randi Reppen

1. Introduction

Like other chapters in this volume, this chapter also focuses on re-occurring multiword units (MWU) of language, but this chapter focuses on a particular type of MWU. The focus of this chapter is on lexical bundles (Biber et al., 1999 pp. 987–1036) and their use in spoken and written language, particularly conversation, classroom interactions, and academic writing. MWU can be identified through two approaches: top-down or bottom-up. Lexical bundles are identified through a bottom-up approach that uses computer programs to identify recurring sequences of three or more words at a certain frequency threshold. Another criterion for inclusion as a lexical bundle is that these sequences occur in more than one text (to avoid idiosyncratic use) and that the sequences do not cross punctuation or turn boundaries.

Both bottom-up and top-down approaches use computer programs to search texts, however, in a top-down approach the researcher enters in combinations of words, or particular expressions that they anticipate finding. For example, in a top-down approach, researchers might enter a sequence of words that they expect to occur, such as, *as big as*. Or, they might use a search expression with a wild card (⋆) as in the search expression: '*as ⋆ as*'. A search with the expression containing a wild card would find '*as big as*', '*as quickly as*', '*as funny as*', if those expressions occurred in the texts. This type of top–down search will likely find some of the same bundles that are found in a bottom–up approach. However, in a top–down search 'non–intuitive' bundles will not be found. It is exactly these bundles that are uncovered by a bottom–up approach where the computer carries out the task of mechanically matching recurring word sequences of a specified length, and counting those sequences for each text to get a total in a collection of texts (i.e., a corpus). It is exactly these 'non–intuitive' bundles, discovered in a bottom–up approach, that help us to better understand some of the characteristics of language, and that uncover some of the surprising differences between the lexical bundles that are typical of spoken and written language.

This chapter uses results from previous lexical bundle research that employed a bottom–up approach to identify four–word lexical bundles that are characteristic of conversation and of academic language (both spoken and written). I did not have to carry out any research; I simply used results from existing research to inform and create the teaching activities presented in this chapter. The lexical bundles described in this chapter come from two sources: *The Longman Grammar of Spoken and Written Language* (Biber et al., 1999) and *University Language: A corpus-based study of spoken and written registers* (Biber, 2006). In this chapter I selected bundles from these resources to demonstrate how we can use existing resources to create activities that reflect frequent features of actual language use that will help our students to become more effective and efficient users of English.

The spoken lexical bundles include both face-to-face conversation (Biber et al., 1999) and classroom language (Biber, 2006). The written lexical bundles include academic language from textbooks and university course materials (e.g., syllabi, reading packets) found in Biber (2006, pp. 133–175), and also published academic articles and books (Biber et. al., 1999, pp. 987–1036). After describing some of the major differences between lexical bundles found in spoken and written language, this chapter presents some typical bundles that are found frequently in conversation and classroom interaction followed by some example teaching activities using those bundles. That section is followed by a section that then focuses on bundles found in academic writing, which also includes example teaching activities with those bundles.

The example activities are not meant to be a complete list, but rather to show a range of activities that can come from the bundles that are presented. Most of the activities presented involve exploring how these bundles are used or how they function to create meaning. Additional activities that have a more granular focus such as vocabulary or grammar activities are equally valuable and can easily be done with the bundles that are presented, but since those types of activities are more typical I chose to include activities that for the most part emphasize use. Of course, how the example activities are actually realized will vary depending on different teaching contexts, different skills-based or content-based courses, and different levels of proficiency.

2. The Spoken/Written Difference?

It seems obvious to say that speaking and writing are different. But some-times things are not that simple. Language is used to communicate and therefore it encompasses many different functions. Communication is complex. Language is strongly shaped by the purpose and the context of the communication event (i.e., the who, what, and when). Take a minute to think about all the different ways you have used language today. Maybe you chatted at breakfast with your family, sent a text to a friend, read a bit of news, chatted with some colleagues when you arrived at work, read an article for class, prepared your lecture notes, asked your supervisor about your upcoming performance review, re-read your notes for today's class, taught class, and then called home to make sure the kids were home and doing their homework. In just that brief and over-simplified snap-shot, spoken and written language was used in both formal and informal contexts and across a wide range of different relationships. So the difference between speech and writing may not be clear cut. Written language can have many characteristics of what we typically think of as spoken language, and prepared lectures can have many characteristics that we typically asso-ciate with written language. Often when we teach, we do not highlight these complex aspects of language that are so shaped by factors such as the mode of communication (spoken or written), the production circumstances (e.g., spontaneous or planned), or the participants (e.g., close family/friend or distant colleagues or strangers). With all these considerations it is not sur-prising that it takes years to become a fluent user of another language! But lexical bundles can provide a valuable resource for us as teachers and for our students as language learners.

In spite of the complexities of language distinctions between spoken and written language mentioned above, lexical bundles offer a nice source of language building blocks with characteristics that are fairly distinct between speech and writing. One of the primary differences between spoken and written bundles is the clausal nature and reliance on verbs found in spoken bundles; in contrast, written bundles are more phrasal and rely mostly on nouns. This trend will become even more apparent in the sections that follow, as we closely look at bundles that are typical of spoken and written language. The bundles from spoken and written language presented below are not the only bundles that can or do occur, rather these are bundles that are highly frequent and therefore ones that our students will definitely encounter in spoken and written language.

3. Some Typical Lexical Bundles in Spoken Language

This section presents some of the bundles that are typical of spoken language in two different contexts: those found in conversation; and those found in university classroom interactions. At first thought conversation and class-room language might seem like two ends of a continuum, however, research has shown that there are many similar linguistic characteristics between these two seemingly different speech events. This similarity is also seen in the lexical bundles found across these two contexts of language use. The bundles used are similar, but the content is different. In most conversations, the focus is interpersonal, while in a classroom context the focus is infor-mational. For example in a conversation the Yes/No starter bundle 'Have you got any ...' is usually followed by a concrete item such as: '*Have you got any tomatoes?*' or by an idea or future activity such as: '*Have you got any plans for dinner?*' or '*Have you got any vacation plans?*'. In a classroom context, this bundle is most typically completed with '*Have you got any questions?*'.

Below is a list of Wh- and Yes/No question bundles that are common in both informal conversation and also in classroom interactions. These question starters or stems provide students with a useable chunk of language to start a question. These stems also provide learners with support when listening to questions, allowing them to be able to have a chunk of language that can be anticipated, and thus focus on what follows the stem or question starter. These question starter lists are followed by example activities that focus application activities with these bundles in conversation. After these example activities, bundles that are typical in classroom interactions are presented along with example activities.

<u>Wh- question starter bundles</u>

What are you doing …
What did you say …
What do you call …
Where are you going …
Where did you get …
How do you spell …
How do you know …

<u>Yes/No question starter bundles</u>

Do you know what …
Do you want to …
Do you want some …
Do you want the …
Did I tell you …
Would you like to …
Do you have to …
Can I have a …
Have you got any ….

3.1 Example Activities with Spoken Bundles

After introducing the bundles to students and providing examples of ways to use the bundle starter stems to generate questions, have students brainstorm a few questions using the bundle stems. I recommend introducing one type of question starter bundle, then other, and then compare and contrast the types of information that the Wh- and Yes/No question bundles elicit.

Activity 1: Using Bundles as Question Starters

<u>Time</u>: 10–20 minutes
<u>Materials to prepare ahead of time</u>: A list of the Wh- question starter bundles. This list can be on the board or a list can be provided for each student.

1. Ask students to generate questions using the starter question bundles. Write the student-generated questions on the board.
2. Have students individually, or in pairs, group questions by the type of question.

    Note: This could get messy. Some students might group questions topically instead of by question type.
3. Point out the patterns in the student-generated questions and discuss the types of information these questions elicit (e.g., people responses to '*who* questions'; place responses to '*where questions*'; explanation or information responses to '*how* questions', etc.). This is an awareness-raising activity that should help students respond more quickly to the different types of questions. This can be the end of the activity, or the student questions can be collected and used in future activities, even as a grammar or spelling correction task – depending on the student level.

Activity 2: Question Mingle

Time: 15–30 minutes depending on the number of students in the class.
Materials to prepare ahead of time: Print out either Wh- question or Yes/No question starter bundles on individual pieces of paper or cards. Another option is to have the students create the cards by writing the bundles.

1. As students enter the classroom, give them one or two cards with question starter bundles.
2. Give students three to five minutes to look at the questions on their bundle cards and to use the starter/stem to write complete questions using the bundle on their card(s).
3. Ask students to mingle around the classroom asking and getting responses to questions using their bundles. Depending on the number of students in the class, this might take 10–20 minutes. Ask students to remember the responses, or to take notes, depending on their level.
4. Bring the class together and discuss the questions and responses.

    Note: This can be a nice mingling activity that can be used in a listening and/or speaking class or as a review activity.

Activity 3: Listening for Bundles

<u>Time</u>: Variable

<u>Materials to prepare ahead of time</u>: Select a conversation to be played in class (make sure it has some of the target bundles!) and have copies of the script of the conversation. Give students a list of bundles (not just the ones that are in the conversation!).

1. Students listen to a conversation twice. The first time students just listen to the conversation. The second time students check bundles off the list as they hear the bundles. Or if the students are more advanced they can write down the bundles they hear.
2. Have students compare their responses with other students. Then pass out the script so students can check their work.

<u>Variation</u>: Teams of students could create and roleplay a conversation for classmates to listen to and identify bundles that were used.

3.2. Some Typical Lexical Bundles in Classroom Language

Classroom lectures and interactions share many of the same question bundles as conversation. In both conversations and classroom interactions questions play an important role. In both situations people are interacting to learn about a person or a topic, so it is not surprising that in both contexts there will be a fairly frequent use of question bundles. In addition to the question bundles that were presented in the conversation section, there are also bundles that are typically found in classroom language, but that are not as common in conversation. Some bundles that are typical of classroom discourse are presented below.

<u>Classroom bundles</u>

it's going to be
and then we can
try to do it
what do you think
if you look at
I wanted to ask
going to talk about
how many of you

if you have questions
or something like that
and stuff like that

Looking at these bundles we can easily see how they are used in classroom settings. Some of the bundles are used to guide student actions or to help them anticipate what will be covered in class, such as *if you look at* or *going to talk about*, while others are vague language used by both instructors and students to extend examples or in response to questions (e.g., *or something like that, and stuff like that*). Some bundles are used to engage students. Instructors often use the bundle *how many of you ....* as a way to include students and relate to their experiences, as in '*How many of you* have ever seen/tasted/done/traveled to …?'. If students are aware of these frequent bundles, then they may be better able to follow lectures and have more opportunities to participate in the fast-paced lectures that often frustrate even fluent second language learners.

3.3 Example Activities with Classroom Bundles

There are many activities that can be done with these bundles: below are a few examples to get you started. Several of these activities provide nice springboards for discussions about language use!

Activity 1: Who Said It?

Time: 15–20 minutes
Materials to prepare ahead of time: Print the list of bundles or write them on the board.

1. Have students make three columns on their papers and label the top row (i.e., Teacher/Instructor; Student; Either). Have students work individually to put bundles into categories by who they think usually says the bundle. That is: Is the bundle usually said by the instructor, student, or either?
2. Next have students work in pairs to compare their responses and come to an agreement about which category to place each bundle in.
3. On the board, the teacher creates three columns for responses: Instructor; Students; Either. Have one student from each pair come to the board and put the bundles into categories.
4. As a class discuss the groups of bundles in the different categories.

Activity 2: Combining Bundles

Time: 10–20 minutes
Materials to prepare ahead of time: Print the list of bundles or write them on the board.

1. Have students work individually or in pairs to combine classroom bundles into longer meaningful units, for example combine 'and then we can' + 'try to do it' to get 'and then we can try to do it'.
2. Give students a certain amount of time (five to ten minutes) to create combined bundles. See how many combined bundles each student/pair has created.
3. Have students share the bundles they created. Check that the bundles are meaningful. This could be done as a class vote or thumbs up/down. Save the meaningful bundles to use in the next activity.

Variation: This could be a timed activity with a competition to see which teams can generate the most meaningful bundles in a given amount of time.

Activity 3: Combining Bundles Follow Up: Grouping Bundles by Functions

Time: 15–30 minutes
Materials to prepare ahead of time: Bundles from Activity 2.
Have students work in pairs to group the bundles by functions (e.g., guiding, eliciting information, etc.). Students can develop or add their own functions. Then share with other pairs. Then share as a class. This can provide a great springboard for class discussion.

Activity 4: Find the Bundles

Time: 15–30 minutes
Materials to prepare ahead of time: Select classroom lecture to be played in class. Make sure the lecture contains the target bundles. Have a list of classroom bundles for each student.

1. Students listen to the lecture twice. The first time students just listen to the lecture. The second time students check bundles off the list as they

hear the bundles. Or, if the students are more advanced they can write down the bundles they hear.

2. Have students compare their responses with other students. Then pass out the script so students can check their work.

<u>Variation</u>: For high intermediate to advanced students.

1. Have students, in pairs, attend a lecture of an introductory course (preferably in a course related to their future major) to listen for the classroom bundles. Make sure each student has a list of bundles so that they can mark each time they hear a target bundle.

   Note: Make sure to arrange ahead of time with the instructors whose courses the students will be attending. Also, do not send more than one pair of students to a class.

2. When the class is finished have the pair meet to compare the list of bundles that each of them heard including how many of each. The pair discusses any differences.

3. In the following class period (back in their regular class – not the class they visited) each pair reports on the bundles that they heard. Discuss the different findings and how they might vary due to the class topic and lecturer's style.

4. Some Typical Bundles in Academic Writing

As we move from spoken to written bundles, a quick look at the bundles below immediately highlights some of the differences in the bundles of language used in speech and writing. As mentioned at the beginning of this chapter, spoken bundles tend to be clausal and with many verbs. They can easily be used as utterance launchers or stems for producing language, much like those expressions found in popular travel phrasebooks. In contrast, written bundles are much more phrasal, typically do not contain verbs, and are not as easily used as utterance launchers, but function more as signposts in a text that help to orient readers or organize the information in a text. Written bundles also frequently include prepositions, which can be particularly challenging for our students. The bundles presented below are examples that are frequently found in textbooks, academic articles, and also in successful student writing. Becoming familiar with these bundles will not only help students become better writers; it will also help them to become more efficient and effective readers.

Most of the bundles presented below serve as signposts that writers use to guide readers. Some of the signals marked by lexical bundles include: how the text or information is organized (e.g., *at the beginning of, at the end of*); expressing relationships among the information being presented (e.g., *as a result of, in addition to, on the basis of*); showing contrast (e.g., *on the other hand*) or highlighting information or processes (e.g., *it is important to*). As fluent readers and writers, we process and produce these chunks of language effortlessly based on our many years of print input. Our students, however, have not had the advantage of many years of print input in English. We can use these bundles to help students to become more effective and efficient readers and writers by presenting and providing opportunities for meaningful practice with lexical bundles that are typical in academic writing/readings.

Academic writing bundles
as a result of
in the case of
in addition to
a great deal of
a wide range of
the nature of the
in the context of
on the other hand
on the basis of
for the purpose of
as part of the
it is important to
at the beginning of
at the end of
at the bottom of

4.1 Example Activity Ideas for Academic Writing Bundles

As mentioned above, our students often face challenges with accurate use of prepositions. In many of the activities provided below additional emphasis can be placed on the prepositions in the bundles.

Activity 1: Putting Bundles Together

Time: 10–20 minutes
Materials to prepare ahead of time: This is a jigsaw activity that highlights the role of preposition choices. Make a card, or slip of paper, that has

each word that is represented in the bundles listed above. Use a subset of the bundles in different class periods, if doing all the bundles at once is too much.

Note: This task can be made easier if words from the bundles are combined instead of given as individual words (e.g., *at the, of the, a wide*).

1. Students work individually, or in pairs. Each student/pair receives an envelope with slips of paper that have the words from the bundles (or groups of words for an easier version of the task).
2. Students work to build four-word bundles using the slips of paper. Depending on the level, students could have seen the list of bundles ahead of time. Do not have the list available while the students are working – or the activity is not as meaningful and simply becomes a copying/matching activity.
3. Once students have finished assembling their bundles, they will compare their bundles with other students.
4. Then compare the student-created bundles to the academic writing bundle list in this section. Be sure to accept bundles that are correctly formed, but that do not appear on the list. These can be added as options. Note that the bundles that are on the academic bundle list need to be retained.

Variation: Instead of providing students with all the words from each bundle make cards, or slips of paper, with the words that are NOT prepositions. Then list the prepositions on the board, or give each student a piece of paper with a list of prepositions (each preposition only listed once!). This is a more difficult task because it requires the students to make more choices about using prepositions versus sorting out and using all of the slips of paper as in the original activity.

Activity 2: Find the Bundle

Time: 15–30 minutes
Materials to prepare ahead of time: A list of bundles for each student.
Make sure students have access to their textbooks, or assigned class readings.

1. Have students scan a text to find bundles. This can be done with each student working on the same text looking for any bundles that are on the list. Or, different texts can be given to groups of students to individually look for bundles in the different texts.

Note: In addition to finding bundles, this activity practices scanning skills that are valuable for reading.

2. Compare results: If all students are working on the same text, results can be compared. That is, did everyone find the same bundles? If students are working on different texts, then a comparison of the bundles found in the different texts can be a good source of discussion.

Variation: Have students look for the academic lexical bundles in texts that they have written. How are they using (or not using) bundles to guide readers?

Activity 3: What Does This Mean?

Time: 20–30 minutes
Materials to prepare ahead of time: The list of academic bundles. Text handouts from textbooks and/or assigned class readings.

1. As a class, talk about the functions of different bundles. Be sure to look at specific text examples of bundles and describe how the bundles function (e.g., to guide the reader, to highlight information, to show contrast).

2. Divide the students into groups of two or three. Each team will take a text and change some of the bundles. This can be done either by using white out (a correction fluid) and writing in the new bundle, or if the texts are available electronically, and students have access to computers, students can delete and replace bundles. Be sure that students know to replace the existing bundle with one that changes the meaning or does not "flow".

3. Groups will trade texts and discuss how the "new" bundles are not functioning as intended and try to replace the "changed" bundle with a bundle that facilitates the meaning of the text and/or the relationship of the information.

Note: The goal of this activity is to demonstrate how these lexical bundles impact text organization and meaning for the reader. Be sure to include discussion of the changes that the students chose to clearly represent the meaning of the text.

Perhaps after trying some of these bundle activities, you are interested in collecting student papers and finding bundles that your students are using or that are being used in class reading materials. The task of combing through and finding bundles is a daunting one, however there are free user-friendly programs, such as AntConc (Anthony, 2018), that can find bundles and then count how often they occur, and also show the bundle in context. This program can also be used to see words in context and to create word list from texts. Online support for AntConc is detailed and easy to use. If you are unsure of how to begin using texts (spoken or written), Reppen (2010) provides clear steps for collecting and using texts and also ideas for developing activities.

5. Wrapping Up

The lexical bundles presented in this chapter can be a rich source of activities and language teaching material. These building blocks of language provide students with chunks of language that can be used to launch utterances, or to signpost writing. In the case of the academic writing bundles, these bundles provide a means to promote accurate use of prepositions.

This chapter has highlighted how results from existing research can be used to provide resources for instruction. The information presented is by no means exhaustive, but is meant to provide concrete examples of how to take information from existing and accessible research on actual language use and create meaningful classroom activities. This, of course, can be extended to developing materials, in addition to creating activities.

In addition to the two resources used in this chapter, there are journals that often publish accessible research on lexical bundles, and other descriptions of linguistic characteristics of language use that can be a source to develop classroom activities and materials. These journals include the *Journal of English for Specific Purposes*, the *Journal of English for Academic Purposes*, *Corpora*, and the *Journal of Second Language Writing*. Some examples of recent publications on lexical bundles found in these journals include Shahriari's 2017 study in *Corpora* that describes lexical bundles frequently found in different sections of research abstracts (i.e., Introduction, Methods, and Results). This information could be used to develop relevant activities for students preparing to write research papers for class, or for graduate students preparing to submit research articles to academic journals. Another example of a lexical bundle study that could be relevant for developing activities is the 2013 *Journal of English for Academic Purposes* article by Staples, Egbert, Biber, and

McClair that explores lexical bundles found in the writing portion of the TOEFL iBT and how those bundles relate to writing development.

A more covert goal of this chapter is to encourage connections between the resources that are made available by research and those that are used to inform classroom materials and activities. Researchers and teachers can work together as a team to create optimal learning resources for students, so that valuable and limited classroom time is optimized to best prepare our learners for the language they will meet and use when they leave our language classrooms.

References

Anthony, L. (2018). *AntConc* (Version 3.5.7) [Computer software]. Tokyo, Japan: Waseda University.

Biber, D. (2006). *University language: A corpus-based study of spoken and written registers.* Amsterdam: John Benjamins.

Biber, D., Leech, G., Johansson, S., Conrad, S., & Finegan, E. (1999). *The Longman grammar of spoken and written English.* Harlow, UK: Longman.

Reppen, R. (2010). *Using corpora in the language classroom.* Cambridge: Cambridge University Press.

Shahriari, H. (2017). Comparing lexical bundles across the introduction, method and results sections of the research article. *Corpora,* 12(1), 1–22.

Staples, S., Egbert, J., Biber, D., & McClair, A. (2013). Formulaic sequences and EAP writing development: lexical bundles in the TOEFL iBT writing section. *Journal of English for Academic Purposes,* 12, 214–225.

Index

a couple of 111, 117, 118, 128
a great deal of 118, 196
a long time 126, 170
a variety of 142
a wide range 128, 182, 196
academic genre 9, 10
Academic Vocabulary List 21
according to the 127, 142
accuracy 22, 46, 119
adjective 19, 42, 49, 65, 76–78, 114
adverb 57, 58, 65, 76–78, 90
amount of 118, 128
apology 5, 8
as a result of 124, 167, 170, 181, 196
as far as 71, 170
assessment 80, 83, 84, 85, 113, 135, 138,
    151–153, 155, 156, 158, 159, 168, 169
at the same time 43, 124, 128, 142, 171,
    181, 182

by and large 32, 133, 142, 165–167, 169, 171
by the way 167

Cambridge English Corpus 24
can I 3, 190
chant 28, 29
communicative breakdown 122, 124
communicative task 26, 86
competence 85–87, 136, 173
compositionality 56, 57, 78
compound 5, 58, 59, 62, 78, 91

conjunction 121
contrastive analysis 31
conversation 4, 7, 8, 9, 12, 21, 22, 27, 91,
    122–128, 131, 157, 166, 170–176, 180,
    181, 186–188, 192
conversational routine 7
corpus analysis 6, 36
Corpus of Contemporary American English
    (COCA) 48, 75, 137, 161
could you 7, 41, 175
creativity 68
culture 3, 4, 8, 24, 85

dictation 30, 40, 121
dictionary 2, 6, 27, 30, 32, 38, 63, 69, 70
dictogloss 30, 126, 129
different from 142
discourse organizer 40, 43, 166, 171
do you 5, 12, 23, 121, 123, 142, 170, 171, 174,
    175, 181, 190
don't think 21, 125, 175

fiction 181
fixed phrase 7
fluency 4, 6, 21, 29, 37, 170
for this reason 124, 126, 128
frequency 11, 21, 23, 24, 33, 38–43,
    45, 46, 49, 64, 67–69, 112, 114,
    119, 124, 125, 130, 168, 170, 171,
    174, 179, 181, 186
function word 11

gap fill 48
General Service List 21
get-passive 9
grammar 2, 10, 11, 12, 37, 56, 58, 64, 68, 76, 90, 109, 110–113, 115, 117, 119, 120, 124, 126, 129, 135, 137, 167, 169, 188, 191
greeting 8, 122, 123

headword 24, 75
hedge 142, 158
how are you 28, 122, 166, 170, 175

I don't know 19, 22, 125, 166, 171, 175, 181
idiomaticity 55–57, 63, 65–68, 79, 80, 81, 83–85, 87, 89, 92
in addition to 128, 196
in order to 171, 172, 182
in other words 41, 142, 170, 180, 182
in spite of 126, 165, 166
in terms of 43, 181, 182
in the case of 124, 171, 181, 196
in the form of 44, 142
inference theory 27
invitation 5, 8
it is important to 124, 171, 196

learning outcome 23, 82, 86, 87
lecture 40, 124, 129, 166, 170, 173–175, 177, 181, 188, 192–195
lexeme 7, 58, 59, 60–62, 70, 71, 78, 91
lexical substitution 45
lexicon 1, 2, 57, 63, 68, 78, 91, 167
listening 21, 37, 39, 41, 47, 48, 77, 109, 112, 114, 115, 122, 126, 130, 168, 177, 189, 191, 192
look into 109, 142, 145

memorization 77, 86
memory 19, 30, 63, 92, 129, 154, 167
metalanguage 42
metaphor 3, 7, 21, 60, 76, 87, 88, 91
misunderstanding 122
more or less 20, 118, 133
morpheme 5, 56, 57, 62, 68, 91
most of the 128
motivation 22, 23, 28, 33

noticing 70, 110–112, 114, 115, 124, 136, 177, 178
number of the 128

on the basis of 44, 128, 172, 181, 196
on the one hand 31, 38, 78, 84, 124, 125, 128, 168

on the other hand 19, 38, 111, 124, 125, 153, 155, 167, 168, 172, 182, 196
one of the 114, 128, 171, 172, 181
opacity 57
Oxford English Dictionary 2

paraphrase 41, 64, 127
part of the 128, 171, 172, 182
performance 68, 83, 84, 86, 87, 92, 151, 188
phrasal verb 6–8, 9, 20, 27, 28, 32, 42, 58, 62, 76, 90, 110, 119, 157
phraseology 1, 2, 58, 65
pivot word 115, 116
poem 29
politeness 8, 171, 175–176
pragmatics 81
preposition 42, 58, 65, 76, 77, 90, 117, 119, 125, 126, 128, 168, 172, 195, 196, 197, 199
present simple 22, 23
productive skill 4, 122
promise 5
pronunciation 48, 168
proverb 1, 2, 8, 26, 31, 57, 62, 65, 66, 70, 76, 90, 91
punctuation 186

reading 3, 21, 25, 29, 36–39, 45, 47, 48, 70, 77, 109–111, 115, 126, 130, 155, 168, 172, 186, 196, 198, 199
recall 30, 63, 84, 177
receptive skill 4, 85, 112
register 68, 75, 80, 170–174, 175, 176, 179, 180, 181, 187
rehearsal 9
relevance 24, 25, 81, 136, 143
repetition 9, 23–29, 49, 70, 120, 121, 177, 178, 182
reporting verb 127
request 5, 8
restatement 129
result of 124, 167, 170, 181, 196
running word 38

saying 2, 8, 57, 58, 62, 76
sentence stem 3, 6, 7, 10, 12, 21, 61
simile 58, 60, 90
simplicity 24
small talk 122
social interaction 9, 170, 175
sociolinguistics 81, 86
song 29
speaking 2–4, 6, 8, 30, 41, 46, 48, 58, 77, 81, 88, 109, 112–115, 117, 121–123, 127, 129, 130, 166, 168, 169, 171, 179, 188, 191

speech 3
spelling 48, 129, 168, 191
spoken discourse 3, 5, 122, 173–175, 181
subordinate clause 6, 88
synonym 31, 32, 47, 115, 147
syntax 58, 78, 81, 86

thank you 12, 28, 116, 118, 123, 125, 133, 171, 181
the end of 128, 172, 176, 181, 196
the most part 165, 166
the way in which 181
thesaurus 27, 32, 38
think about 180, 183
TOEFL iBT 200
translation 30, 31, 57, 68, 79, 168, 177, 179, 182
transparency 57, 77
turn-taking 8

vagueness 142
very sorry 170, 175

what do you 121, 175, 181, 190, 192
what time 121, 129
word family 20
word list 21, 38, 39, 43–45, 48, 50, 199
would like 125, 130, 174
would you 1, 5, 7, 28, 125, 175, 190
writing 2–4, 9, 10, 11, 36–38, 45, 46, 48, 77, 79, 81, 88, 109–112, 114, 117, 126–130, 135, 141, 153, 155, 157, 166, 168–173, 179, 180, 181, 186–189, 191, 195, 196
written discourse 3, 9, 80, 127, 130, 174

you know 43, 113, 116, 130, 170, 182, 190
you mind 5, 12
you think 175, 183, 185, 192

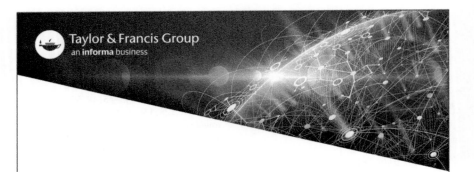